THE

RIGHTFUL REMEDY.

ADDRESSED TO

THE SLAVEHOLDERS OF THE SOUTH.

By EDWARD B. BRYAN.

"I CANNOT tell what you and other men
"Think of this life; but for my single self,
"I had as lief not be, as live to be
"In awe of such a thing as I myself."—*Julius Cæsar*, *Act* 1.

PUBLISHED FOR THE SOUTHERN RIGHTS ASSOCIATION.

CHARLESTON:

STEAM POWER PRESS OF WALKER & JAMES.

ERRATA.

Page 15, for "*at the first shock. The two small cities,*" *&c.*, read at the first shock, the two small cities," &c.,

Page 21, for "*Pertual Slavery,*" read "perpetual slavery."

Page 32, chap. 6, line 5, for "*immortality*", read "immorality.

Page 54, line 11, for "*means*" read "meanings."

Page 60, line 3, (from bottom,) for "*mostly*" read "most costly,"

Page 60, In note at bottom of page, for "*see page* 70," read "see page 27."

Page 87. line 24, for "*deducted*" read "deduced."

Page 93, line 2, for "*a shot cold,*" read a shot could."

Page 111, line 12, for "*a co-equal*" read "a co-equal state."

CHAPTER II.

"I grant this argument is old, but truth
No years impair; and had not this been true,
Thou never hadst despised it for its age:
Truth is immortal as thy soul, and fable
As fleeting as thy joys."

To appreciate the merits of an institution, and to comprehend the claims of any custom to the respect of society, it is essential that we should be well acquainted with the history and the object of them. Let us then distinctly understand the nature of slavery, and for this purpose glance at its history, that we may become acquainted with it in all its bearings. The leading questions which would naturally occur to most minds would seem to be, when and where did slavery originate? What caused it, or how was it brought about? And what are the leading features of it?

It is impossible to determine positively, how and when slavery first occurred, there being no conclusive evidence to be had on the subject. But so far as human reasoning is to be relied on, it appears evident that it must have arisen *out of the nature of things.* On the authority of ARISTOTLE we can unhesitatingly say, that "in the natural state of man, from the origin of things, a portion of the human family must command, and the remainder obey; that the distinction which exists between master and servants, is a distinction at once natural and indispensable; and that when we find existing among men, freemen and slaves, it is not man, but nature herself, who has ordained the distinction." As to *how* this relation could have arisen out of the nature of things, it can easily be conceived. At the expulsion from Paradise of our first parents, they and their descendants were ever condemned to earn their bread by the sweat of their brow. That is to say, it was ordained, that man to live must labour. But as the family increased, we have evidence, there was a *division of labour;* some tilling the earth, and others keeping flocks. Moreover, at this early period man had no instrument but his hand, and no science to guide him; yet he was compelled to subject the earth to cultivation, and to labour industriously. Now this labour must have been, to a greater or less degree, shared by the whole family, and as the result of nature, the child must have been taught and compelled by the parent to labour as he increased in years. Thus every child, as he became older, was required by his *natural superior* to labour according to the directions he received. The parent having supreme authority over his child, possessed in him a slave as implicitly obedient as any African slave of the present day; and that the younger were not compelled to perform the more servile and menial offices for the older can hardly be supposed.

But in order to come up to the more extended views of the present-day philanthropy, let us take a more enlarged view of primitive society, and see if reason does not bring us to the belief that slavery must have sprung from the very nature of things.

However thoroughly convinced the abolitionist or philanthropist of the present day may be, that the interests of the great mass of poor people, as well as the amelioration of their miserable condition, *ought* to be the care of the powerful and wealthy; it is nevertheless an absolute truth, that such is *not* the state of affairs in any primitive condition of society. And no further evidence of the absolute necessity of slavery, in some form or other, for the comfort and well being of the human race, in its earlier stages of society, can be desired, than the well known universality of its existence in every nation of every climate since the world began.

But few words are sufficient to account for this truth. When man was in his primitive state he possessed no property except the few necessaries he derived from the store of nature. Such a thing as capital, or a "value of exchange," was utterly unknown. Man's capital was his mind and body, his profession or occupation was that of appropriating to his use the few articles his body craved, and which nature supplied him with in return for his efforts; and the only value these few articles could possibly bear was the "value of use." In the course of time, however, the race increased, and the habitations of man were gradually extended along the pleasant streams and valleys of the neighborhood, until a day's journey would perhaps intervene between the abode of the nearest relations. The development of mind successively called for new exertions of the body; space was passed over; new scenes became attractive, new fruits were plucked, new homes were made, and, apace with all, new men were born, who lived to extend the migrations their fathers had commenced. But whilst time served to develop these circumstances, it served also to create many necessary accompanyments, conspicuous among which was the transfer of those articles which were originally appropriated from the bounty of nature, and which may be styled the *transfer of property.* Soon followed the exchange of these articles, or of this property, and then immediately springs up a new value in these articles, and that is the "*value of exchange.*" Then comes the idea of traffic, and its result, a desire to accumulate these articles to an amount over and above the demands of the individual body; this property brings influence, and this influence is a guarantee of power. But since property has thus become an object of life, the accumulation of these articles is the aim of all; avarice and ambition germinate apace; those that are honest adhere to the old custom of appropriation and industry, and those who are wicked steal. Some become rich, some remain poor. But the rich have influence, and they have the power to assist and protect the poor. Now the vicious poor do violence to their weaker neighbours, through envy, hatred or malice, or for the purpose of plundering their scanty stores. The rich are appealed to by the injured poor, or may be the helpless poor are rescued by the sympathising rich; but however that may be, the rich and poor thus brought together, make common their cause; the poor that they may be protected by the influence or the power of the rich, and the rich that they may derive new sources of wealth and new fountains of power, from the grateful hearts and willing hands of the relieved poor.

Property becomes more insecure, and violence more universal; there is no safety for the weak and the poor, but with the rich and powerful. This lower class then glides surely into the power of the higher class, which is in such a state of things *at least practically* the superior of the two. What then must be the inevitable result? Let the philanthropist look into the heart of man, and see whether this higher class will concern itself for the care and protection of the lower, without exacting *at least* what is deemed an *equivalent* for the security and comfort bestowed. Who will dictate terms. The high or the low; the strong or the weak; the rich or the poor; the secure or the insecure; the unruffled giant in his quiet abode, or the panic stricken wretch who pleads for life under his most redoubted protection? What will the terms be? And—what, according to modern philanthropy is worse than any terms of miserable dependence—what specious name will be given to the relation thus springing out of the course of these events. The answer is slavery. Slavery *at least in fact,* let it be what it may *in name.*

Argument is not needed to convince the plainest intellect of this unavoidable result. It must be remembered that in the primitive times to which we allude, because "humanity, justice, and policy; so powerful in civilized ages, are then unknown, and the sufferings of the destitute are as much disregarded as those of the lower animals;" and because "compulsion is the *only* power which can render labour general in the many ages which must precede the influence of artificial wants, or a general taste for its fruits;" it follows as the inevitable result, that supreme power over, or a clear right of property in "the person and labour of the poor is the only inducement which could be held out to the opulent to take them under their protection."

Now either of these relations of the person and labour of the poor is inseparable from the idea of slavery. In the first case where one man has supreme power over the person of another man, we would certainly say the one was the master and the other the slave. And likewise in the second case, where one man has the right of property in the person of another, he not only has supreme power over the person, but can transmit or resign that power to another at his discretion, and can set his value (of exchange) upon the property. This would assuredly be called slavery. If this then is slavery, and the conjectures we have laid down as to primitive society be correct; we can feel no hesitation in saying that slavery originally sprung out of the circumstances of society, and was the unavoidable result of man's nature and relations. Nor are we, upon the whole, loath to extract from the works of a distinguished historian* who decries slavery, the following very comprehensive remarks. "The varieties of human character, the different degrees of intellectual or physical strength with which men are endowed, the consequences of accident, misfortune, or crime, the destitution and helpless state of the poor in the infancy of civilization, early introduce the distinction of ranks, and precipitate the lower orders into that state of dependance on their superiors which is known by the name of slavery. This institution, however odious its name has now justly become, is not an evil when it first arises; it only becomes such by being continued in circumstances different from those in which it originated, and in times when the protection it affords to the poor is no longer required." And "how miserable soever the condition of slaves may be in those unruly times, they are incomparably better off than they would have been if they had incurred the *destitution of freedom.*

Let us return to the question, when and where did slavery originate? Where shall we look for an answer but into history, and what history more ancient, or more to be relied on than the Pentateuch. There then let us search for any evidence on the subject of the origin of slavery. From the first chapter to the middle of the ninth of Genesis, is the only history of the world, before the flood, now extant, and in it there is no mention of any thing like slavery. But immediately after the ebbing of the waters of this mighty deluge, we find a distinct and unequivocal *creation of slavery;* a clear and comprehensive decree, ordination, and injunction of that relation of servant and master which we call slavery. It is in these words:†

"And the sons of Noah that went forth of the ark, were Shem, and Ham and Japheth: and Ham is the father of Canaan. These are the three sons of Noah; and of them was the whole earth overspread. And Noah began to be an husbandman, and he planted a vineyard: and he drank of the wine, and was drunken; and he was uncovered within his tent. And Ham, the father of Canaan, saw the nakedness of his father, and told his brethren without. And Shem and Japheth took a garment and laid it upon both their shoulders, and went backward, and covered the nakedness of their father; and their faces were backward, and they saw not their fathers nakedness. And Noah awoke from his wine, and knew what his younger son had done unto him. And he said, cursed be Canaan; *a servant of servants shall he be unto his brethren.* And he said, blessed be the Lord God of Shem; *and Canaan shall be his servant.* God shall enlarge Japheth, and he shall dwell in the tents of Shem; *and Canaan shall be his servant.*"

Here is the earliest record of the institution of slavery that could possibly be

* Allison's History of Europe, Vol. 2, No. 1.

† Genesis, chap. ix, 18.

desired. For what wild dreamers has ever dreamt of going back into the anti-diluvian world to search for the history or traditions of society so primitive and remote, or in hopes of finding ought concerning a custom, which we may reasonably suppose was not known by any distinct appellation, though universally existing.

Though there can be no doubt as to the existence of slavery before the flood, yet in the absence of any authority for a positive assertion on the subject, we will be content to confine ourselves to the post-diluvian world; and with Moses as our venerable authority, we say, that Noah instituted, created, or ordained slavery: and Canaan the innocent offspring of his own loins, was by him *made a slave.* All this was done by the delegated authority of God himself. We are then fully prepared to answer the question, when did slavery begin, by saying it began in the year 2348 before Christ, which is the date of Canaans curse. Can any abolitionist deny this?

It may be urged here, by those disposed to be foolish, that the word *servant* does not imply *involuntary* servitude, or what we term *slavery* at the present day. It is true the word of *itself* does not always imply African slavery, or any other kind of bondage, but taken in the present connection it can imply nothing else than *involuntary servitude.* "Cursed be Canaan, a servant of servants *shall he be etc.*" There is no choice in this, there is no appeal from this severe mandate; Canaan is cursed for his father's sin, and the nature of the curse is that he *shall be a servant*, willing or not though he be.

Assuming this to be the beginning of slavery, let us follow up the records; for it is important that every Southern man should be acquainted with the history of an institution of such vital consequence, and which bears so powerfully upon the very existance of his State, the peace of his family, and the dignity of his birthright. And we must not be astonished to find that the descendants of Canaan, for hundreds of years after the curse was pronounced by Noah, were the slaves of the descendants of Shem; the very one in whose tent Canaan was condemned to be a slave. We must not be astonished to find that even as late as the time of Moses aud Joshua—1490 years B. C.—and nearly *one thousand years after* Canaan's curse, his descendants. became the miserable slaves of the descendants of Shem. We say we must not be astonished, for it was the unalterable will of God; and *his* will on *this subject* has never been disputed till the superb refinements of the nineteenth century sprang up to put it to the blush.

But to return to history. The next mention of the subject we meet with, of any material consequence in our present purpose, is the sale of Joseph by his brothers, in the year 1729 B. C. The affair is thus related:

> "And Judah said unto his brethren, what profit is it if we slay our brother and conceal his blood? Come, let us sell him to the Ishmealites, and let not our hand be upon him; for he is our brother, and our flesh; and his brethren were content. Then there passed by Midianites, merchantmen; and they drew and lifted up Joseph out of the pit, and sold Joseph to the Ishmealites for twenty pieces of silver: and they brought Joseph into Egypt," and "the Midianites sold him into Egypt, unto Potiphar, an officer of Pharoah's, and captain of the guard."*

Thus it appears, at this early period it was not only customary to hold men in bondage, but also *to buy and sell them as articles of traffic;* for it must be evident to all, that the idea suggested by Judah was no new thing; on the contrary, we have every right to suppose that it was a common custom to buy and sell men the same as other kinds of property; for if it were not then a common custom, would all of Joseph's brothers so readily have consented to the measure? Would the merchantmen so readily have purchased him? Or would

* Genesis, chap. xxxvii. 26.

Pharoah's officer have dared to purchase him from the merchants, if it was not lawful to traffic in slaves. These conclusions are borne on the very face of the occurrence.

We hence date our first accounts of the slave traffic as far back as the year 1729 B. C. And though we have every reason to believe that this traffic was carried on long before this date, yet in the absence of positive evidence to that effect, we are willing to say, the slave trade existed in the year 1729 B. C., and has been carried on ever since.

This feature in slavery, that is the slave trade,* seems to have drawn down the especial indignation of present-day philanthropists. Indeed this is the principal objection urged against the system we practice at the South, and it is in fact the only material difference between African slavery at the South, and European slavery in Europe, or Northern slavery at the North. And though it is so much objected to, we find in the records of Moses that it is the oldest distinctive feature of slavery; and, moreover, that one of the sublimest evidences of God's omnipotence, the conducting his chosen people to the promised land, in connection with his curse on Canaan, the final realization of which took up a space of nearly one thousand years. All this we find, turns on the selling of Joseph, a slave, into Egypt. Joseph, a descendant of Shem, sold into bondage, that the curse of the Almighty upon certain of Hams descendants, might be fearfully executed four hundred years after, under the inspiration of Moses and the guidance of Joshua.

After experiencing various vicissitudes, we find him exalted to wealth and honor, and in the enjoyment of the confidence of the King himself. But every body knows how Jacob, his father, (also called Israel,) was induced to visit Egypt, and how Egypt became the abode of the Israelites for a few hundred years, and how they finally migrated to the promised land. And it must appear evident to every reader of the history of those remote ages, that even from the time of the dispersion of men after the flood—God had a peculiar regard for certain of Shem's descendants who were afterwards to be called his own; and that he also directed the steps of Canaan's descendants, with a view to the fulfilment of the curse pronounced by Noah. He pointed out the country which *the former* were to inherit; he caused to be possessed by another laborious nation, who applied themselves to cultivate and adorn it, and to improve, by all possible methods, the future inheritance of the Israelites. He then fixed, in that country, the like number of families, as were to be settled in it, when the sons of Israel should, at the appointed time take possession of it; and *did not suffer any of the nations, which were not subject to the curse pronounced by Noah against Canaan, to enter an inheritance that was to be given up entirely to the Israelites.*†

And, in confirmation of all that has been said, it is remarked by an American writer,‡ whose work is compiled from those of the most eminent commentators of the Scriptures, that "Noah on a memorable occasion was inspired to declare the future condition of his sons, and of their posterity. Moved by the spirit of God to utter his holy oracle, Noah said, 'cursed be Canaan, etc.'" * * * * *

Japheth was the eldest son of Noah, and his name signifies enlargement, and his posterity have been surprisingly extended; for they have peopled Europe, Asia Minor, part of Armenia, the whole of the regions north of Mount Taurus, and probably of America.‖

* When we use the term "slave trade," we mean the legitimate trade, the bona fide exchange of a bona fide slave for a bona fide equivalent. The African slave trade, *properly speaking*, must of course be included in the general term "slave trade," but the thefts and abductions, frauds and violence, said by abolitionists to be practised in Africa, are of course unworthy of the term trade, and is, therefore, not alluded to when we speak of the slave trade.

† Rollins' Ancient History, vol. 1.

‡ Sears' Bible Biography.

‖ Genesis, chap. x, 2–5.

Shem signifies renown, and his fame has been truly great, both temporally and spiritually. His descendants occupied the finest regions of upper and central Asia, particularly Armenia, Media, Persia, Syria, etc. Shems chief renown, however, consisted in his being the ancestor of Abraham, and the nation of Israel, and especially of the Messiah, the seed of the woman, to which it is thought that Noah might allude, when he exclaimed—" blessed be the Lord God of Shem!"

Ham or Cham, signifies black or burnt, perhaps indicating the sultry regions which his descendants should occupy, or the dark complexion they should possess, or both. * * * * * *. Canaan and his sons occupied Syria, Canaan and Palestine; and the sons of Misraim* peopled Egypt, Lybia and Africa.†

Ham and his son had dishonored their venerable father, and upon them he pronounced the prophetical malediction: cursed be Canaan, etc. In accordance with this denunciation, the devoted nations which God destroyed before the Isrealites, were descended from Canaan: so were the Phœnicians and the Carthagenians, who were subjugated with the most terrible destruction by the Greeks and Romans. And the African nations, whose miseries have become proverbial through the world for the last three centuries, and even to our times, by the operations of the horrible slave trade, are also descended from Ham, the son of Noah."

The next feature we observe on this subject, is one which would naturally follow from the first; for if we would sell a slave, it would be but a modification of the same act to sell his services for a given time, or in other words, to *hire* him to another. This custom of hiring slaves, we find recorded in a very early age. Let it however be distinctly borne in mind what a marked difference there is, between hiring one's self for one's own personal benefit, and being hired for the benefit of another. Thus, a freeman may hire his services to another, and receive the wages of his labor; yet his freedom is not permanently effected, it is only conditionally qualified, he is only in part, and for a time a slave, and that too voluntarily, for it is a voluntary agreement, or, at least, is to be supposed so.

On the other hand, if one man hires the services of another to a third person, and bargains for and receives the wages, regardless of the will of the individual hired, why that individual is no party in the contract, he is the matter under contract, the material upon which the others operate, and is a slave in the broadest sense of the term; he must be either a bondman, or else a freeman in a most slavish position.

It is to this species of hiring we allude, when we say we find it recorded in the history of the most remote ages. This feature ranks next in antiquity to that of buying and selling. As to the other kind of hiring, where a man who calls himself free, is forced through dire poverty to render himself the menial of another for a miserable support; where a free born man condemns himself—or rather, we should say, is condemed by the circumstances which surround him—to serve, and plod, and drag out a miserable existence, performing the most menial offices, submitting to the most degrading and demoralizing conditions; or else living in a state of half starvation, and in rags; shivering in the poverty, disease and vice flowing from the most unpardonable idleness and ignorance; a stranger to the common decencies of life; unconscious of the meaning of the grand word *liberty*, so constantly in his mouth; in some instances absolutely ignorant of the existence of a God, and a perfect stranger to the rays of the sun: glorying in his freedom, rejoicing over his liberty, notwithstanding he that very day bartered his vote, the index of his liberty, at the ballot-box; all these are the results of modern refinement, the glorious results of wisdom and philanthropy. It is an exalted

* Misraim was, according to Rollins, the first King of Egypt.

† Genesis, chap. x, 6 20.

system of *hireling slavery*, far above the kind we allude to, and perhaps better suited to the tastes and the pockets of those who conduct it, than any other could possibly be.

The first mention we have seen made of hiring slaves, was at the building of Solomon's Temple, about one thousand and fourteen years before Christ.

Solomon having determined to erect this grand edifice, immediately set about to gather his workmen, and collect all the material requisite for so vast an undertaking. Being a wise man, he soon perceived that his own people could not carry out his views without the assistance of others better skilled in the art of building, and hewing timber. Being also on the most friendly terms with Hiram, King of Tyre, he first communicates his intentions to that monarch, and then proceeds in the following words: "now therefore command thou that they hew me cedar trees out of Lebanon; and my servants shall be with thy servants: and unto *thee* will I give hire for thy servants, according to all that thou shall appoint: for thou knowest that there is not among us any that can skill to hew timber like unto the Sidonians. * * * * * * And Hiram sent to Solomon, saying, I have considered the things which thou sentest to me for; and I will do all thy desire concerning timber of cedar, and concerning timber of fir. My servants shall bring them down from Lebanon unto the sea: and I will convey them by sea in floats unto the place that thou shall appoint me, and will cause them to be discharged there, and thou shalt receive them: and thou shalt accomplish my desire in giving food for my household. So Hiram gave Solomon cedar trees and fir trees, according to all his desire. And Solomon gave Hiram twenty thousand measures of wheat for food to his household, and twenty measures of pure oil: thus gave Solomon to Hiram year by year."*

Now it may be supposed by those who have read the account of this transaction as it is recorded by Josephus, that the servants here spoken of were not bondmen, but that the word is used to signify subjects.† It is true they were two powerful monarchs who were negotiating, and they may well have termed their subjects servants. It would, however, be an error to suppose that such was the application of the term in this case, for in the sacred record of the affair—which must be admitted as the highest authority—we are distinctly informed that *bondmen* were employed, and we are, moreover, told that Solomon collected workmen from among the conquered Canaanites who were under Noah's curse. This being more than thirteen hundred years after the curse was uttered. "But of the children of Isreal did Solomon make no bondmen;" from "all the people that were left of the Amorites, Hittites, Perizzites, Hivites, and Jebusites, which were not of the children of Israel, their children that were left after them in the land, whom the children of Israel also were not able utterly to destroy, upon those did Solomon levy a tribute of bond service unto this day."‡

The natural subjects of Solomon, the tribe of Israel, furnished his armies, and offices of trust and honour;‖ and, in the building of the temple, they supplied the superintendants and overseers. "These were the chief of the officers that were over Solomon's work, five hundred and fifty (children of Israel) which bore rule over the people that wrought in the work." Here, then, we have the grandest building the world ever saw, the finest specimens of art and ingenuity, the noblest applications of mechanical philosophy, all the work of hired and domestic slaves, whose operations were performed under the immediate superintendance of free overseers; though under the general direction of the wisest man of the times. And there can be no question, in view of innumerable facts,

* 1 Kings, 5, 6.
† See Josephus, Vol. 2, page 140.
‡ 1 Kings, ix, 15, 23. 2 Sam. 5, 9. Ps. 51, 18. Jos. 16, 10-17, 11-and 19, 36.
‖ Josephus, vol. 2, p. 159.

that the same decree which kept the descendants of Canaan in slavery, for so many series of ages *then*, has served the same end since, serves the same end *now*, and must continue in the fulfilment of his designs until the author of it sees fit to suspend its terrible effects. That the negro slaves of the South can be the descendants of any other than Canaan, is too improbable to be discussed.

Thus far, we have ascertained beyond doubt,

First, That slavery existed, *by virtue of law, four thousand one hundred and ninety-eight years ago.*

Second, That the *slave trade flourished three thousand, five hundred and seventy-nine years ago.*

Third, That the custom of *hiring slaves prevailed two thousand, eight hundred and sixty-four years ago.*

In view of this, we are prepared to assert that the Southern slaveholding States, in defending themselves against the innovations of Northern legislation, are not only defending what remains of their independance and sovereignty, but they are defending *the oldest, and most time-honoured institution of society.*

Let us briefly examine the practice of it, as it existed in the civilized nations of every age, and compare it with our own. And, in doing this, we will not fail to see that, whatever may be the condition of man, his composition is still the same—his nature is unchanged, and his prime motives have always been the same. His system of government, and particularly that department which relates to slavery, though frequently changing, is but the perfection of what it was in its primitive state.

In taking this cursory glance at the history of the world, for the history of slavery is nothing else, let us be content to look into the more prominent circumstances; for, if we find a continual resemblance and identity of principle in the most important points, we may disregard those of minor consideration, and attribute discrepancies among them to local causes, or the incidents of the times.

The principal causes which have brought about slavery, are, first, *crime*, either against the State or against the Creator; of this nature was the cause of Canaan's condemnation. In ancient States, on account of crime, some were condemned to temporary, and some to perpetual slavery.

Capture has been a most fruitful source. Prisoners taken in battle were, in most cases, made slaves, either to serve the conquering governments on the public works; or were distributed among the victors, as private property; or they were sold to fill the public coffers; or were ransomed. It was one of the effects of the laws of chivalry, first, to set the captives at a certain price for their ransom; and more latterly, it became the practice for belligerent powers to exchange their prisoners, on fair and equitable terms.

Debt has also been the cause of slavery, sometimes temporary, sometimes perpetual.

Theft, treachery, or misrepresentation have, in some instances, been the cause of it. The case of Joseph's sale, by his brothers, comes under this head.

Birth has doomed millions to this state of subjection. Children born of slave parents, as a natural consequence, inherit their parents' state, and are slaves themselves. At the present time, this is the chief cause of slavery in the civilized world.

It was an *Egyptian* law, of great antiquity, that wilful murder should be punished by death, whatever might be the condition of the murdered person, whether he was freeborn or otherwise.* And, in this respect, the equity of the Egyptians was similar to ours, and superior to that of the Romans, for they gave the master the absolute power, of life and death, over his slave. In fact, this law

* Rollins' Ancient History, Vol. 1, p. 127.

was peculiar to the Egyptians, and was a distinguishing feature in the regulations of slavery, from those of other ancient States.

Among the Ancient *Jews*, slaves were acquired as captives in war, and those thus obtained appear to have been kept in bondage for the remainder of their life. Theft was sometimes punished with temporary bondage.† The creditor of an insolvent debtor had power to enslave the family, as well as the person of the debtor,‡ in a similar manner as in the preceding case of a theft: that is, until the debt was, in some way, made good, or the equivalent of the stolen property was restored. Slavery originated at birth, among them as among us: that is to say, children inherited the condition of their mothers, just as, at the present day, in our land. Slaves were not permitted to give evidence in a court of justice,§ for it was supposed that improper motives might induce them to give false testimony. So, in our courts, slaves are not permitted to appear as witnesses against a free white man, nor is any *oath* administered when they are brought to give evidence in a case where those of their own condition are concerned.

It was enjoined that no freeman should marry a slave, however desirous such a union might be to the parties concerned:‖ for it was considered disparaging to the one, and detracting from the requisite discipline incidental to the condition of the other. So with us, such a thing is not tolerated, as a white man marrying a slave.

A remarkable point of resemblance between the Jewish and our system of slavery, is the fact, that slaves were originally brought from abroad: "Both thy bondmen and thy bondmaids, which thou shalt have, shall be of the heathen which are round about you: of them shall ye buy bondmen and bondmaids. And ye shall take them as an inheritance for your children after you, to inherit them for a possession; they shall be your bondmen forever."¶

Now, in some systems of slavery, certain descriptions of slaves had the right, under certain circumstances, to claim their freedom, at the expiration of a certain time, or when they became able to pay a certain sum of money, as a ransom; and in some, the death of the master was a signal for the emancipation of the slaves. But in the Jewish, and in our systems, slaves were procured from abroad. The Jews possessed themselves from the heathens round about them; we from the heathens of Africa—all being the descendants of the same Canaan. The Jews handed down this species of property, from father to son, and the property was confined to the same race, from generation to generation. We inherit, from our fathers, this same kind of property, and it has been confined, for generations, to the African race. In short, we find every important principle, of law or custom, which existed in the earliest ages of slavery, either entirely preserved, without change or modification, or else merely shaped and moulded in conformity with the principles of christianity.

The religion, policy and government—the customs, manners, social habits prevailing among men—their very languages, arts, sciences and amusements—*all* have changed; but man is still the same, and the fundamental essence of slavery is unaltered and unalterable, whether it be viewed with regard to the physical or moral world.

In ancient Greece, slavery existed to a very great extent, and the laws regulating it were more rigorous than those of the Jews, or of our times. Slaves were obtained by conquest in battle, by a voluntary sale of themselves, for the means of support, in payment of debt, by purchase from abroad, and by inheritance.

In Sparta, slavery sprang up with the city, and is almost as remote in its origin, as a civil institution of the State, as the foundations of the town: for, in the

† Exodus, xii., 2, 3. ‡ II. Kings, iv., 1, Mat. xviii., 25. § Josephus, vol. i., p. 264.
‖ Josephus, vol. i., 268. ¶ Leviticus, xxv., 39.

earliest days of Lacedamonia, a city not far from Sparta, called Elos, was captured, and the inhabitants reduced to slavery.* The Helots, or slaves, were, in the first instance, for political purposes, treated with extreme rigour, and afterwards were the miserable victims of the misguided philosophy and the heathen superstitions of their masters. They were, unquestionably, an oppressed people.

The freemen of Sparta, devoting their time entirely to the pursuits of war, or the affairs of State, left the very necessary management of agriculture, and the raising of stock, and all other domestic concerns, almost exclusively in the hands of their slaves. The number of slaves in Greece varied from ten to twenty times that of the free citizens. Spartan slaveholders seem to have had, at least in some instances, the power of life and death over their slaves. But we are inclined to think that this was an abuse, and not legal usage.

In their tribunals of justice, slaves were not permitted to bear testimony, nor to defend their cause personally; but, as in our courts, the master could always secure competent legal defence for his slave. On some occasions, of extreme emergency, a portion of the slaves were armed, and assisted in the common defence. But it has ever been the exclusive prerogative of the freeman to conduct battles and campaigns, both in ancient and modern times. This principle has never been permanently departed from since slavery began.

Among the Athenians, the code of discipline was less rigorous than at Sparta. Slaves, there, were allowed to participate in many of the ordinary pleasures and amusements of the times, and were permitted to acquire property and hold estates, always, however, paying a tribute to their masters. In cases of aggravated cruelty, the temple of Thesus was an inviolable sanctuary. If a slave received injury at the hands of any individual, he was, under his master's control, permitted to proceed, by a course of law, to seek redress before the public tribunals.

Society, in Athens, was divided into three great classes—citizens, strangers and servants.

A citizen could only be such by birth or adoption. To be a natural denizen of Athens, it was necessary to be born of a father and mother both free, and Athenians.†

A stranger was one who, being of a foreign country, came to settle at Athens, or in Attica, whether for the sake of commerce, or the exercising of any trade. He took no share in the government, could not vote in the assembly of the people, and could hold no office.

There were two classes denominated servants. Those were free, but not able to earn bread by their labour, and were consequently obliged, by the wretched state of their affairs, to go into service; and those who were involuntarily forced into service. These latter were slaves, who had either been taken prisoners in war or bought of such as trafficked publicly in them. Part of their master's estate consisted in them, who disposed absolutely of them, but generally treated them with great humanity. Demosthenes assures us, in one of his harangues, "that the condition of servants was infinitely more gentle at Athens than any-where else." And the equitable treatment which the Athenian slaves experienced is to be attributed chiefly to the natural suavity and good temper of their masters, which was so different from the austere and cruel severity of the Lacademonians, in regard to their slaves.

On the island of Crete, when the laws of Minos flourished—from which, it is supposed, many of Lycurgus' were framed—the land was cultivated by slaves and hirelings, who were called Periæci, apparently from their being people in the neighbourhood, whom Minos had subjected. As an evidence of the spirit of

* This originated the term Elotæ, or Helot. See Rollins.

† Rollins' Manners and Customs of the Greeks.

the institution, in those remote times, among the Cretans, Rollins tells us a custom anciently established in Crete, from whence it was adopted by the Romans, gives us reason to believe that the vassals who manured the lands were treated with great goodness and favour. In the feasts of Mercury, the masters waited on their slaves at table, and did them the same offices as they received from them the rest of the year.

The history of Syracuse, from the time of Gelon down to its subjection by the Romans, is an unbroken series of alterations, from slavery to freedom, and from freedom back to slavery. It was sometimes enslaved by the most cruel tyrants; at others, under the government of the wisest kings; sometimes abandoned to the capricious will of a populace, without either government or restriction; sometimes perfectly docile, and submissive to the authority of law and the empire of reason. It passed, alternately, from the most insupportable slavery to the most grateful liberty—from a kind of convulsions and frantic emotions, to a wise, peacable and regular conduct. When left to themselves, the Syracusans allowed the liberty they enjoyed to degenerate into caprice, anarchy and phrenzy; and, when subjected to the rule of others, they were the most submissive and degraded slaves.

The empire of the Medes and Persians was nothing more than a vast community of slaves, and the peculiar characteristics of the Asiatics, in general, was servitude and slavery.* As for the Persians, so great was the distance between the king and his subjects, that the latter, of what rank or quality soever, whether satrapæ, governors, near relations, or even brothers to the king, were only looked upon as slaves; whereas, the king himself was always considered, not only as their sovereign lord and master, but as a kind of divinity.

The condition of the Asiatic slaves were, however, mitigated by the peculiar manners of those countries; and, to this very day, the condition of a slave, in all the Eastern empires, differs but little from that of a domestic servant in modern Europe;† even the enfranchised poor of France and England would find something to envy in their situation. Succour in sickness, employment in health, and maintenance in old age, are important advantages, even in the best regulated States; but, duriug the anarchy of ancient times, their value was incalculable.

But here we must stay our pen, to insert a reflection which forces itself irresistibly upon us. It has been so frequently urged, that slavery, as a political institution, is sure to weaken, and eventually ruin, the most powerful government, that many of the most enlightened advocates of abolition regard the proposition, with whatever collateral circumstances it may be attended, as an axiom. But, upon a careful consideration of all the glorious events of Grecian history, and particularly upon a review of those unparalleled struggles between Greece and Persia, first under Darius and afterwards under Xerxes, when "all Asia, armed with the whole force of the East, overflowed on a sudden, like an impetuous torrent, and came pouring, with innumerable troops, both by sea and land, against a little spot of Greece, which seemed under the necessity of being entirely swallowed up and overwhelmed at the first shock." The two small cities, of Sparta and Athens, with the immense number of slaves they possessed, were able, not only to resist those formidable armies, but to attack, defeat, pursue, and destroy the greatest part of them. Can it be said of those cities, that the slaves they possessed were a weakness to them?

When it is remembered, that at no time during the palmiest days of Grecian glory and power, was the number of freemen one-half that of her slaves, can it be maintained that slavery was a cause of political evil, or a source of military weakness? Greece never declined from the lofty eminence she obtained, because

* Rollins.

† Allison.

she held slaves. The cause of the declension of the Grecian States is ascribed, by every historian, to have sprung out of *the disunion which rose up amongst themselves.* When they became divided by domestic jealousies, and turned those armes against themselves which had made them the masters of the world, they wrote in blood, on the indelible pages of history, a gloomy chapter, which should be read in tones of thunder to the miserable fanatics who are now sundering every tie which ever bound the States of this Union in one confederacy.

Among the *Romans*, slavery was the result of each of the causes already mentioned. Captives in war were divided into two classes: those who surrendered without resistance, and those who resisted till they were conquered. The latter were generally those who were sold into bondage. Insolvent debtors were sometimes given to their creditors, in a species of slavery, but their bondage was not as absolute as in other cases.

Among the Romans, we also find that, as in our system, the children of female slaves were the undisputed and natural property of the master; and this kind of property was inherited from generation to generation. Owners had unlimited power, and in many cases the power was abused; and, before the light of christianity was effectually shed upon them, the master sometimes exercised his right to the extent of murder.*

Workhouses, partaking of the nature, though not entirely resembling those in use among us, were in use among them. Slaves were not permitted to appear as witnesses before a court of justice; nor could they inherit property. No action by the civil law was given to a slave, nor could he personally appear to a suit, or suffer condemnation. Slaves were never enlisted in the armies of Rome. There were slaves attached to the soil, and public slaves, differing, in many respects, from domestic slaves.

Any further research, as to the practice of slavery among the Romans, may be dispensed with by us, as an able expounder of the law,† writing in the *Commercial Review*, of 1846–7, has exhibited every point we would wish to expose. We will therefore close this portion of our sketch by borrowing his own instructive remarks.

Among the Romans, "very rigid and important provisions existed with respect to fugitive slaves. He who concealed a fugitive slave was declared to be a thief; and the highest reward given to those who, finding them in their possession, without delay conducted them before a magistrate, or surrendered them to their masters. By a constitution of Constantine, a severe penalty was incurred by concealing a slave. The party was forced to restore a similar slave, or to pay twenty pieces of gold. The military were authorized to enter into the country houses, and upon lands of senators, and into the cottages of peasants, in search of fugitive slaves. Letters of the prince required magistrates to protect such persons as searched for these persons, under the penalty of one hundred pieces of gold, which was also the penalty prescribed for opposing them. Masters had also the right to demand the assistance of magistrates and the military, in aid of their recovery, and of the punishment of persons concealing them. The presidents of provinces had power to authorize a search into suspected mansions, and to prescribe a penalty in case of a refusal; and even the pleasure house of the prince was not exempt from the scrutiny.

"One arresting a fugitive slave was bound to convey him immediately before the magistrate, who was required to guard him in such manner as to prevent his escape, and, for this purpose, he was authorized to cause him to be chained. Great care was taken to identify such fugitives. Their names, descriptions, and

* This power of the master over the slave was also possessed by the father over his family.

† The Hon. B. F. Porter, of Alabama.

the name of the masters to whom they were reputed to belong, were submitted to the magistrates; and very particular directions were given as to their marks, which referred to a practice, common to the Romans, of impressing letters or marks, called *stigmatæ* or *subverbustæ*, with a hot iron. These formalities were evidenced by a public writing, or one affixed upon the place of their seclusion. A singular rescript of Antoninus Pius declared, that if a fugitive slave was delivered up for combat in the public games, he was not, in being thus exposed to death, withdrawn from the power of his master, but should be delivered up to the master, either before or after he had encountered the wild beasts; for often, says the rescript, slaves love rather to enter into combats of the arena, than into the hands of their masters, and be punished for their robberies and other crimes.

"If fugitive slaves were not claimed by their masters, they were sold by the prefect of the night guard; and, if recognized by the owner within three years, the price for which he was sold was surrendered. There seems to have been additional punishment, in case the fugitive slave passed himself as a freeman. A species of international provision also existed, by which it was made the duty of foreign nations, in case fugitive slaves were arrested within their limits, to condemn them to the mines or some similar punishment.

"In the sale of such slaves, the rule *caveat emptor* prevailed; to evidence which they were sold publicly, bound hand and feet.

"The State retained the power of making slaves of persons born free, in the case of soldiers deserting in times of war, of persons guilty of high capital offences, where such condition was imposed as part of the sentence, and of a free woman amorously affected towards a slave, &c.

"There was one provision, with respect to slaves, among the Romans, which might be profitably adopted, as a regulation, by individuals of our own society. It was, that slaves should not be permitted to be interrogated upon matters concerning their masters, but in cases of incest and conjuration. If this were strictly enforced, it is probable that more than half of the gossip and slanders agitating communities would be cut off.

"By the law we are considering, the seller of a slave was held to guarantee not only his bodily, but also his moral soundness, and he was likewise bound to expose their deficiencies, if known. In truth, each slave carried to the public place for sale, had attached to his person a writing, upon which was set forth all his good, as well as bad qualities. The consequences resulting from the condition of enciente women were exceptions to this principle of guaranty. If a slave committed theft, on the instigation of his master, the slave was punished in proportion to the theft, or the damage resulting. This seems to be the better reading of the 105th law of the twelve tables.

"It deserves consideration, while upon this subject, that, notwithstanding severe and unjust strictures are indulged in against slaveholding communities, very beneficial laws are found to exist among them in our day. For instance, it is held that the owner of a slave is under moral and legal obligation to supply his necessary wants; nor can he avoid the obligation thus to provide for him by permitting the slave to be absent. So the hirer and owner are both liable for the value of medical attendance furnished the slave—a decision reflecting very honourable distinction upon the humane court making. Gibson *vs.* Andrews, Ala., R. 66, Hogan *vs.* Carr, 6 Ala., 471. So, if a hirer refuses to provide medical aid for the slave, and insists on his labouring when physically unable, his owner may take him into possession, provide the necessary attention, and still hold the hirer liable for the sum stipulated. Ibid. The contract of hiring, covers also an agreement that the slave shall be honestly employed; and, if a hirer incites a slave to any immoral or dishonest act, the master may rescind the contract of hiring. Rasco. 5 Ala., R. 38. We are surprised, at every step into an investigation into the subjects of the civil law, to find how much of the principles of that law has become, without the authorities knowing it, parts of our slave law. In illustration of this position, it may be affirmed that the principle of the case of Rasco *vs.* Willis, cited as above, is the fruit of the civil law; for, in book xlv. of the Pandects, tit. 3, § v., we find the following:

"'Male fidei possessori servi, ex nulla causa per servum acquiri potest.'

"'He who possesses a slave in bad faith, ought to acquire nothing by the slave.'

"The right of holding slaves was defended by the Romans on two grounds: 1st. That the custom of nations had made enemies, taken in war, slaves to the conquering power; and 2d. That men who had no property to exchange for the means of subsistence, had authority to sell their liberty for the subsistence thus furnished by others. And, as was the condition of the parent, so should be the condition of the child."

These few remarks are sufficient to point out the leading features of an institution which flourished so universally in all the States of antiquity of which we have any authentic accounts. We cannot, however, leave this part of our subject without quoting an English work, which was designed to disparage the institution.* It is remarked that even the famous Roman, Cato, a man celebrated in all ages for his exact observance of the nicest rules of justice, in his conduct to his slaves seems entirely to have overlooked them. Notwithstanding his slaves had been very faithful and serviceable to him, when years came upon them, and they were no longer capable of hard labour, he made no scruple of turning them away, without the means of sustaining nature. True or not, as this assertion may be, how delighted the writer would be to learn, that in the *Southern States* there is no such thing allowed as *turning away* a slave because he is disabled, or for any other reason; and that, so far from turning them away when they become sick, old, or infirm, they are carefully nursed, and receive the best medical attendance the neighbourhood affords.

We do not attempt to deny that such cases may occur in the Northern States, among hireling slaves; but they never do in the Southern States, among domestic slaves. The sick factory hireling, the crippled or superannuated labourer, may suffer for want at the North; but not so the Southern slave. At the North, the streets may be infested with beggars—imposters, taught from infancy to impose upon the credulity of the unwary Southern stranger; but at the South we have no imposter beggars, excepting, perhaps, a few who escape from the *free soil* of the North, to learn a nobler calling in a more congenial clime. It is a notorious fact, that no slave at the South is a beggar; and how many hundreds, and even thousands, have spurned the hypocritical offers of starving freedom presented them by the North, through the contemptible emissaries sent among us by their abolition associations.

* Copley's History of Slavery.

CHAPTER III.

"This world is not for aye; nor 'tis not strange,
That even our loves should with our fortunes change;
For 'tis a question left us yet to prove,
Whether love leads fortune, or else fortune love."

From the decline of the Roman Empire to the middle of the fifteenth century, is a space in the history of Europe which demands but a passing glance. For the purposes of our present undertaking, it merely affords a connecting link between ancient and modern times. During this period, slavery was universally practised, and possessed, as all institutions must, local peculiarities.

In Italy, during the reign of the Roman Emperors, agriculture was the chief occupation of the great majority of the slaves; and here it may be remarked, as a fact worthy to be remembered, that *agriculture and slavery, as national characteristic s, have in all ages been companions.*

When the Northern Barbarians, as history terms them, invaded the southern parts of Europe, they carried off numbers of slaves as booty, and disseminated a system, already existing among them, all over the continent, and the whole of Europe fell into a colapsed state of barbarity, ignorance and superstition.

In Russia, Poland and Germany, slavery was perpetuated. In the former, it was a species of hereditary slavery or feudal vassalage. In the latter it originated in captivity, birth of slave parents, or by voluntary contract.* In the German States the system was in no respect burdensome; slaves were not sold out of their own State or province. They all pursued agriculture, and we only occasionally find that they were called upon to serve in the more domestic offices.

When the barbarians had reduced the Roman Empire to a state of subjection, land and slaves, as well as all other property was transferred into the hands of the conquerors; and society was divided into two grand classes, those who defended, and those who supported the Commonwealth; or, in other words, those who pursued the arts peace, and those who pursued the arts of war; of the latter class all were free, of the former the great mass were slaves, the nature of whose bondage varied in different regions. This thorough revolution in the affairs of the whole of Europe developed in the course of time, what is every where known as the *Feudal system*, a few vestiges of which are still to be found in some countries.

This system, a more rigorous one than which never existed, seems to have been practised among the Northern hordes long before their invasion of the Roman Empire. It is of higher antiquity than is generally supposed;† the rights of the feudal lords not having been originally acquired by usurpation, but derived from the primitive establishment of their people. For when the Barbarians gradually extended their work of spoliation, they also gradually changed the practice of slavery from that of the old Roman to their own; which, after the lapse of a few ages, was universally adopted and permanently established. By the tenth century this change was complete, and by the close of the twelfth it was in its greatest vigour.

History assures us that the inhabitants of the vanquished States were sometimes reduced to such extremes of distress that they voluntarily submitted to bondage as the price of life, and sought in slavery the only protection which could be obtained from the violence by which they were surrounded.‡

* Copley Hist. of Slavery.
† See an able article on the subject in the Southern Literary Messenger, of 1838.
‡ Allison's History of Europe.

That the hardships of the feudal system were perhaps greater than those of any which has prevailed since the world began, is owing, we think, chiefly to the spirit of the times during which it prevailed. For in those days the steel-clad Baron, perched on his steepest hill, and shut up in his strong castle, surrounded by his faithful retainers; alike ready to defy his king or his vassal; was wholly indifferent to the ravages going on in the valleys under his grim old castle walls. He felt none of the sufferings of his distracted bondsmen, nor was he annoyed to see his villages wrapt in flames, and his helpless serfs carried away captives from beneath his frowning bastions by the exulting invader. This was but the welcomed challenge, the resentment of which was destined to cover a whole generation with imperishable fame on many a bloody field.

The iron-hearted knight, cased in his armour from head to foot, and let loose at the head of his devoted followers like some raging lion; dealing death and desolation, wielding his massive instrument of war, both to the right and left; would break through the thickest ranks of the astonished peasants with nearly the same ease as he would mow down the ripening wheat of an adjacent field. He sought no end but glory, and knew no friend but fame. As to his dependant slaves they were fortunate in having his protection, and for *that boon*, they must needs be content with such a life as never-ending feuds afford. There was, indeed, no law for the weak and poor, but to submit to the overpowering demands of stern necessity. They, in accordance with the times, had but little consideration and still less sympathy extended to them; they were the devoted material with which the more fortunate nobles were enabled to enact those fearful dramas upon which later ages look back and are amazed.

The serfs or slaves of Europe, during these ages, were held under the sternest discipline, and were the recipients of the poorest remuneration. The ravages of the Normans, and the cruelty of the Huns, excited but little compassion, while it was wreaked only on the slaves of the country.* Notwithstanding, even at the time of Charlemagne, only a few thousand freemen were to be found interspersed among as many millions of slaves; yet, the slightest attempt to rebel against their stalwart masters was but the signal for the most unsparing retribution, and the severest regulations. Even the insurrections of the Jacquerie in France, of the peasants under Wat Tyler, in England, and of the Flemmings, under the brewer of Ghent, were repressed, says Allison, " with a cruelty of which history affords few examples."

This system has, however, given place to another, and all Europe is more or less changed. The haughty Baron no longer rears up his castellated towers, that he may unfurl the banner of defiance, oppression or rebellion. The grimvisaged retinue of the invading knight no longer dashes through the peaceful village, striking terror to the hearts of the affrighted serfs.

The feudal system has passed away from the nations of Europe, to make place for the stranger one which now prevails among them. Money has now taken the place of arms; duplicity the place of rank; cunning the place of courage; avarice the place of ambition; vice the place of folly; and mockery the place of superstition. This, however, like all the great changes of nature, was accomplished by slow degrees and imperceptible additions.

There is one truth in regard to the several changes which have taken place in the institution of slavery, which we should always remember, and it is this: In all the great changes which have taken place in any nation, in that relation of society called slavery, we find they have been brought about by the derelict conduct of the masters, and have never been instigated by the will of the slaves. The decay of the feudal system is thus truly accounted for by a historian of no

* Allison.

little celebrity.* He says, "the power of the nobles, incapable of being subverted by force, was undermined by opulence; and the emancipation of the people, for which so many thousands had perished, in vain, arose at length from the desires and follies of their oppressors. The Baron was formidable when his life was spent in arms, and he headed the feudal array which had grown up under the shadow of his castle walls; when his years were wasted in the frivolities of a court, and his fortune squandered in the luxuries of a metropolis, he became contemptible."

During those turbulent ages it cannot be expected that much respect was paid to the requirements of *civil* law; they were *military* ages, the strong right arm was the arm of justice, and the sword was the magistrate who settled all disputes. The physical world was in the ascendancy over the intellectual. There were, however some very equitable laws regulating slavery even in these unsettled times.

The children of slave mothers were slaves; and in whatever way slaves were acquired, they could be sold at the pleasure of their owners; the conditions of the transaction being regulated by different laws in different States. Slaves never gave evidence in the courts or tribunals. For some misdemeanors and crimes there were distinct laws for the two grand divisions of society. What would be a scriminal offence in a slave, would not necessarily be such in a freeman. There are such laws among us, for instance, an "assault and battery," where the parties are both white persons, is punished by fine or imprisonment; but if the offender is a slave he is to suffer death, unless the assault is so triling as to render the punishment obviously unjust.

This law is particularly denounced by abolitionists, and is not favourably regarded even by some slaveholders themselves. But we think the justice of it, and to a certain extent, the absolute necessity of it, can be demonstrated by the most ordinary reasoner. Among the great catalogue of crimes, there are two grand classes, one of which affects the rights and privileges of individuals only, whilst the other affects the peace of society, the well being of the State, and either directly or indirectly, the very existence of both. And what would be more certain to destroy the best regulated State, than such laws as would punish a slave for an offence in which rebellion is added to assault, in the same way, as a citizen would be punished for an affence which, though embodied in the same act, is simply an assault, and has no connection whatever with th eidea of rebellion.

The Roman yoke was withdrawn from Britain in the early part of the fifth century; and about a hundred years after, the Saxon heptarchy was permanently established. During the existence of this government, which lasted about two hundred and fifty years, England was a slaveholding State, and the slave trade was extensively carried on, reaching frequently even as far as the Roman marts. Parents would not unfrequently sell their own offspring into pertual slavery in a foreign land.

In the year 693, slaves were exempted from labouring for their masters on Sundays. It has been estimated that during the Saxon period, there were upwards of a million of slaves in England, by whom the land was cultivated; these were called *national slaves*, and could not lawfully be sold out of England. The children of these slaves inherited the condition of their parents. Among the domestic slaves of this period, were those who performed the menial duties of the household and farm, and all others, from the clown or jester down to the humble swineherd. They were transferred or bequeathed at the pleasure of their masters; but the agricultural, or national vassals were transferred or bequeathed only with the estates on which they lived and laboured.

* Allison.

CHAPTER IV.

"Oh, man ————
Thy love is lust, thy friendship all a cheat,
Thy smiles hypocricy, thy words deceit!
By nature vile, ennobled but by name,
Each kindred brute might bid thee blush for shame.

We now come to that part of the history of this institution which leads to our own system, and will perhaps be more interesting to the reader. We allude to African slavery.

As far as we have any information, it appears that within the limits of Africa, slavery has always been a universal practice; and there is probably little exaggeration in saying, that with the exception of a few colonies and settlements, every man in Africa is either a slave or a master. And that negroes have been to a greater or less extent, imported from Africa into other countries, for centuries past, for the express purpose of being enslaved, is apparent from the history of every nation which has flourished in the South of Europe. We will, however confine our observations to the *Atlantic* trade chiefly.

Owing to the mildness of the climate, the fertility of the soil, and the barbarism of the population, that part of Africa from which our negroes were originally brought, is a country in which labour is comparatively unknown. From the Prince down to the meanest slave, the wants of the African are few aud of easy gratification; on this account there is little necessity for *co-operation* in labour. Each individual being in a great measure independent of the assistance of others, but like roving herds, each one depends alike on unassisted nature for support. In such a state of things it can easily be supposed that the disappearance or loss of a portion of a tribe, would, in time of peace, be productive of no essential inconvenience to the remainder; neither would the acquisition of numbers be an essential gain. But on account of unbridled passions, and universal idleness, the invariable accompanyments of a savage state, many serious feuds must necessarily arise between individuals of different tribes; these feuds soon take the form of local quarrels, and out of these spring the most sanguinary wars between neighbouring princes. In the battles which are fought, a number of prisoners are taken by one, or both parties; but these prisoners, which in times of peace would be of no advantage to the tribe, in times of war become positive burdens. From motives of revenge they are not liberated, and from motives of self preservation, and with an eye to the incumbrance which prisoners always are, especially in savage warfare, it becomes necessary that they should be disposed of.

Precisely in accordance with these truths, we find it was formerly the universal practice to sacrifice these victims to their heathen gods; and not until the idolatrous victors could be induced to forego the imaginary approval of their gods for the sake of trinkets and European novelties were the captives rescued from death, to be bought into slavery in some foreign land. It has now become the fashion, however, among philanthropists, to think that if the matter were left to captive to decide, he would infinitely prefer death to slavery; this fashionable opinion may be correct, but we can only say, that so far as the ordinary principles of untutored nature is concerned, it is highly probable that as these prisoners by being transported, only change savage for civilized masters, they would rather prefer this change to the dubious allurements of death. And even if after this change is effected they still have a longing after death, it is not probable any moral or religious compunctions would prevent their resorting to it.

There is a vast difference between the several tribes of the African race, both in point of civilization and mental endowments. The most superior are the Jolofs, and those of Guber and Hausa, who are said to have made some advances towards civilization when first discovered by the Portuguese. The Ashantees, a powerful tribe in the interior of the North of Africa, were the chief people to supply the Spaniards and Portuguese with slaves (captives taken in war,) when the trade became one of notoriety. The district along the South-western coast of Africa, commonly called lower Guinea, has always been a great slave mart. The negroes brought from this region, usually known as Congos, have always been considered the most valuable, on account of their being susceptible of some slight education in mechanical and other arts. The Eboes and Mongullas, commonly called among themselves Gullas, are inferior to the Congos on account of their unconquerable laziness, and the impossibility of teaching them any higher art than that of breaking the sod with a hoe; they are, however, susceptible of more endurance in a hot climate than any other branch of the human race. There are some other tribes who have never been disturbed by the Christians, for purposes of trade, because of their supreme barbarity and utter worthlessness.

In the fifteenth century there arose an extraordinary spirit of enterprize, and love of adventure on the sea. Navigation had become a science, and among other nations, the Portuguese the most expert in the management of maratime affairs; to this nation we are indebted for the African slave-trade.

It is said to have originated in the following way. In the year 1440, while the Portuguese were exploring the coast of Africa, a captain, named Anthony Gonzales, seized some Moors near Cape Bajador, on the Western coast, a little to the South of Barbary, and just at the entrance of the great desert. Two years afterwards their celebrated Prince, Henry, commanded Gonzales to carry his prisoners back to Africa. He did so, and landing them at Rio del Oro, a little farther South, received from the Moors in exchange, a quantity of gold dust, and ten negroes, with which cargo he returned to Lisbon. These negroes had perhaps been taken captives in war by the Moors, who, according to the usages of barbarous nations, felt themselves at liberty to dispose of their captives at the best market, or in exchange for their own countrymen. But the speculation proving profitable to Gonzales, others of the same nation soon embarked in it, and the Moors found many purchasers for their captives.

Towards the close of the same century, the Spaniards discovered and took possession of the West India Islands, and having, in their inordinate thirst for gold, compelled the wretched natives to labour in the mines of Hispaniola, till their race was nearly exterminated, and the sources of their wealth in consequence, closed, a vehement desire to pursue their lucrative, though laborious projects, inspired the thought of procuring slaves from Africa. Accordingly, about the year 1503, a few slaves were sent by the Portuguese to the Spanish colonies. In 1511, Ferdinand the fifth of Spain, allowed a larger importation of them. They were, however, found unfit for the labour which they were destined; and as numbers of gold mines then began to be wrought in Mexico and Peru, those of Hispaniola were the less regarded. The labour of the slaves was therefore turned to agricultural pursuits.

This trade was encouraged by Charles the fifth, the successor of Ferdinand. He granted a patent for the annual importation of 4000 negroes into the West India Islands.

In the French colonies, during the reign of Louis the thirteenth, African slavery was introduced on a large and extensive scale.

The importation of negroes into the British American colonies commenced during the reign of Queen Elizabeth, under the immediate supervision of Sir John Hawkins. During the succeeding reigns of James 1st, Charles 1st and 2d, the slave trade in the British colonies steadily and rapidly increased; and Great

Britain far outstripped any other nation in the world, in the extent to which she carried the trade.

In the year 1793, Great Britain imported more than half the number of slaves imported by all the European powers put together. From the year 1700 to 1786,* the number of slaves imported by British subjects into the Island of Jamaica alone, was *six hundred and ten thousand;* or about seven thousand one hundred every year. In the year 1771, *forty seven thousand one hundred and forty-six* negroes were imported into the British colonies, in British ships alone.

Is it not difficult to believe that Great Britain, who so short a time ago, was the most extensive and cruel slave-trader in the world, is the same Great Britain who is now the greatest suppresser of that very trade? The entire number of negroes said to have been enslaved, (that is transported and landed in the British colonies, for those who died on the voyage across the Atlantic are not included) by Great Britain is over *three millions.*

For the great majority of negroes now in the United States, English traders are to be thanked. Let us, therefore, before we utter our thanks, examine our affairs and see to what extent these thanks are due.

The census of 1790 affords us the earliest information as to the number of negroes in the country at the close of the revolution; and though there will be error, yet the error will not be very material, if we adopt that census as indicating the true number in the States at the close of the war.

The population of the free States was then as follows: Whites, 1,852,116. Free coloured, 29,435. Slaves, 49,257.

The population of the slaveholding States was: Whites, 1,201,351. Free coloured and Indians, 28,265. Slaves, 646,183.

In *Vermont* there were 85,268 whites, 255 free coloured, and 16 slaves.

In *New-Hampshire* there were 141,197 whites, 630 free coloured, and 158 slaves.

In *Massachusetts* the negro trade had been prohibited in 1778, and there was not a slave (that is a negro bondman) in the State. There were 373,324 whites, and 5,463 free negroes. In this, as in other New-England States, there was comparatively little necessity, and less profit, for the peculiar labour to which the African disposition is adapted, viz: agriculture on a large scale; for the negro is dissatisfied on a farm, his predilection is decidedly for the large plantation, on which reside fifty or a hundred of his associates; he there has every facility for that merry and blithsome intercourse, the love of which is a striking characteristic of the race; whereas, the lonesome life he would lead on a small New-England farm would be distressing to him. The climate of these States is against the health and comfort of the negro; his native home is under a tropical sun, and notwithstanding he can endure, without serious inconvenience, the extreme degree of heat incident to such a climate as Africa's, he is utterly averse to the frigid blasts of winter. There not being any means by which money could be made in these States, through the medium of slave labour within their limits, is the chief cause of its never having been resorted to on a larger scale.

In *Rhode Island* the slave-trade was always extensively carried on until prohibited by law. The rum distilled in the West Indies was carried to Africa to purchase negroes, and the negroes purchased in Africa were carried to the West Indies to purchase rum; this profitable trade was continued by those interested in it, to the latest possible period.* It was the source of wealth to

* Copley's Hist. Slavery. Winterbotham's States of America.

* Winterbotham, vol. 2d, p. 233—239.

many of the people of New Port. The population of this State was 64,470 whites, 3,407 free negroes, and 948 slaves.

In *Connecticut* there were 232,374 whites, 2,810 free negroes, and 2,764 slaves.

In *New-York* there were 314,142 whites, 4,654 free negroes, and 21,324 slaves.

In *New-Jersey* there were 170,954 whites, 1,762 free negroes, and 11,423 slaves. For about six or eight years previous to 1790, there had been a remarkable increase in the number of slaves, and an equally remarkable decrease in the number of free negroes. But for a space of over forty-five years, it is to be observed that the increase of the black population (including both slave and free) was at the same rate as that of the white population. At this time the principal pursuit of the people of New-Jersey was agriculture, and that on a small scale; a kind of farming not calculated to enhance slave labour, though perhaps able to support it. And it is said by a writer, who travelled all over North America and the West Indies, when preparing his history;† that agriculture (in this State) had not been improved to that degree, which, from long experience, we might rationally expect, and which the fertility of the soil, in many places, certainly encouraged. Evincing either a want of enterprize on the part of proprietors, or a fault in the system of labour; the latter cause is perhaps that which may most reasonably be assigned, for no one can impute the energy and enterprize of the people of New-Jersey. This is a good instance of the unprofitableness and misapplication of slave labour in the Northern States.

In *Pennsylvania* there were 424,079 whites, 6,557 free negroes, and 3,703 slaves.

In *Delaware*, which is more assimilated in climate and natural resources with Maryland and Virginia than any other State, lying as it does, in the same latitude, and possessing similar natural features, we find a greater proportion of slaves than in any State North of it. There were 46,308 whites, 3,899 free negroes, and 8,887 slaves. This is the last of the free States which then held slaves.

Since that census was taken, all the 45,371 slaves held in these States have disappeared, and the current which swept them away, has borne along with it we cannot tell how many times that number from the Southern States, through the agency of those good abolition gentlemen, who never fail to let "charity, in golden links of love, connect them with the brotherhood of man;" the essence of which golden links of love is the golden rule, "rob Peter to pay Paul," or rob white to pay black. In all these States the white population has regularly and rapidly increased; but the negroes, where are they? Some have been sent to their father land, *Liberia*, to set up a model republic, and to enlighten and amend the civil code of Ethiopia. Some have gone the way of all flesh, through sheer want of that same thing, wherewith they might have been nourished and kept alive, but for the want of it. Some have emigrated Westward, and the glory of their enlightened minds have shed lustre on the name of Ohio. Some choice spirits among them are the pride and boast of divers Northern penitentiaries and alms-houses. And some remain, the sportive imps of fun and frolic, in the large cities of the North; and have their annual and semi-annual exhibitions, for the benefit of their gaping brethren of a paler hue; of the spontaneous effervescence of the spirit of liberty fresh from their American bosoms. And for the rest, they are among the most *influential* and *respectable* citizens of the Northern community.

† Winterbotham.

In *Maryland* there were 208,649 whites, 8,043 free negroes and Indians, and 103,036 slaves.

In *Virginia* there were 442,117 whites, 12,866 free negroes and Indians, and 292,627 slaves. It must be remarked here, that the increase of the slave population of Virginia, for fourteen years preceding this census, was less than it had been for a century before; owing to the fact, that about 30,000 slaves died of the small-pox or camp-fever, caught from the British army; or were inveigled off, while Lord Cornwallis was roving over the State.

In *Kentucky*, then in its infancy, there were 61,133 whites, 114 free negroes, and 12,430 slaves.

In *North-Carolina*, there were 288,205 whites, 4,975 free negroes and Indians, and 100,571 slaves.

In *Tennessee*, there were 5,813 whites, and 1,161 slaves.

In *South-Carolina*, there were comparatively more slaves than in any other State; the population being 140,278 whites, and 107,094 slaves. A great loss in slave property was incurred by this State during the revolutionary war, and was, comparatively speaking, about three times as great as that met with by Virginia. During the three years the British were in possession of Charleston, they stole away and sold in the West Indies, no less than 25,000 negroes.

In *Geoıgia*, there were 55,156 whites and 29,264 slaves. The circumstances connected with slavery in the early settlement of this State, present a striking contrast with those of Massachusetts and other New-England States; in these latter, slavery was originally introduced and considerably practised, but as the population increased, hired labour took the place of slave labour. In Georgia, exactly the reverse was the case. The original "board of Trustees for the settling and establishing the colony of Georgia," consisting of twenty-one opulent and humane gentlemen in England, prohibited the use of *negroes* in the colony, and the importation of rum.* By this one ruthless stroke of philanthropy, the settlers of Georgia were deprived the two-fold blessing enjoyed by their more fortunate neighbours of Rhode Island; *they* could accumulate wealth by trading in Africans and rum, but Georgia was designed for a *free* State, and Africans were not to be used, neither rum. This was about the year 1732. The plan was a theoretical one, and was, perhaps, the worst that could have been adopted; it was certainly productive of the most pernicious consequences to the prosperity of the colony. The paramount object of the trustees being to raise silk and wine, they deemed it inexpedient to introduce slave labour. And in addition to this, the colony being, at this early period, a kind of barrier between Carolina, on the one side, and the Spanish settlement at St. Augustine, on the other, the trustees fell into the very general, though equally erroneous belief, that negroes would rather weaken, than strengthen, its defensive powers. These were the chief reasons why the settlers were prohibited from employing slaves; but the absurd restriction had a visible effect. It was found impracticable in such a climate, and without African labour, for the colony to flourish; the enterprise, therefore, proved a failure. In a country so rich, with a climate so favourable, and a soil so productive as that of Georgia, the colonists, nevertheless, gradually disappeared, and effectually deserted the enterprise; because they were convinced they could never succeed under such impolitic restrictions.

The trustees finding that the colony was languishing under their trans-atlantic care, resigned their charter, in the year 1752, to the King of England, and the deserted colony became a royal government. History informs us that, at this time, "the vestiges of cultivation were scarcely perceptible in the forests, and in England all commerce with the colony was neglected." But, immediately on the

* See Winterbotham's States of America.

government being changed, the people became possessed of the same privileges which their neighbours enjoyed; prominent among which, was the privilege of cultivating their rich lands, by the only profitable means, which is no other than slave labour. Several years elapsed, however, before the value of the lands became generally appreciated. And about the year 1760 a sprit of enterprise sprung up, which has ever since been a characteristic of this State. And it should be particularly observed, that no portion of the population, under the new laws, increased so rapidly, and no system of labour became so generally disseminated, as that of the African slave.

The experiment has, therefore, we think, been farily tried, both North and South have had ample opportunities to discover the interest and policy of their respective sections. All the New-England States have tried slave labour, but it was not found profitable and was abandoned. In the South, the State of Georgia was, for a period of twenty years, not only a *free*, but decidedly a *white* colony. White labour was here found to be incompatible with the climate; slave labour was introduced; and in the short space of thirty years, nearly thirty thousand slaves were actively employed in the pursuits of agriculture. And, at the present day, slaveholding Georgia will favourahly compare with any State in the Union.

Now, "facts and dates are stubborn things," and the facts cited with regard to the expulsion in one quarter, and the introduction in another, of slave labor, are two *stubborn* facts. They are the legitimate effects of the same remote, but stubborn cause, *necessity*. And all the abolition societies, colonization societies, and Wilmot Provisos in Christendom, can never change those facts. The Congress of the United States may violate the constitution, and, in its corrupt and faithless career, it may abolish *law*, right and justice, but it can never abolish these facts; for, as long as the climate, soil, and all the physical causes at the South remain unchanged, just so long must that soil, if cultivated at all, be cultivated by the negro slave. And precisely the reverse proposition is applicable to the North; all sylogistic ravings and abolition pulpit-exhortations to the contrary, notwithstanding.

We have now finished our brief historical sketch of slavery. We have glanced at a few of the leading features of the institution, and have become sufficiently acquainted with it to learn that it is a momentous subject, and one that involves a profound inquiry. It may be viewed in a moral and in a religious, a political, economical, and a comparative view; also, in a *States rights* point of view. Each of these views of the institution we will briefly lay before the reader, and then call to mind some of the chief combinations of causes which have effected its abolition in some countries, and tend to effect it in others.

CHAPTER V.

"What opposite discoveries we have seen!
[Signs of true genius and of empty pockets,]
One makes new noses, one a guillotine,
One breaks your bones, one sets them in their sockets."

THIS chapter will be devoted to the "opposite discoveries we have seen." It will contain some of the "signs of true genius," which point out the English and American philanthropists of late days, as the lucky people, who are, of all others, most likely to produce the *philosopher's stone*.

The English people are perhaps the most astonishing race of biped animals inhabiting the known world; excepting only, perhaps, that tribe of men, each of whom, is said by a French explorer, to be provided *with a tail*, and which may be found in some of the unknown parts of Africa. They are, with this obvious exception, probably the most astonishing bipeds in nature. They do such queer tricks, they have such queer whims, and are with all such queer fellows, that it makes us feel quite queer to talk about them. But the queerest thing these queer people ever did, remains to be told, and it can be told in very brief terms. Once upon a time, as I've been told,

> "The King of France with 3,000 men,
> Marched up the hill and then marched down again."

This was a very funny thing, and every body laughed; it was *so droll* in the king, and *so like him too*. But after all, what the King of France did was nothing to what the people of England did! Why, they with 3,000,000 *men!!* marched *down* the hill, and then marched *up* again.

It has already been said, that the people of England have, from first to last, enslaved 3,000,000 Africans. The magnanimous generosity of their enlightened minds induced them to sell these three millions of slaves for the highest price they could obtain; the higher the price the slave could bring, of course the better would be the condition of the slave; and though the seller's purse would be all the heavier for it, yet such a consideration was quite overlooked. No Englishman, in the days of the slave trade, or at the present time either, would, for a moment, consider the value of a few guineas, when he had an African to sell. After having pocketed the rich proceeds of this immense traffic, the great Englishman's good heart sickened; and having violently precipitated himself first half way down the hill, then slowly dragging himself down the other half, he stopped to take breath, and then, when it was alas too late, it in a very forcible manner appeared to him that he had done wrong in going down so far; so he roused himself, and, feeling all those delicate compunctions of conscience so peculiar to himself, he took up his line of march up hill again. Through the purest motives of Christian humility and charity the English people brought down upon their nation the admiring eyes of all the world, by cheerfully emancipating the helpless and untutored slaves of their defenceless colonies.

The old system only gave way for a new kind of slavery, which was still more congenial with English humanity. As might be expected in all great changes of society, where the aggrandizement of a small portion only is consulted, this change was of no benefit to the great mass of people concerned; it advanced neither master nor slave. The old slaveholder, now politely called the employer, not being bound, as formerly, to support and keep in health those in his service, but being left with the power of procuring labor at the lowest possible rate, that of barely keeping soul and body together, became unmindful of all other considerations, save only that of gain. This new system of slavery is peculiarly English, but it is, to a certain extent, becoming Americanized. The principal distinguishing features are these: in the new system, the slave is mocked by being called a freeman; he lives in rags and misery, filth, drunkenness and vice. In the old system, the slave was exempt from the absurd mockery of the new; he was well clad, lived in comfort, sobriety, and comparative morality. In the new, he shares his squalid hut with cattle, swine and poultry, or his damp and noisome cellar with innumerable rats. In the old, even in the British West Indies,* he shared his comfortable cot with his family, and partook his evening meal in contentment and happiness; and always knew that let what would come, *he*, at least,

* Winterbotham.

would be provided for on the morrow. In the new and improved system, the child of seven or eight years is put to hard labour; and once located, poverty (the overruling genius of the system) condemns him, for the remainder of his life, to the most burdensome state of slavery; that is, the slave of destitution, ignorance and disease; and what is more cruel than all, the slave of an avaricious, disinterested master, who cares little for his welfare, and as little for his life. In the old system, the slave-born child knew nothing of labour, till he became sufficiently old to endure it; the fourteenth year being the usual age at which one was set to work. He was not the victim of poverty, but rather the recipient of plenty; not the blind dupe of ignorance, but rather in the enjoyment of useful instruction; not the shattered wreck of disease, but rather, as is proverbially the case, one of the most robust, healthy, long-lived of the human race; not the hireling of a master to whom his life and health was of no consideration, because it was of no value, but the slave of an interested master, who was compelled by law, policy and common interest to promote the health and long preservation of his property.

A thousand other comparisons might be drawn, to show what an *improvement* the new system is, and how far superior it is, in every respect, to the old.

The people of England are all philanthropists; it would appear they do every thing for the good of mankind in general. They amuse themselves at the expense of other people, and in spite of fate, they amuse other people at their own expense. Among the first class of amusements, is a kind intimately connected with our present undertaking; and it will, probably, amuse the reader to see the gross absurdities in which these queer bipeds have for ages indulged. We allude to the African slave trade, as conducted by them, and the horrid abuses of the laws of slavery as practised by them. And among the second class of amusements, is the grand farce which they so comically performed, when they abolished slavery in the West Indies with one hand, whilst with the other they were making slaves in the East. Truly of them it may be said, the right hand knows not what the left is doing.

We cannot be otherwise than astonished, when the Englishman tells us seriously that millions were sold by their own countrymen, at a profit of from three to four hundred per cent., not for the sake of gain, but for the civilization of the slave. We are told that the natives of America being unable to endure the hardships of labour to which they were forced by the white race, and to which they were entirely unaccustomed, became, in a short time, almost extinct; and their places in the gold mines, and in the fields, were filled by imported Africans. Now, the part the English people took in this business, was *not* for the sake of the profits, it was exclusively the offspring of that noble liberality peculiar to the English breast. It was all done for the sake of the slave, and the merchants or traders pocketed the profits, merely because 'tis somewhere said, "riches are not to be despised." But virtue is its own reward, and the Englishman has the consolation of knowing, that his nation has far outstripped all others in the African slave trade. This is sufficient compensation, and all that can be desired; for, as to that sordid ore, that dross, that filthy lucre, that *gold* which was the price of the slave, it could not circulate in all England; the very idea would offend the English breast; and it may be very well doubted, whether there is a single pound of such capital to be found within the British realm.

The grand results of British abolition, will be recorded in their proper place. For the present, it is enough for us to know how the Hawkins' have become Clarksons; how the English thief has become the English benefactor, by first pilfering, then generously restoring what he has no further economical use for; how England has made millions of slaves, and how England has made as many freemen; and how all was done for the benefit of the human race *generally*, and the

African race in particular; how England colonized America, and how she trusted to the profits of slave labor, for the support of her colonies, and for a large contribution to her own revenue; how she waxed too greedy, and wished to exact more than her share of the said profits; how the colonies had a consultation, and how they determined to rid themselves of such a domineering and bullying, though always great and good connection; how the two parties did lay on the hard knocks in the tug of war; and how the colonies were victorious, and became a distinct government; and how the citizens of the new government determined to continue in the same pursuits, and to perpetuate the same institutions, among which was slavery, which were taught them by good old England; how poor old England, after being quite crippled in the wars, took a while to refresh herself; and how when she put her hands in her pockets, she missed so much of that filthy lucre, the produce of slave labour; and how she raved and tossed about for a while, and finally swore she would liberate her slaves, because it was really a pity to keep the poor creatures in service; how she cajoled herself about the immense generosity of her nature, and how she set herself up as a model for all Christian nations; how she waxed envious of the new republic, which retained its slaves and prospered; and how she would give any thing to get her slaves back again, *even if they came from Calcutta*, but which alas she could not do; so she suddenly dries up her tears, and seeks to be amused by abusing America; for doing what? The same thing she had industriously taught America to do.

Nothing is more delightful to the great mass of English cockneys, than to collect together at Exeter hall, or some other place, and rehearse the "tempest" *in the tea-pot.* To talk loud, and look sour, to bully and bluster about slave labour in America, forgetting all the while how totally unaware the unconscious Americans are of all the grave proceedings conducted so bravely across the sea. They abuse and falsify the Americans on account of slavery, notwithstanding the produce of slave labour enriches thousands of their countrymen, and is perhaps the chief source of their own support. The blustering cockneys however forget this fact, the system of slavery practical among us, is a legacy from England. She enslaved the African, she introduced him among us, and now cannot sufficiently abuse us, because we retain what she taught us to possess.

It has been suggested in more than one quarter, that the capital now circulating in England, and which was originally accumulated from the *slave trade*, could, if applied to that purpose, purchase all the slaves in America. And this is no random remark, it is the result of calculation. Almost every negro who was ever brought from Africa to this country, was so transported by English or Northern slave-traders, and all we say with regard to Englishmen, applies also to the Yankees. The great mass, however, was the subject of British trade. We will, therefore, state the proposition. Where a slave was worth, on an average, $200, when the trade was conducted by the English people, he is now worth $300. On the other hand, the natural increase of available slave population is not more than about *two* per cent per annum; whereas money, the money which was originally paid for the slaves, is at the lowest calculation, always worth *three* per cent.. Any increase in the value of slaves, is therefore fully counterbalanced by the greater natural increase belonging to money. And it is a matter from which all possible doubt is removed, that if the capital derived from the slave trade, could be collected and appropriated as above mentioned, there would not only be a sufficiency for the purpose, but there would be *an immense surplus which could be judiciously laid out in donations to the poor of Ireland.*

Now as it is the earnest desire of all true Englishmen to promote the liberation of every African slave, why is not this capital appropriated for the purpose? It cannot be urged as a reason, that it would enrich the slave-holder to purchase his slave, for the very capital in question came originally from the purse of the slave-holder; the slave he now owns is but the equivalent of the money he has put in the Englishman's pocket. It cannot be given as a reason, that it would impoverish the Englishman; such would involve a contradiction, and the conclusion would be an absurdity. We all know, and the Englishman tells us, he is penitent, and grieves at what he has done; his heart's desire is to liberate the poor African he has enslaved; then surely he would be rejoiced to retrace his steps and undo what he has done. The last thing he did for the African, was to sell him and pocket the proceeds, the first he should now do, would be to buy the African and disgorge the proceeds which have so long been accumulating in his pocket; then having returned the money, and received the negro back into his possession, he could dispose of him as becomes a sinner who has repented of his sins. Who can doubt, that if our slaves could but be transferred back to the English people from whom we got them, they would be immediately liberated *sans recompense.* Time will no doubt prove that our estimate of English philanthropy is correct, and we would sincerely advise owners of slaves who desire to sell their property, not to be precipitate, but wait a short time till all this British competition is brought into the market.

What has been said of England, is equally true of the non-slave-holding States of America. The people of New-England particularly resemble those of Old England, they must always have a hobby to ride; for without such a thing they could not live. The King of France marched up the hill and then marched down, the English hosts marched down the hill and then marched up, but the Yankee people *compromise* the matter, and they march round and round the hill; being mounted on their hobby, they never tire.

The people of New-England must always have some class or sect of people at whom they can aim their squibs, and over whom they can exult and bully. When they were driven by persecution from their European homes to the unsettled wilds of America, they had scarcely located themselves securely in their new homes, before they fell into the same course of persecution, from which they had so recently fled. And calling themselves free, solemnly ordained in their public assembles, that no person who was not a member of some church within their limits, should be entitled to the privilege of a freeman.* Thus New-England, a worthy copy of the original at that time, in some matters at least, was not only the curtailer of liberty within its limits, but was the religious oppressor.

Whilst Old England was manufacturing slaves by theft and corruption, New-England was eliminating freemen by the enactment of laws based on the ground of religious superiority. About twenty-five years after this pious and charitable law was enacted, the whole force of it seems to have fallen upon the society of friends, or Quakers. Why they should have been the particular objects of persecution, does not appear; but, perhaps, they proved to be the tamest hobby, and for that reason could be ridden with whip and spur, without danger either to the life, or limb of the rider. Be that however, as it may, it is certain the united colonies of New-England, petitioned some of the neighbouring colonies to co-operate with them "in taking effectual methods to suppress the Quakers, and prevent their doctrines being propagated in the country." This, of course, was all right; but it would be very wrong for any Southern slave holding State, or any number of them, to take effectual methods to suppress the *abolitionists*, and prevent *their* doctrines being propagated in the country. This would immediately be styled an offensive and unlawful proceeding; and the poor Southern State which was so reckless as to commit the error, would be chastised by the whole christian community of the North, and perhaps any citizen of such a State, who was so unfortunate as to be within the limits of a Northern State, would be vio-

* See Winterbotham's States of America.

lently seized upon and retained as a hostage, a prisoner of war, a living witness of the valorous resentment of the North.*

The people of New-England and the other Northern States require a hobby, but it must be one that grows, and in its growth supplies new sources of amusement. It must be one whose wounds and bruises heal rapidly; for it becomes tiresome to them to ride, unless they can always find a fresh spot upon which to lay the lash. These people were perhaps never better accommodated than when they mounted the South sixty years ago. In the South, they found their very beau ideal of a hobby; it was strong, it was growing, it was gentle and easily broken to the harness; it was fat, happy and content, and wholly indifferent to the burden of the North. It was like an unsuspecting lazy horse, and bore the pale-faced rider patiently enough through many a boggy spot over which the rider never could have passed without him. Of late, however, the equestrian has grown prodigious, his ease, comfort and high keeping, have brought on dropsical symptoms; his weight has become enormous, and his huge legs encompass the tired animal from Maine to California. The hobby sometimes seems to be waking up, then relapses to its torpor. Mr. Wilmot's thorny switch awakes it for a while, but Mr. Clay's composing drugs restore its sleep again. The noisy clatter of contending jockies arouse it from a dream, but the croaking chorus of some degrading compromiser receives it back to sleep. At one time the infatuated hobby did seem to have an eye partly opened to the day, there was some evidence that it felt the mighty weight and overgrown pressure of its gormandizing rider. We thought we heard its impatient stamping, and its pawing up the earth; there was something like the white foam of its anger rising from the valley of the Mississippi, and the snuffing of his nostrils was heard at Nashville. But the rider still rides on, and *the hobby hobbles on.*

CHAPTER VI.

"Cal—Cal—Cal Caliban,
Has a new master—get a new man."

There is a manifest inequality in the conditions of mankind, and this inequality is evidently not artificial, but the natural, the necessary state of man. The first point then to be decided, is the extent to which this necessary inequality extends. It has frequently been the error of persons who attempt to discover sin and immortality in slavery; unwittingly to take men in a savage condition to be in the state for which nature intended them; or what is much the same, to assume the savage condition of man as a standard, and from it to remodel the civilized portion of the human race; and because the roving savage, whose means of subsistance are derived chiefly from fishing and hunting, has neither inducement nor means to encumber himself with a retinue of slaves; they leap to the conclusion that slavery must be an artificial state, and could never have been that in which the God of nature intended man to be placed.

Others fall into the opposite error, and being disgusted at the barbarities of a

* During the summer of 1849, upon its becoming known in the city of New-York that an abolitionist, named Barrett, had been lodged in jail in South-Carolina, for circulating incendiary papers in the State, it was proposed among the people, and announced in one of the papers of that city, that a distinguished citizen of South-Carolina, there on a visit, should be forcibly retained as a hostage.

savage condition, present to their minds a most pleasing contrast, by summing up all the civil and moral advantanges of a civilized state, entirely forgetting to enumerate a single vice, or disadvantage belonging to this state of society. But it appears to us, that in order to discover the real essence of man's nature, and to form a correct idea of the *necessary extent* of that inequality belonging to his race, we should proceed in the same way we would, for the same purpose, with regard to any other race of animals, or class of created beings, viz: examine his history for centuries back, and if practicable, from his very origin. Discover what have been the chief characteristics of the race, and having once become acquainted with these, we may rely on their continuing unchanged. If we find that the predilections, pursuits, faculties and propensities of man, have always tended to produce the same results; we have no reason to suppose that this tendency will ever be changed. If we find that the human family has always been divided into classes, whose privileges and enjoyments have been unequal at all times, we conceive of no reason why this inequality should cease to exist, and indeed we know of no possible means by which it could be obviated.

If the laws of nature remain unchanged, we have no right to suppose that this one law of inequality of condition can ever change; but it would be difficult to conceive of a community of men, wherein there was not an inequality of condition; in fact, history affords no instance of the kind.

Was not the mind of Newton entitled to vastly more consideration, in the intellectual world, than that of his cook or butcher? Would not the accomplished, well trained and accoutred knight have commanded more consideration, in the physical world, than his awkward and untutored groom? In short, is not genius one condition and idiocy another? The huge athletic man one condition, and the miserable dwarf another? Are not amazing inequalities *necessarily* found, both in the intellectual and physical structure of man? Can it then be said in view of these unalterable and stubborn facts; that vast inequalities do not necessarily exist in the several relations and conditions of man? And are not these inequalities manifestly the *sacred will of God?* The human family is then naturally and necessarily subjected to inequalities of condition.

As to the *African*, there can be no doubt that he will long continue to be enslaved by the white man; for it is absolutely certain, that long before European ships began to explore the coast of Africa, negroes were carried away by Arabian caravans to be put in bondage by the white race of the North. It is a historical fact, that "ancient Egypt was at one period the principal seat of science, literature, arts and civilization, and that the various nations or tribes of the African race were in close contact, and had a pretty extensive intercourse, not only with the Egyptians, but also with the Phœnicians, and afterwards with the Romans.

What did they profit by this association? Literally nothing. For while the then almost equally barbarous people of Greece, Asia Minor, and Magna Græcia, raised themselves, in a comparatively brief period, to the highest civilization and refinement, the negro race of Africa continues, with but one single solitary exception, down even to the present day, immersed in the greatest barbarism.

It is not possible that during the space of *four thousand years*, opportunities have not been afforded some of them to make some slight advances in the scale of human improvement. Is there any proof that they have had the sagacity that is inherent in the Caucasian family, to profit by contact with more favoured nations? It appears to be a fact, that Africa has not produced a single name worthy to rank with the heroes and sages of the world."

From the remotest antiquity, they have been "hewers of wood and drawers of water" for others; and from the fact, that during these thousands of years they have made no advancement towards civilization and self-government, whilst other nations under the same circumstances invariably have; the obvious inference is, they are incapable of so doing. That "as a body, they are incapable of living in a civilized state, except in the condition of servitude to their more favoured fellow men." There is, and ever has been, a marked inequality between the African and European races; and until it is demonstrated that this inequality is at an end, we cannot do otherwise than expect its continuance.

Whilst we maintain that the African race is now, and probably will ever continue to be, an inferior race, we do not for a moment agree with those writers who pronounce that race a distinct species. We are, on the contrary, glad to have at our elbow a late argument in favour of the doctrine of "the Unity of the Human Race; and will, with the greatest satisfaction, borrow a few remarks from one who unites in what he says, the twofold authority of the philosopher and the christian.*

"The ways of God are dark and inscrutable to man—he converts evil unto good, and often causes the wrath of man to praise him. If Africa is ever destined to become civilized and christianized, the first dawn of light to all human appearances has been reflected on her from the Southern States of America. On the other hand, if the negro by his constitutional adaptation to labour in situations where we would find only disease and degeneracy, contribute to our wealth and comfort, then is he also our benefactor, and hence we will mutuallly have reason to bless the wise provision of heaven in constructing the human frame in the various races of man, that they in their several gradations can mutually benefit each other, by cultivating every soil, the products of which are so necessary to the support of man, and by this means binding together the whole human family in one bond of universal dependence and brotherhood.

These people are the peasantry of our southern land—they are the members of our household—they have been the nurses of our mothers and wives, and they are the playmates of our children. If the efforts to degrade them into a different species, incapable of receiving the truths of christianity are countenanced from political motives, they must inevitably fail, for they are not only unwise and unphilosophical, but being an embodiment of a scientific error with a political folly, it never can unite us in sentiment. If we however, assume the higher grounds of christianity as our authority, we will stand on a foundation which cannot be shaken. Here we may all be united in knowing and defending our rights, and learning our obligations. The master is here directed how to perform his duties with humanity, and minister according to the best of his abilities to the temporal comforts, and spiritual wants, and the enduring happiness of his humble fellow men, and the servant is here taught the duty of obedience and gratitude to his earthly protectors, and of accountability to God.

Although we were born in a slave-holding State, and have never resided in a State where the African did not, at the time, exist both as a slave and a freeman, yet our observations were made on two widely separated latitudes, New-York and Carolina; in the latter State, we have resided for the last thirty-five years. From these opportunities so amply afforded us, we have been irresistibly brought to the conviction, that *in intellectual powers the African is an inferior variety of our species. His whole history affords evidence that he is incapable of self-government. His inferiority, however, in intellect, does not prove that he is not a man.*"

With such high authority as this, we feel fortified in our assertion that there is a *natural* inequality in the conditions of men. And if this is true, the theory of abolitionists is completely overturned. The whole theory of abolitionists is based upon the idea that all men are by nature equal, that is, all men come into this world endowed with equal powers, equal rights, equal privileges, and equal claims upon society. It is this idea we wish to explode.

* The Rev. Dr. Bachman of South-Carolina.

In the first place, it is essential that we should understand the difference between natural rights and privileges, and political rights and privileges; we must draw the distinction between natural equality, and political or conventional equality. It is certain that when a child is born, its rights and privileges are of a very dubious kind, and whatever rights it may have, it is utterly unable to claim the least of them. To be sure it has the power of inhaling a portion of the atmosphere which surrounds it, but this is nearly all that can be said of its power of claiming and exercising any rights or privileges. It is born with the right to live, and the privilege of living, provided it has the power of doing so. This we conceive to be the sum total of man's natural and inalienable rights *at the moment of his birth;* and so far as they only are concerned, we are free to admit, all men are born equal. But, immediately upon their being born, the *one life* which each child has, becomes qualified by the state of things around him. One child is covered with silken down, another with scanty rags. One becomes on the instant, and by virtue of all the laws of nature and society, the heir to wealth; the other, by virtue of the same laws, is the heir to poverty. One is pampered with every luxury that wealth affords, the other is stinted by all the privations which poverty imposes. One is taught from its earliest lisp to breathe the sentiments of haughty confidence, and acknowledged power, the other learns by instinct to keep the humble sphere its parents seem to hold. One is instructed in all that can be desired, and every effort of his mind at self-development, is followed by the most assiduous exertions of art to assist and lead it, the other spends his days in the mechanical imitation of his industrious sire, but he is poorly instructed, and none of the auxiliaries of wealth, art and polished society, come to assist a single effort of his mind. One reaches manhood and finds himself in the lap of plenty, and in the atmosphere of pride and power, the other finds manhood but another name for constant labour and scanty support. One is seized on the decline of life with the torments of disease, he sinks on a bed of down, every artifice of wealth is resorted to, to soothe his dying hours; but he dies, and is nothing more than a mere body of matter of certain dimensions, and certain composition; the other is also seized with disease, he sinks on his hard pillow, and amid the poverty of his whole life he also dies, and he is also a mere body of matter of certain dimensions, and certain composition. They are equal now perhaps, but were they equal all their lives? They each brought one life into this world, and they each carry one life out of it; they were each born supremely helpless, and they are each now a lifeless carcass. This is the beginning and the end of their equality. Society, the laws of nature, and the universal voice of humanity, gave each of them that position among his fellows which his parents occupied before him. But the respective positions which these parents occupied were not equally elevated, they were distantly removed from each other; how then can any power give them their just inheritance from their parents, and yet make them equals. If one is born of rich parents, he must inherit riches; if the other is born of poor parents, does he not inherit poverty? He that is born of white parents is white, and he that is born of black parents is black. If he is born of English parents is he not English? If he is born of French parents is he not French? If he is born of Catholic parents is he not Catholic? And if he is born of Jewish parents is he not Jewish? If he is born of free parents is he not free? And if he is born of slave parents is he not also a slave? Does not the child take the *name* of the parent, and does not nature stamp the very *features* of the parent upon the child? Is not the child actually a part of the parent, is he not the enlarged and invigorated secretion of the parent's own loins? If, therefore, there are two parents in this world, whose powers, rights, privileges and claims upon society *are not equal*, and if these parents have children, it follows that these children are also not equal. It is only necessary then in order to refute the proposition, that all men are born equal, to show that there have been two parents in the world who were not equals; and, to see such, we have only to look upon the first two individuals we meet with.

Now it is maintained by thousands who pass for sensible people, that though the child should inherit the property of its parents, and though every feature of the parent is impressed on the child—though the child of free parents should be free—yet there is one single, solitary, isolated condition, which should not be transmitted from the parent to the child, and that is slavery. Though numerous diseases to which parents may be liable, must necessarily be transmitted to the child, yet the single condition of servitude to which the parent has been unalterably subjected, is never under any circumstances to be transmitted to the child. All men it is said are born free, yet there is not a more abject and dependent object in nature than a new born child.

It does not matter how we acquire property, it is universally acknowled that when we die, as we cannot make any further use of our possessions, they should be inherited by our children. But if that property happens to be a slave, they say the rule does not apply. Abolitionists maintain that though we may legally purchase a slave, and have a legal right to her person and services forever, yet we have no right to claim her children as ours also. Is it denied that the babe is ours at the moment of its conception in the mother's womb; the mother is ours, the whole person of the mother, each and every part of her belongs to us; the infant in her womb as being *a part of her* is also ours; but in the course of nature the infant and the mother are separated, and one body becomes two, those parts which were *one* yesterday, have to day become *two*. Does this change which has taken place in their relation to each other, effect their relation to us? If they both belonged to us yesterday when they were one, why do they not both belong to us to-day, when they are by the course of nature become two? Because, says the abolitionist, all men are born free. Suppose then we admit the proposition; all infants are free; this mother is ours, but this child is not; we want the mother elsewhere, we must take her away, but we must leave the child, it is free, we have no right to touch it, we would be infringing upon its *rights*, we would trample on its liberty to carry it away with its parents, it has expressed no desire to be moved, therefore we must let it remain where it is. How long will the babe, thus left to its helpless state of freedom, live to enjoy its liberty; and what would abolitionists say to such treatment? Why the language could not signify their pious indignation. But if the free infant is not to be abandoned, who is to rear and support it; why, we are to do it, of course. And who is to recompense us for our care and expense, no body, to be sure. Then our house is to become a foundling hospital for *free* infants, where the milk of human kindness is to flow spontaneously and in pure gratuity, whenever our *slave* thinks fit to bring a *freeman* in the world. We are to dispense our substance for the growth of these *free and equal* babes, without claiming even the obedience we receive from our own offspring. Who is so fanatical as to enjoin such a course? Yet if all men are born free and equal, such a course would not be altogether unavoidable.

The writer of an article, to which we have already adverted,* very justly remarks, "if it be true *now*, that all men are born free and equal, it must have been true in all ages from the beginning of time. And if this doctrine were true in the early ages of society, the fathers of the primitive families would have been assassinated by their descendants whom they held in bondage—masters by their servants, lords by their vassals, sovereigns by their subjects; the foundations of

* See an able argument in the Southern Literary Messenger, 1838, addressed to the late Hon. Hugh S. Legaré, of South-Carolina.

society would have been broken up before the social edifice was erected, and the earth would never have been subdued or colonized.

This philosophy was the natural offspring of the French revolution and of the school of unbelievers; it is a doctrine of blood and pillage, and utterly subversive of that order, which forms the bond of social institutions. False as it is, when shall we cease to teach and to believe it? Shall we continue to dismember and overturn, by inculcating a theory which has already corrupted many of the most gifted of the sons of men, which has arrayed people against their rulers, which has covered the earth with the ruins of the social fabric, and which has turned loose upon the face of the earth a spirit of licentiousness, insubordination, and riot, that continue to shake to their deepest foundations all existing establishments?

Let us concede the stern, but unwelcome truth, that the existence, as well as the universality of slavery, is to be attributed to the labour required in the infancy of man to subdue the earth, from which he has been doomed to reap fruit in the sweat of his brow—that it was wisely ordained by the author of nature himself, and is therefore founded in the very nature of things, and of man. It is only when we have lost sight of this sublime truth, that we proclaim our absurd systems of equality, in a state of nature.

In considering this question, it is essentially necessary that we should accurately distinguish between the natural condition of man, and those principles of political equality, upon which free civil institutions repose, and which, like those of this country, are regulated by a moral compact. And the most couclusive evidence of the propriety of this distinction, is exhibited in the formation of our federal compact, which declares all men to be free and equal, and yet expressly recognizes the existence of slavery, maintains and protects the natural right of the master over the slave, and makes the slave himself a constituent part of the basis of representation. All the parties to this contract are free and equal, but no one will be so frantic as to contend, that by this declaration of the fundamental principle which governs our political compact, it was designed to deny the right of slavery either in this free country or elsewhere. The charter itself legalizes, defends, maintains and protects slavery. It is the confusion of ideas, which springs from this intermingling of conventional and political equality with the natural rights of man, that deludes us. It will scarcely be affirmed that Thomas Jefferson, the author of the declaration of independence, the great apostle of democracy, and the strenuous advocate of popular rights, deeply imbued as he was with the philosophism of the eighteenth century, designed to repudiate slavery when he declared all men to be free and equal. To his understanding, the distinction was clear between the conventional or political and the natural rights of man; and he well understood that in the formation of a political compact, the slave, from his inability to contract, could be no party." The idea that all men are born with equal rights, equal privileges, or equal claims upon society, is to our apprehension a mere fancy, an abstract delusion, and the foundation of the wildest and most impracticable theories. It has been from the very beginning the universal practice of the human family, to leave to custom, convention and policy, to determine, constitute, and classify the rights and privileges of men. We therefore believe there is a natural and a necessary inequality in the condition of men; and the question how far this inequality necessarily extends, is one well calculated to rack the brains of the wisest philosopher.

For our present purpose however, it is sufficient to know that these inequalities must, and consequently do exist. And it would seem the best way to dispose of the matter, is by the following brief, but correct course of reasoning. There must be naturally either an equality, or an inequality in man's condition. If equality is his natural condition, it would be usurping nature to bring about an artificial inequality, and during the thousands of years that have transpired since the creation of man, his condition would have by this time been undisputed, and his natural equality would have displaced any artificial inequality which may have been instituted. But, on the other hand, if equality is the natural condition of man, then it is the duty of all men to submit to this inequality; and for the good of all, it should be the object of each to lighten the hardships of the others' condition. But we have already seen that all men are not, and never have been, upon an equal footing in society; that there still exists, as there always has, a vast natural inequality in the condition of men. We therefore conclude, that a distinction of classes will necessarily exist as long as the laws of nature remain unchanged; and that it is the duty of all men to submit to these laws, always however endeavouring, if they please, consistently with the laws of society, to lighten their burdens as much as local circumstances will permit.

Let us now see if the people of the South are recreant to their duty. Our fathers have determined for us how society should be divided in our country; they have most permanently established two grand classes. Both at the North and at the South, *all over the country*, the whites and the blacks *always have been two distinct classes*. The white man has invariably occupied the most eminent, and the negro the most menial positions. Why this should have been, it is not our business to enquire, it is sufficient for us to know that these two classes have always existed in accordance with the principle of inequality of condition; and we also know that in keeping with the same principle, the burdens of the negro's condition have been very much lightened by the superior intellect of the white man.

Now it would be unreasonable to suppose that one class would sacrifice every consideration for the sake of another, which is materially removed from it in every respect, accordingly we find that our northern friends in *ameliorating* the condition of their colored brethren, have not consulted the good of their sable brothers exclusively, but have been decidedly careful in consulting their own interests. When free labour became cheaper than slave labour, of course the people of the North adopted the cheapest, and for doing so they cannot well be blamed, provided they liberated their slaves in a humane manner, and by so doing violated none of the established laws of society. For what government or community will not invariably exercise economy, and what item involves a greater source of economy than the price of labour. We believe, therefore, that the Northern States did no more than what was right when they emancipated their slaves, if they found free labour cheaper, provided always, they confined their operations strictly within their respective limits; but when we say they were right, we would be understood to mean, they were right as far as it effected the white slaveholder, or the employer of labourers, whether it materially improved, or decidedly aggravated the condition of the slave, we will endeavour to learn.

In the South, the same principle has ever been at work, the higher class has not failed to consult its own interest, and in doing so it necessarily consults that of the lower. But the same external causes, among which are climate, soil, productions, and the growth of population, do not operate at the South as they do at the North. The white population of the South has never been so proportioned to its capital, as to be compelled to labour cheaper than the slave; nor will the climate of the South permit white labour to be brought in competition with slave labour, *even if other circumstances did*. Slave labour continues, therefore, to be the cheapest, it is carefully fostered, and ever will be as long as it is profitable. But is not this inequality, this division of society into classes, this system of slavery, then absolutely necessary? It was bequeathed us by our ancestors, all external causes tend to perpetuate it, and until these causes change, what is to terminate it, who is to say this distinction must not be preserved?

When, on the contrary, these causes change and become so reversed, as to be the same as those existing at the North, there can be little doubt that similar effects will appear.

Now as regards the *moral obligations of individuals* of different classes, we must be satisfied to dispense with their consideration; not because such considerations would militate against slavery, but because they would be out of place; for we speak of slavery always as a public, a national affair. And we trust we are not so wanting in good sense, as to suppose that this institution is any less liable to abuse, on the part of individuals, than others are. We are free to admit also that the institution is attended with some serious, but unavoidable evils; but what institution, or system, calculated to replace it, is not equally inconvenient?

The following remarks are those of one of the greatest champions of political reform that France could boast during the last century.* He says, "it has been supposed that I proposed to violate the laws of nature, by proposing to establish the use of slaves in Europe: but are not these holy laws violated in States, where some citizens possess every thing, and others nothing. I beg to remark, that the liberty which every European thinks he enjoys, is nothing more than the power of occasionally breaking his chains, in order to get himself a new master. *Necessity makes him a slave, and his case is the more lamentable, inasmuch as nobody provides for his subsistence. It is mendicity that degrades men, and that is inevitable in every country that does not set bounds to the cupidity and the fortunes of its citizens. It is an insult upon common sense to pretend, that every man is free in a country, where one citizen employs another citizen to serve him, and condemns him to the vilest, the most laborious, and the most disgusting occupations.*"

Before we pass to other considerations, we cannot but remark, that in all the publications deprecating slavery that have met our eye, existing evils have been maliciously exaggerated, and abuses, in themselves of trifling consequence, and rare occurrence, have been represented as being the result of absolute law. And, strange as it may appear, these absurd falsifications so invariably come in the garb of truth and pious concern, that some, even in a Southern community, who have no excuse for not knowing better, throw aside the truth which they every day see, to take up the falsehood of latest importation. Abolitionists, both in England and America, are continually conjuring up some rare instance of cruelty, and asserting that such is the common mode of treatment which all slaves receive. They too frequently indulge in *imaginary* humanity, at the expense of their own *substantial* veracity. They denounce an institution, on account of a few accidental abuses to which it is liable. Why, the Christian religion had better be denounced, because it is liable to be the occasion of crusades, civil wars, persecutions and schisms. Does the abolitionist denounce slavery because slaves have been cruelly oppressed by a few brutal masters? As well might the infidel denounce christianity, because Christians have been cruelly tortured by a few Roman emperors. Yet this system of reasoning has its advocates.

A moral and religious view of slavery brings no remorse, nor produces no terrors to the mind of the slaveholder; for no deductions follow which are calculated to stagger the conscience of the most consciencious slaveholder. Every body knows, who is conversant with Scripture, that "slaves existed, under the divine government, among the Jewish people.† The Scriptures distinctly set forth the rules by which they shall be made, by which they shall be governed, by which

* Monsieur L'Abbé de Mably, (Droit Public de l'Europe.) See Southern Quarterly Review, 1828.

† A pamphlet called "Slavery at the South." Anonymous.

they shall be punished. They are described as bought for a price; as the property of their masters; as subject to his will; as beaten with stripes; as marked; as sold; as manumitted; as placed in every possible position to which the condition of slavery is liable. Slavery, then, is recognized, permitted, enjoined by the Old Testament; but that which is recognized, permitted, enjoined by the divine law cannot be sinful." Again, "when our Saviour taught, slaves were every where about him. He frequently makes allusion to their condition; he denounces every form of sin around him; he reproves Sadducee and Pharisee without scruple; but he uses no expression that can be tortured into a condemnation of slavery. The apostles were in the midst of slavery, in its worst forms and abuses, in Asia Minor, Greece and Italy. It could not, therefore, elude their observation. They taught the new converts to christianity not only the great truths of religion, and the rules of morals, but many minor observances incidental to their situation, many regulations of behaviour, and even of dress, becoming their new condition and profession, and rebuked any infringement of them with severity. If slavery were a sin, it could not, therefore, escape either their notice or their condemnation. But there is not, in the New Testament, a single expression, which even insinuates a condemnation of slavery." In view of these facts, it cannot be said that slavery is either immoral or sinful.

Whatever is immoral must be sinful. If, therefore, slavery is immoral it must be sinful. But if it is sinful it must be an offence against the laws of God. To learn, then, if it is an offence against those laws, we must first know what are the laws of God. The laws of God, according to our understanding, are those mandates, precepts, regulations and commandments, recorded in the Old and New Testaments, which were delivered through Moses and the prophets, and afterwards through Christ. But none of the mandates, precepts, regulations or commandments delivered by Moses, the prophets, or Christ and his apostles, prohibit slavery, but rather enjoin and regulate it. Slavery, then, is not a sin; and, as it is not a sin, it therefore cannot be immoral.

Many persons, however, maintain that slavery is a sin; and, in deference to their better judgment, we will waive that point, and reason thus: It must either be no sin, or it must be a sin; that every body will admit. If it be *no sin*, then it may with propriety be practised in a christian community, and abolitionists are wrong to oppose it, on the grounds of its being sinful. But if it *is a sin*, then not only Moses, who *delivered* the law, but Christ, who came to *perfect* the law, and his apostles, who were taught to *practice* the law, sanctioned and regulated a violation of the law. And if *they* countenanced this sin, why should Christians of the present day be afraid to do the same? As they approved of the commitment of this sin, no Christian should hesitate, from consciencious scruples, to commit this sin, which is so clearly fostered by their divine sanction and regulation. It would certainly be presumption in any man, to be ashamed to do that which received the sanction, and operated under the regulations of the divine founder of his creed. Thus, while we do not here attempt to say whether slavery is a sin or not, we *do* say that, if it *is* a sin, the Redeemer of the world holds out an inducement for man to commit it.*

Nothing affords a stronger inducement for man to commit this so-called sin—or rather, no portion of Scripture affords better evidence to the sane mind, that slavery *cannot be a sin*—than that text which relates to our Saviour's healing the centurion's sick servant. After recording the centurion's application to Christ for an instance of his mercy, to be bestowed upon a sick servant, St. Luke gives us the answer, in these words: "When Jesus heard these things he marvelled at

* See the 7th chapter of St. Luke.

him, and turned him about and said unto the people that followed him, I say unto you, *I have not found so great faith, no, not in Israel.*"

This great faith was found in the centurion who was the master of the sick servant. The greatest faith which our Saviour found in Israel was in the bosom of a slaveholder. Now, if slavery was a sin, it would have been a sin for this centurion to own a slave. But Christ, himself, tells us that this centurion had greater faith than any other in Israel; and we all know that he who has *faith* must necessarily avoid sin in every way he can; and one having such a superior degree of faith as this centurion, must have been peculiarly exempt from sin. But this centurion, who was thus peculiarly exempt from sin, was a slaveholder. Therefore, we conclude that, as the man who had greater faith than any other in all Israel was a slaveholder, and that, so far from being rebuked by Christ for being a slaveholder, he was extolled for his superior faith, slavery cannot be a sin; or, if it is, it is such a sin that Christ extols the faith of one who commits it.

CHAPTER VII.

"Cæsar, beware the ides of March."

As a political institution, slavery can hardly be called an evil; for, though there may be evils belonging to it, yet there are so many benefits to society resulting from it, that the good of it has a vast preponderance over the evil of it. "To say that there is evil in any institution, is only to say that it is human." But it would be folly to say that any political institution is an evil, because there are a few evils which cannot well be separated from it. With regard to the system of slavery practised in the Southern States, the folly of such an assertion would be superlative. For no custom which invariably, and with the utmost degree of certainty, promotes, and actually *causes* the civilization of the human race, even though it be accompanied with a variety of inconveniences, can be esteemed an evil. And if there is one custom of society which has served, in all ages and in every climate, to civilize the human race, more effectually than any other custom, it is slavery.

It has been remarked, by one of the ablest jurists of the age,* that, "if any thing can be predicated, as universally true, of uncultivated man, it is, that he will not labour beyond what is absolutely necessary to maintain his existence. Labour is pain, to those who are unaccustomed to it, and the nature of man is averse to pain. Even with all the training, the helps and motives of civilization, we find that this aversion cannot be overcome, in many individuals of the most cultivated societies. The coercion of slavery, alone, is adequate to form man to habits of labour. Without it, there can be no accumulation of property, no providence for the future, no taste for comforts or elegancies, which are the characteristics and essentials of civilization. He who has obtained the command of another's labour, first begins to accumulate and provide for the future, and the foundations of civilization are laid. We find confirmed by experience that which is so evident in theory. Since the existence of man upon the earth, with no exception whatever, either of ancient or modern times, every society which has attained civilization, has advanced to it through this process.

"Will those who regard slavery as immoral, or crime in itself, tell us that man was not intended for civilization, but to roam the earth as a biped brute?"

* Chancellor Harper, in his "Memoir on Slavery."

Cicero tells us, "there is a true law, a right reason, conformable to nature, universal, unchangable, eternal"—a law which "is not one thing at Rome, another at Athens, one thing to-day, another to-morrow; but, in all times and nations, this universal law must forever reign, eternal and imperishable." Such a law is the law of nature, upon which the law of society is based, which makes one man master and another slave. Can the institution which springs from such a law be an evil? or, if it is an evil, can it be avoided?

As for the Southern States, they can have, literally, nothing to apprehend from their domestic institutions. Slavery, as a political institution, is the result of such a law as Cicero describes. Wherever there is a political community it will be fortified against usurpation, and secured against popular tumults of all kinds, by a well-regulated system of domestic slavery; *and, where a distinction of* RACE *can be made to accompany that of rank, the advantage is two-fold.* All civilized society will necessarily settle down into two grand classes, one of which will comprise all capitalists, and the other all labourers. We think we have already shown that the former class *will own* the latter, either under one set of laws or another; either as hireling slaves or as domestic slaves. In England, and at the North, the labourers are hireling slaves; at the South, the labourers are chiefly domestic slaves. In taking a political view of the subject, then, we merely have to determine whether our system of domestic slavery insures public tranquillity, private rights, and the general welfare, in an equal or a greater degree than the hireling system.

In every possible stage of society, there must be individuals who perform the duties and discharge the various offices of society; some of these duties are agreeable and exalted, others are disagreeable and humiliating; some offices are enviable and honourable, whilst others are servile and degrading; but they are not the less discharged on these accounts—they must be performed, and the individual members of society must perform them. Those who perform the higher offices are regarded by the individuals of the community in which they live, as somewhat exalted; and those who perform the more menial are regarded as being somewhat degraded. The different offices of society are, then, naturally classified in two grand divisions: those which are deemed honourable and desirable, and those which are regarded as servile and degrading. Of course, capitalists will discharge the former, and labourers will discharge the latter offices. But, as soon as the individuals of society and the offices of society are thus arrayed in such unmistakable positions as they must necessarily assume, their relative merits immediately appear; and the idea of superiority on the part of capitalists, who are either masters or employers, and of inferiority on the part of labourers, who are either slaves or hirelings, becomes permanently established. The latter class is generally looked upon as a *degraded* portion of society, and, in *comparison* with the former, it certainly is degraded. If, then, this degraded class constitutes a portion of the *political community*, it may be said that it is in part a *degraded community*, and a degraded element is certainly introduced into the body politic. But if this degraded class is excluded from the political community, the superiority which is attributed to the individuals of the other class attaches itself to the community of which these individuals constitute the entirety. Moreover, it has been found, in all ages, that the introduction of such an element as we have termed a *degraded* element, into the body politic, is also the introduction of a *dangerous* element; for such an element invariably tends to violate the rights of property, to usurp the supremacy of law, and to overturn government itself. Now, in the system of hireling slavery, which is practised in England, Franee, and at the North, this dangerous element is admitted into the political community; but, in the system of domestic slavery, practised at the South, this dangerous element is *not* admitted into the political community.

The consequence of these facts is perfectly obvious, and equally well known. At the South, where this element is excluded from the body politic, no obstinate contest can ever arise between capital and labour. At the North, and wherever this element is admitted into the body politic, capital and labour wage eternal wars against each other; and these wars must eventually destroy the stability of all governments where universal suffrage prevails; for they never fail to convert the gravest senate into the wildest mob, or the most conservative power into the most absolute despotism. At the South, it is impossible for such conflicts ever to occur. Capital and labour are indissolubly united; the labourer is himself capital; he has no opportunity to retard the progress of government, or stay the execution of law, by the promulgation of those detestable agrarian principles, which have with such startling rapidity, of late years, taken possession of the Northern people. Why then should we be astonished to hear it come from the lips of a consummate statesman, that "slavery is the most safe and stable basis for free institutions in the world."* And from another, that "domestic slavery instead of being an evil, is the corner stone of our republican edifice."†

It is unquestionably true that the efforts of abolitionists to frighten timid young men, and terrify nervous old women, with the horrors of rebellion, have not always been without their effects. There are innumerable pamphlets constantly pouring from the press of the Northern States; some containing what are called *sermons*, some containing addresses, some letters, some the proceedings and debates of abolition conventions, some the testimony of travellers and residents in the slaveholding States, and some got up expressly for the benefit of California and New Mexico; but all teeming with the grossest sophistry and the most wholesale falsehoods. These publications find their way to every town or village in nearly every State in the Union. The boldest efforts are made to alarm the slaveholder, by laying before him, in the most glaring colours, the eminent dangers of his situation; the minds of enthusiasts are excited into frenzied zeal in the *glorious* cause; the ignorant are duped, and the curious puzzled by the horrors of slavery and the glory of universal emancipation; the understanding of the slave himself is confounded, and his own senses contradicted by these never-ending tirades. The unlettered slave, as he spells his way, word by word, through the obscure and unmeaning sentences of the pamphlet before him, or as he listens to the jargon of his deluded associate, conceives but a vague idea of the subject before him. He believes there is some good coming, but the nature of what is to come he does not know. He believes for the while, that he has better friends elsewhere, than he has at home, but who they are, and where they are, he does not know. He believes he is an injured man, but what is the nature of the injury he has never been enabled to conceive. His anxiety is aroused, his curiosity is excited, his hopes raised, and his vanity flattered; but all for what, he really does not know. He becomes restless and impatient, his industry is ruined, his contentment gone, his temper is soured, and his happiness forsakes him. He first becomes idle, then surly, impertinence and disobedience follow, till retributive punishment recalls him to his senses. What, then, are the effects of these publications? They do not, in the slightest degree, benefit the community. They destroy the happiness of the slave altogether; for they not only banish contentment from his once grateful heart, but compel the master to be more rigid in his discipline, and more guarded in his indulgences. Municipal regulations are more strictly observed, and the vigilance of the police is constantly redoubled, till the overt act of some deluded victim brings him to the scaffold, and thus, for a time, recalls the neighbourhood to its former tranquillity.

These causes and these effects have so long been in operation, that some of the

* Mr. Calhoun in the Senate, January, 1840. † Mr. McDuffie.

most troublesome of them are beginning to disappear; though we are still compelled to view with distrust and severity those slaves, whom we would otherwise be disposed to regard with confidence and leniency. Yet the evils which might formerly have been feared, on account of the ignorance, impulsiveness and improvidence of these people have considerably disappeared.

It is a truth which cannot be questioned, that "hope long deferred maketh the heart sick," and it is illustrated in the long deferred hopes which abolitionists have for fifty years been holding out. "Forty years ago," says a fluent writer from Georgia,* "any thing looking to the emancipation of our slaves, was spoken of only in whispers, and was printed only in asterisks; now, we all talk as openly and freely about the abolitionists and their aims, as we do of almost any other subject. The truth is, they have heard so long, and so much about abolitionism, and seen so little good result from it, that they begin to think you really care nothing for them, or that your friendship is not worth having. The soundest philosophy that ever emanated from a negro's brain."

The whole result of the abolition agitation, so far as it effects the social and political condition of our slaves, is thus summed up by an able advocate of Southern rights.† He says: "Of late years we have been not only annoyed, but greatly embarrassed in this matter, by the abolitionists. We have been compelled to curtail some privileges; we have been debarred from granting new ones. In the face of discussions which aim at loosening all ties between master and slave, we have, in some measure, to abandon our efforts to attach them to us and control them through their affections and pride. We have to rely more and more on the power of fear. We must, in all intercourse with them, assert and maintain strict mastery, and impress it on them that they are slaves. This is painful to us, and certainly no present advantage to them. But it is the direct consequence of the abolition agitation. We are determined to continue masters, and to do so, we have to draw the reign tighter and tighter day by day, to be assured that we hold them in complete check. How far this process will go on, depends wholly and solely on the abolitionists. I do not mean by all this, to say that we are in a state of actual alarm and fear of our slaves; but, under existing circumstances, we should be ineffably stupid not to increase our vigilance and strengthen our hands." And may we not add a truth, which has now become evident to all, that there is a point at which this process would become suicidal; *and whenever this point is reached, we will be compelled, in self-defence, to direct our measures, no longer against the slave, who is but the victim of a strange delusion, but against* THE RESPONSIBLE AGENT, *the true aggressor, the abolitionist himself.*

There is one measure lately adopted by Northern abolitionists, which, as a combination of consummate impudence and open falsehood, is perhaps superior to any thing which has ever been levelled against the South. It is entitled, "*An Address to the inhabitants of New Mexico and California, on the omission by Congress to provide them with territorial governments, and on the social and political evils of slavery.*" Published in New-York, for the Am. and For. Anti-Slavery Society, in 1849. The object of this address, was to induce the people of those territories to exclude slavery by every possible means they could resort to; and without caring to inquire whether it has had any material effect upon the minds of those to whom it was addressed, it affords a good specimen of the untiring efforts which are constantly made by the people of the North to degrade the South in the eyes of all who come within their reach. For the sake of attaining these ends, the signers of this address broadly denounce the *feelings* of slaveholders, the state of religion in our community, and the piety of our ministers, and even

* "A Voice from the South," signed "GEORGIA," published in Baltimore, in 1847.
† Gov. Hammond's Letters to Thomas Clarkson, p. 12.

cast odium upon the *state of morals* at the South, though they would not dare to compare it with that of the North. They impute to us a total disregard for human life, and for *constitutional obligations!* They ascribe to us a desire to annihilate the liberty of speech, as well as the liberty of the press, because we will not allow the open promulgation of treachery and rebellion. But what is equally absurd, though perhaps more glaring in its falseness, they attribute to us a degree of military weakness, which would make us contemptible, if there was the least truth in their assertions.

They commence to discuss our "military weakness," by giving the remarks of "a distinguished foreigner," but without giving us the *name* or the *nation* of their distinguished traveller, that we may be enabled to judge for ourselves as to the weight of his authority. They say, "a distinguished foreigner, after travelling in the Southern States, remarked that the very aspect of the country bore testimony that, defenceless and exposed as they are, *it would be madness to hazard a civil war;* and surely no people in the world have more cause to shrink from an appeal to arms. We find at the South no one element of military strength.*" They then go on to say, that those classes of society which, in other countries, would supply material for armies, are regarded at the South as the most deadly foes. And, as an evidence of the weakness they impute to us, they attempt to show, that during the revolutionary war a considerable portion of the Southern militia was *withdrawn from the defence of the country, to protect the slaveholders from the vengeance of their own bondmen.* How much it is to be regretted that these abolitionists are not more explicit in what they say. If they could only accompany their assertions with something like an evidence that what they say is true, their remarks might then claim the serious attention of the reader. As it is, however, we merely advert to a few, because we believe the majority of our readers but seldom see the calumnies which are heaped upon them by the Northern press.

These abolitionists go on, in their address, which is to enlighten so many unwary Californians and Mexicans, to say, in plain language, that an invading enemy would strike the first blow at the slave system, and thus aim at revolution—a revolution that would give liberty to two and a half millions of human beings; and that such a war would be very embarrassing to the slaveholders, and the more horrible, because, as formerly in South-Carolina, a large share of their military force would necessarily be employed, not in fighting the enemy, but in guarding the *social system;* meaning, we suppose, by the term social system, the system of domestic slavery. Then comes the "unkindest cut of all." No persons, say they, are more sensible of their hazardous situation, than the slaveholders themselves; and hence, as is common with people who are secretly conscious of their own weakness, they attempt to supply the want of strength by a bullying insolence, hoping to effect by intimidation what they well know can be effected in no other way. This game, they say, has long been played, and with great success, in Congress. And, finally, they remark that the slaveholders, whatever may be their vaunts, are conscious of their military weakness, and shrink from any contest which may cause a foreign army to plant the standard of emancipation upon their soil. "*The very idea of an armed negro startles their fearful imaginations.*"

These are a few of the slip-shod assertions, under the head of "military weakness," which appear in this patriotic address. They will not be disputed here, but when we come to discuss the military resources of the South, we will be enabled to learn whether they are true or false. It must not, however, be supposed that the writers of this address have referred to a single authentic document, to prove what they assert with regard to Southern militia, during the revolutionary

*** Alluding, we suppose, to the event of a war between the North and the South.**

war. And, although their production teems with extracts from the speeches or writings of worthier men than themselves, yet, on the score of military weakness, they have not advanced the least authority, nor the slightest argument, to maintain their position. It is true, they have inserted a paragraph from the *secret journal of Congress*, but it affords no proof, it amounts to nothing. We will presently see the true state of things in this respect.

Certain English and American abolitionists have slandered the African character to no small extent. They impute to their sable brothers the dark crime of ingratitude. And we would not stop to exonerate the Africans from this charge, did we not believe many of them to be vastly the superiors of their white traducers. It is constantly said that, during the revolutionary war, the great mass of the slaves were so overjoyed at the prospect of escaping from their owners, that they flocked by thousands to the British standard, and the few who were not so fortunate as to escape, required a considerable portion of the Southern militia to be withdrawn from fighting the enemy, to keep down rebellion among the slaves. Perhaps no falsehood could be a more open contradiction to history than this. And it is a fortunate circumstance, that the present generatiou is not compelled to rely solely on *written* history for their information on this score; but we have all had abundant oppertunities to learn from the lips of those who were actors in the scene, the *truth* as regards the conduct of the slaves they had about them, and which Messrs. JAY & Co. would have us believe they stood in so much awe of.

We are told that, during the revolutionary struggle,* the British carried off according to Ramsay, "25,000 slaves from South-Carolina," and from Georgia, according to McCall, one half. But these States were long held as conquered provinces, and the slaves *seized and sold to the West Indies.* Those who *joined* the British, under *promise of freedom*, were mostly carried to Nova Scotia, and afterwards sent to Sierra Leone. Clarkson computes the number at Nova Scotia, after the war, at upwards of 2,000, men, women and children,† but only 1,131 were ever sent to Sierra Leone. No doubt, a large proportion of these renegades were native Africans; and that the number was, under the circumstances, so small, is a strong proof that in time of war we should have little to fear from the seductions of an invading army. We are inclined to think that, as things now stand, the abolitionists annually kidnap and seduce more slaves away, than could be taken from us in a campaign on our soil.

In fact, our history, like that of the ancient republics, shows, that in war our slaves have been found faithful allies. Numerous proofs of this might be given, did our space permit. As early as 1747, the provincial legislature of South-Carolina passed an act for enlisting slaves, to the number of one-third of the males, and in Charleston one-half. The preamble of that act is conclusive evidence, of the highest authority, of their well-tried fidelity. It begins thus: "Whereas, it has been found *by experience* that several negroes and other slaves have, in times of war, behaved themselves with great faithfulness and courage, in repelling the attacks of his majesty's enemies, in their descents upon this province, &c."

Mr. Madison, afterwards President of the United States, placed so much reliance on the faithful adherence to the interests of his master by the African slave, that he once advised the enlistment of slaves to serve in the armies and to defend the country.‡ Yet, the cry in every bodies' mouth, is rebellion! insurrection! Why, thousands upon thousands of armed soldiery, with the most blood-thirsty violence, have not been able to subdue the hireling slaves of Europe, yet there is

* The North and South, by Elwood Fisher.

† 2,000, out of a population of about 500,000, is indeed a small proportion, and evidences no very great desire to escape, or to rebel.

‡ See Madison's Papers.

no such force required here. If the spirit of insubordination existed among our happy slaves, why has there never been a necessity for such armed forces?

During the revolutionary war, when whole districts of country were left entirely to women, children, and slaves, with nothing but an overruling power to preserve discipline; not one active white man within fifty miles; with British promises of the most enticing nature, and with the most sedulous instigations to revolt, the African slaves, "so far from proving treacherous, or deserting their masters, continued their labours upon the plantation, and no faithful watch-dog was ever more true in giving the alarm, on the approach of an enemy, or, if needed, to assist their master's family to escape to a place of safety." And we are told by British writers themselves, that "slaves were often pressed into the service of the British, and those that would not promise to renounce slavery for liberty, were made to work on the fortifications. They obeyed through necessity, until an opportunity offered for them to return to their masters; and but few of them left the country with their benevolent liberators; and even some who did, afterwards found their way back from Novia Scotia, and joyfully returned to the comforts of slavery."

And where, let us ask, has any stable government ever been overturned, or in any way seriously injured by the rebellion of its slave population? Surely not in the insurrection at St. Domingo! That island was not a sovereign state, nor had it ever a stable government, it was the mere colony of a distracted state. That insurrection was not the creation of *slaves*, it was the work of the "Amis des Noirs," in France, and the abolitionists in England, as we will see in the sequel. We solemnly believe, that let the number of our slave population be what it may, the Southern States have no danger to apprehend, but *the evils arising out of the too close connection we bear to the Northern States.*

As to any danger arising *solely* out of our system of domestic slavery, we are as safe as man can be. The entire history of man is but a succession of bloodshed and revolution; we continually meet with rebellions and insurrections of people whose political rights have been trampled under foot, and whose condition has been rendered insupportable by oppressive laws. The revolution of the American colonies was a rebellion, and a very proper one, of a free people, whose political rights and privileges had been grossly abused; but there was nothing in that struggle which partook, in any measure, of the nature of a servile insurrection. And, as to any of those local insurrections which may have occurred among the ancient Greeks, they were nothing more than the result of religious superstition—the miserable slaves of those ages were sometimes deluded by imaginary signals from the gods. But, what is very certain, the signal for rebellion invariably proved the signal for the disastrous defeat and fearful massacre of the unwary dupes.

Even on the score of the elopement, or the abduction of slaves from the frontier slaveholding States, we are astonished to find how comparatively futile the efforts of abolitionists have been. In the frontier counties of Maryland, adjoining Pennsylvania, there are 10,000 slaves. In many of these counties there are as many, and in some more, free negroes than slaves, and perhaps more anti-slavery white men than slaveholders; "yet the slaves here adhere to the service of their masters with nearly the some fidelity that they do in the interior counties of South-Carolina."* And in the river counties of Kentucky, bordering on Ohio and Indiana, the slaves, instead of escaping and diminishing in numbers, have increased more than three-fold in forty years, notwithstanding, there are persons ever ready to facilitate their escape.

* See DeBow's Commercial Review, of 1849.

It is, however, absolutely necessary that we should keep an ever watchful eye on the doings of our Northern neighbours. And the only source from which danger arises, even in that quarter, is the too close connection which exists between them and us. If all the Northern States formed one confederacy, and all the Southern States formed another, each, being a distinct government, would enact its own laws, without having to consult the other. Thus, the Northern republic could adopt as many Wilmot provisos, in its own territories, as it pleased; and the Southern republic could adopt whatever measures, within its own territory, as it pleased. In such an event, instead of the constant wrangling which is now kept up in our national legislature, the subject of slavery would be forever abandoned from the politics of the North, and calmly considered in the councils of the South.

In the present state of affairs, however, the South and the North are yoked together, practically, and perhaps avowedly, the most unwilling associates. While we maintain that slavery is not a political evil, and would assure the North that we are satisfied to remain under the dominion of customs we have always cherished; the people of that more enlightened land cannot allow us to persist in an error, which is, to their microscopic eyes, of the most gigantic import. But, after all, how are we to estimate the merits of our political and social institutions, unless we compare them with those of other nations. Now, to carry out such a comparison to its full extent, would be the occasion of an elaborate volume, so we will leave that task to the reader himself, after inserting a few remarks.

If our domestic slavery *is* a political evil, let us see if it is a greater or a lesser evil than the hireling slavery of the North and of Europe. In the first place, we will take it for granted, that any institution, to be a political evil, must serve to enervate, degrade, or corrupt the political community in which it exists, and, if it does produce these effects in the community, they must, sooner or later, appear in the government under which that community exists, *especially* if that government is a popular one, such as ours is.

It is fashionable, at the North, to declaim violently against slavery, and to make every assertion of which the language is susceptible, as well as many which can belong to no language at all, calculated to impress upon the minds of people that it is the greatest combination of crimes that the world ever saw; and these assertions have so long been in vogue, that their falseness and absurdity are completely forgotten by the credulity of men. We were never more thoroughly convinced of this than we were a short time ago, during a temporary sojourn in the city of Cincinnati. Whilst there the "Minutes of the Christian Anti-Slavery Convention" was issued from the press. This convention was a convocation of abolitionists, which was called for the purpose of considering "the connection of the *American Church* with the sin of slaveholding." Sermons were preached, prayers delivered, committees appointed, resolutions adopted, and finally, a grand address delivered to the "American Churches." We would not pay this convention the compliment of a passing notice, were it not that its proceedings come to our assistance in illustrating the style and temper of the fashionable jargon which every day becomes more and more in vogue in the Northern States. We will insert but one example. The *address* proceeds to say,* "Slavery is evil in all its tendencies—a Bohon Upas, that poisons the moral atmosphere all around it. The injuries it inflicts on the oppressed are returned, if possible, with double vengeance, on the head of the oppressor. It pollutes the morals of a rising family, depraves and degrades society, and engenders a spirit of violence and blood. Slavery is a crime which is, at this moment, working immense mischief in the moral, social

* See page 36, "Minutes of the Christian Anti-Slavery Convention, convened in Cincinnati, in April, 1850.

and religious interests of our country—waging a deadly war against the principles of righteousness in the church, *and of liberty in the State*, and threatening to overthrow all that our fathers toiled and bled for—a crime which, according to the established laws of God's moral and providential government, exposes our nation, most fearfully, to the terrible judgments of heaven, and, unless repented of, the sure presage of wrath and ruin."

In another part of the North—in the city of Boston—the pulpit of the Twenty-eighth Congregational Church was the rostrum from which the following political discoveries were gratuitously published to the astonished world:*

"In the day when the monarchs of Europe are shaken from their thrones; when the Russian and the Turk abolish slavery; when cowardly Naples awakes from her centuries of sleep, and will have freedom; when France prays to become a republic, and in her agony sweats great drops of blood; while the tories of the world look on, and mock, and wag their heads; and while the Angel of Hope descends, with trusting words, to comfort her, shall America extend slavery? butcher a nation, to get soil to make a field for slaves?" And afterwards, the more astonishing discovery: "Slavery has already been the blight of this nation, *the curse of the Nor h* and the curse of the South. *It has hindered commerce, manufactures, agriculture.* It confounds your politics. It has silenced your ablest men. It has muzzled the pulpit, (surely not *this* pulpit) and stifled the better life out of the press. It has robbed three million men of what is dearer than life; it has kept back the welfare of seventeen millions more. You ask, Oh Americans, where is the harmony of the Union? It was broken by slavery. Where is the treasure we have wasted? It was squandered by slavery. Where are the men *we* sent to Mezico? They were murdered by slavery. And now the slave power comes forward, to put her new minions, her thirteenth president, upon the nation's neck? Will the North say 'Yes?'"

These specimens will suffice; but if every production of this kind could be collected together, there is no roof on the continent that could cover them. Let us now come to the reality of things. If, reader, you are a resident of any of the Southern States, you must be already acquainted with the state of the political community of the South; and if you are a resident of any of the Northern States, we have no desire to inform you on the subject, for we are not addressing ourselves to you, and care but little for your opinions.

We have already endeavoured to show how exempt the Southern States must be from anything like a war between capital and labour, and how certainly such wars must occur in countries where domestic slavery is excluded. For actual instances of such contests, we have only to look at the State of France, and even the condition of some of the Northern States is familiar evidence of the soundness of our doctrine. A variety of causes have been, for some time back, aggravating this cruel war between capital and labour, in many European States; but in France the consequences have been marked. There the essence of modern liberty seems doubly concentrated, in the glorious principles of socialism and red republicanism; law, order, society, decency, government, and even religion, must there bow down to the shrine of *liberty* as it is tossed about by the convulsions of a mob. In France, the spirit of agrarianism, and the rule of mobs have "swept away government after government, like the waves of the sea; one dictatorship has followed another—now an emperor, now a king, now the *bourgeoise* capitalists, and now mere numbers, all equally unstable. And all this, despite the fact that France has been, under all dynasties, since the first revolution, eminently democratic in her civil laws. The reason is not hard to discover. At the bottom of

*** See "A Sermon on the Mexican War;" by the Rev. Theodore Parker. Published in Boston, in 1848.**

4

French politics—and the same idea applies with equal truth to the free States of the North—ljest he idea that *might makes right;* in other words, that a majority of mere numbers has a natural, indefeasible, and absobute right, to govern the minority. No matter about the injustice and oppression of the rule, the minority has no remedy, short of civil war."*

"France is the living and unhappy proof of all our reasonings. The reaction against the tyranny of the numerical majority, *as public opinion*, produces the multitude of 'false doctrines, heresies, and schisms,' the growing infidelity, the Grahamites, the Fourierites, the Mormonism, and Millerism, and all those wild vagaries of fanaticism, to which the people of the free States are so prone, but which cannot live beneath our Southern sun. The reaction against the tyranny of the numerical majority, *as government*, begets the proclivity to mobs and tumults, the instability of all constitutions and laws, which we see manifesting itself in the free States. The only rebellion ever known in the United States, against the exercise of undisputed constitutional authority, was in Pennsylvania. In Rhode Island, the Dorrites would have waged civil war, if their leader's courage had not failed him at the crisis, not for any great principle, but only to determine, by a trial of actual physical force—a most rational and logical test—which party was the sovereign numerical majority. Federal authority had to be invoked. When has a Southern State ever had to call in foreign aid to settle her domestic difficulties? The legislature at Harrisburg had to be brought to order by a military force; and the senate of Ohio, after one or two hundred ballotings, lately elected a speaker, who has since been forced to resign, for bargain and corruption. The State was near being thrown into a state of anarchy last year, by the inability of the legislature to determine who were its members. In the chief cities, mobs dispute the right of private citizens to consult their own taste in a play actor; they set fire to convents of helpless females, and they tear down the house of God, because it shelters the wretched emigrant from their brutal fury. And yet, when a citizen-soldier has the nerve to fire upon them, and vindicate the majesty of the law—an example of moral courage, alas! too seldom found at the North—instead of receiving the thanks of the whole community, his house is the mark of the midnight incendiary, and all the public avenues of public honours are forever closed to his approach."

"The love of true liberty, and manly independence of thought, cannot flourish in such a community; the greediness of office, and the love of power, take their place; there is an eager courting of popular favour, a feverish fear of differing in opinion from the majority, a making haste to leave the few and join the many. Hence, the politicians of the free States have always been wanting in the comprehensive views necessary to found governments or parties, and in the moral courage, the energy, and administrative talent, requisite to conduct them with success."

In that Agrarian community, the laws of the land which ensure to the citizen the peaceable enjoyment of his property, are openly, and with impunity set at defiance; so much so, that in many parts of the North long leases of land are rarely heard of, for they are distrusted, and there are just grounds to fear that tenants with such leases would refuse to surrender the property at the close of their term, and the landlord, perhaps, be unable to find sufficient law in the land to compel them to do so. "whole counties have united in refusing to pay rents, which were justly due, and the officers of the law, while in the execution of its mandates, have been deliberately murdered. *And these violators of the rights of property and life; of the laws of God and man, had strength enough to elect a governor, whom they could force to pardon the convicted murderers.*"

Which, now, is to be considered the greatest political evil, our domestic slavery

* See a pamphlet recently published, called "the Union," by a citizen of Virginia.

or their hireling slavery. That which has never occasioned a mob, or that which is ever doing so; that which has never destroyed a church or a convent, or that which has repeatedly done so; that which has never infringed upon established rights, or that which is eternally doing so; that which has never required the interposition of federal authority to ensure tranquillity, or that which has; that which has never required military force to organize its civil government, or that which has; that which is supported by civil law and moral influence, or that which is maintained by physical force and monied influence; that which is based upon the immutable laws of nature and of reason, or that which is founded upon selfish arrogance and delusive passion?

There can be no doubt as to which governments or which communities are the most degraded or corrupted, or the most enervated by their political institutions, those of the North, or those of the Southern States. For it cannot be denied that when any branch of a government becomes so disorderly as to be quelled by a military force, so dubious in its formation as not to know its own constituent parts, so corrupt in its composition that its chief members are forced to resign on account of bargain or corruption, or else forced by a lawless mob to stay the action of the law in the execution of convicted felons; that government is more degraded and corrupted than another which has never had such hurtful contingencies to arise during its whole political history. But such governments as the former are to be found in every direction at the North, while such as the latter characterize every slaveholding State in the Union. And the same we have said of the *governments* applies with redoubled force to the *communities* of these respective sections. No more must be said then of the political evils of slavery, it is almost as absurd to speak of that as it is to speak of all men being born free and equal.

We have, a few pages back, suggested that a separation of the South from the North would surely end the discussion of what is commonly called the "slavery question," in all our public councils, and thereby terminate the disgraceful and dangerous events which have been gradually crowding themselves upon us ever since the Constitution was adopted. Let us then, for a moment, suppose the Union was dissolved, leaving the *manner in which it should be dissolved* to be a matter of future consideration. Many have asked what will the South do then? What *can* the South do *then*, which it cannot do *now*? Why, let us see.

It is every where known that this entire Republic of thirty States is, more or less, the offspring of thirteen States, *all* of which were originally in their colonial state, slaveholding communities. At the time of the adoption of the Constitution, some of these thirteen progenitors had abolished slavery within their limits. The opinions of society at that time, from causes which will hereafter appear, leaned to the belief that slave labour was destined with peculiar certainty, and at no very distant period to be abolished throughout America. So powerful was the influence of this opinion, that in the framing of the Constitution, we see manifest indications of timidity, or at least a want of confidence on the part of Statesmen, when they approach the subject of slavery. Moreover, among the contracting parties, there were those whose *interests* and *opinions* agreed in condemning slave labour; on the other hand, there were those whose interests and opinions *did not agree* in condemning slavery. What was the consequence? The subject was avoided as much as possible, every allusion to slavery was as obscure as could be; so much so, that in the whole Constitution the word *slave* is not to be found. A singular infatuation seems to have taken hold of those great men, when they so studiously avoided using a plain word whose meaning is unmistakeable, but must substitute for *slaves*, those obscure terms, "other persons," or "persons bound to labour," &c., none of which can be considered as adequate definitions of the term they are meant to replace. The matter then which was evidently the subject of conflicting opinions among the contracting parties, was thus left for posterity to decide upon. It is true some arrangements were agreed upon, and were called *compromises*, but the subject was *left open to discussion*. The questions involved in it were not *permanently* settled, it could not reasonably be expected that they could then have been settled, they never have heen settled, and if they ever are settled, they must be settled either *now* or at *some future time*. Then seeing as we do, that this matter could not be arranged when the Constitution was framed, because there were two parties to the contract, whose views and interests rendered such a thing *impossible* And knowing that the very evil which our fathers wished to avoid by *avoiding the subject*, has now appeared in a monstrous form. Is there any doubt as to what the South *should* do, if it is in self-defence forced to separate from the North? If the South is forced to dissolve the contract, because institutions essential to her very existence cannot safely exist *under the contract*, is it not the result of common sense to suppose that she would immediately erect her own government, so framed and constituted, that those institutions which are essential to her existence *can* safely exist under it, and that the causes which dissolved the old compact, could not exist under the new. The question then comes up, can the South accomplish this? We answer, yes; and by the same simple process, that a burnt child avoids the fire. After the division is effected, the slaveholding States would, without doubt, form a republic similar to the present, and the Constitution of that Republic would be essentially a copy of the Constitution of the present Republic. But there would be this difference among others. Where the Constitution now leaves the subject of slavery one of dispute and discussion, there would undoubtedly be some clause in the Constitution of the new Republic which would set that matter forever at rest. We cannot doubt there would be something in spirit and substance like the following introduced into that instrument, viz:

Whereas, It has been found by experience in the affairs of the late Republic of the United States, that it is inexpedient and dangerous to allow the discussion of such subjects as rest wholly on the prejudiced opinions of a small minority, who consider slavery wrong, and who have no connection and no legal right to interfere with the custom they undertake to condemn, in the halls of a National Congress; because of the inevitable tendency it creates to sectional animosities and Geographical parties. And, whereas, It is believed to be out of the province of governments to intermeddle with such deep-rooted customs of society, as the mode of worshipping, the mode of living, the mode of dressing, the mode of labouring, the mode of purchasing labour, the mode of commanding, the mode of obeying, or the mode of classifying the relations of society; except in so much as may relate to a wholesome regulation of the same.

And whereas, Slavery is, in all civilized communities, *a usage of society* which should be left to the opinion, interest, policy, and economy of the *society in which it exists*, to abolish or continue it; and which has been a fundamental principle and a characteristic feature in the domestic relations of society *in each and every State here represented*, from the beginning of their very existence.

Therefore, All propositions, petitions, resolutions, bills, or any other measures relating to the subject of slavery in any of these States, or in any territory now belonging to, or hereafter to be acquired by these States, are prohibited in the Congress of this Republic; except in such cases as may require the incidental advertance to the subject, or may relate to claims for indemnity for the loss of property, or otherwise acknowledging the right of property possessed by the master in the slave, and the consequent right of the master to carry his slave into any territory which, at the time, belongs to this Republic.

Provided, Nothing herein prohibited shall be so construed as to prevent the action of any State, with regard to slavery, *within its own limits* and *and among its own people.*

Now, what is to prevent the adoption of such a clause as this? If every State is a slaveholding State, every State must agree to it, at least in its essence. It does not interfere with the prerogative of the States. It is not inconsistent with the Constitution of any of the slaveholding States. It does not *perpetuate* slavery any more than the present Constitution does. It does not prevent the abolition of slavery by the only proper authority, the sovereign people as represented in their *State Government.* But it *does* prevent the insulting and obnoxious discussion of the subject in the *Federal* Government. It *does* obviate the dangers of sectional and geographical jealousies, and it does most effectually guard against any infringement on the rights of the States, the dignity of a Congress, and the stability of the new union of States.

If this is done by the South *then*, will it not be something which the South cannot do now? Would it not be something which our fathers could not do sixty years ago, because they could not reconcile conflicting opinions and interests. And would it not be doing *something*, to do what they could not do?

This division of the States, if properly consummated, is, under the existing state of things, most earnestly to be desired. It would certainly be an advantage to the South. The great reason why this division should be accomplished as soon as possible, is. that unless some *miraculous* interposition of Providence creates a thorough revolution in the political affairs of this government, it must lead to a separation of the South from the North, or a total subjugation of the former to the latter, at some future time. Another reason is, the longer this crisis is delayed the more cruel will be the contests of the occasion. Another is: It would be doing wrong to our children to leave them to perform a task which we ourselves can accomplish with half the ease. It would be disgraceful in us to entail a revolution upon them, which will at least be doubtful in its results, whilst we, with good prospects of success, shrink from it because it is troublesome. The longer this crisis is delayed the greater will be the population of the North, in comparison with that of the South, and consequently the greater will be the political as well as military strength of the North in comparison with those of the South. The longer it is delayed, the longer will the North grow rich off the slave labour of the South, and the longer will the South be the theatre of constant watchfulness and apprehension lest new insults be added to new injuries.

CHAPTER VIII.

Romeo.—"The world affords no law to make the rich;
Then be not poor, but break it, and take this."
Apothecary.—" My poverty, but not my will, consents.
Romeo.—" I pay thy poverty, and not thy will.

The economy of slave labour in the Southern States is a matter which has long since been determined by those competent of judging from experience. And the fact of its so long continuing in prosperity, notwithstanding the relentless endeavours that have been made to crush it, is no slight evidence that slave labour is *politically* economical. We say politically economical, but it must not be supposed that we do not also mean it is *domestically* and *individually* economical. For no enterprize which, by its own nature, proves unprofitable to the *individuals* concerned in it, can at the same time be profitable or advantageous to the *com-*

munity at large; neither can that enterprize which enriches the individuals concerned in it, at the same time impoverish the community. The wealth and prosperity of a political community is, after all, nothing more than the aggregate wealth and prosperity of the individuals of the community. And when we speak of the political economy of slavery, we refer to *practice* only, no vague theories of utilitarianism, philanthropy or money circulation, enter into our ideas of economy, for none of them are necessarily involved in the definition of the term. Great national wealth may exist without a correspondingly great amount of *money;* therefore, it must not be expected when we assert how much wealth there is at the South, that we will sum it up in dollars and cents. Wealth and money have very different means. Nor would it be correct to judge of a nation's wealth by what is seen in one or two cities. Single instances of large fortunes possessed by individuals, or a great amount of capital concentrated in a single city, afford no conclusive evidence of the general wealth of a nation. Therefore, in estimating the merits of slavery, as it concerns political economy, we must look to general practical results, and descend to particulars only with a view to illustrate or contrast.

We have already seen, that in the year 1790, when the United States began to be settled and confirmed in its new form of government, the population in the Northern and in the Southern States were nearly the same, and their wealth and resources was also about equal. Since then, however, the North has obtained a decided superiority in some respects, and that superior degree of political influence and aggregate wealth which *may have* accrued there from, has to no small extent given rise to the belief that slavery was a check on the progress of the South. This opinion among the great mass of citizens, who have heretofore thought but little on the subject, may appear a plausible one, for to the superficial observer the only essential and striking difference between the South and the North, is that one is slaveholding and the other non-slaveholding, and in view of the great discount to which philanthropy has fallen in these late days, it is not difficult for people to be persuaded that any difference existing between the two sections, in any of their resources, is entirely owing to the difference of domestic institutions belonging to the two. Such a belief, however, involves a most egregious error.

It is a palpable feature of man's nature that he must be made to feel the effects of any cause before he can be brought to investigate the cause itself. The aid of medicine is not resorted to before the symptoms of disease admonish us; neither can a remedy be applied before the evil is discovered. It is on account of this fixed principle in our nature, that monstrous political errors sometimes mislead a community for ages, for they are destined to remain uncorrected till sluggish man finds the burdens they impose absolutely insupportable. Such an error has been that of supposing the *apparent* superior advancement of the North is owing to its, so called, free labour being more economical than our slave labour. The time has come, however, when men begin to suffer from the pernicious effects of this error, so long indulged; and they have accordingly begun to investigate the causes.

Why should it be said that the difference in the affairs of the North and South is to be attribted to their different systems of labouring? As far as the wealth of the two is concerned, it may truly be said that convenience is the sole cause of the assertion, for truth and reason have no share in it. Every intelligent being must be aware that the wealth of different countries, and even different sections of the same country, arises from very different circumstances. That enterprize which would be profitable in one quarter, would not necessarily be so in all others. That system of labour which is cheapest in one quarter, is not necessarily so in all others. Because hireling labour is cheapest at the North, it does not follow that slave labour is not the cheapest at the South. In that country where nature has been pleased to provide a fertile soil and a genial climate, where agriculture is the most favoured and most profitable pursuit, it would be folly to urge that agriculture should be abandoned for the pursuit of commerce or manufactures because they outstrip agriculture in other countries; and in the same way, in that country where nature has been sparing in her bounties, by leaving the soil barren and the climate harsh, but in which there are admirable facilities for commerce and manufactures, it would be folly to urge that they should be abandoned for agriculture, because agriculture outstrips them in other countries. In that country where nature breathes an atmostphere poisonous to one race, but not so to another, it would be folly to argue that the race which endures the climate without injury, should not be made to gather the rich harvests which no other hands could gather, but which are necessary for both races in common; and likewise, in that country where the atmostphere bears no poison on its breath, where every race can bear exposure with equal chances, because one race in this climate reduces the wages of labour to a lower standard, (absolutely considered,) than another race in another climate is able to, it would be folly to contend that the labour which is cheapest in the first climate, must, if transported to that other climate, necessarily be the cheapest there also; on the contrary, the very poison which pervades that other climate renders such labour the most costly that could be had, in as much as the wages of labour *would then be death.* It may, therefore, be premised that, in any country, that system of labour is cheapest, which all things being considered, promotes best the general wealth and prosperity; without any regard being necessarily had to the number of dollars and cents bestowed in *wages.*

It is an invariable rule, where great wealth has been accumulated from commerce and manufactures, that profits in these departments will regulate profits in agriculture. For "as the price of those commodities, raised at the least expense, will regulate, in ordinary circumstances, the price of others, in the same department of production, so will profits follow the same general law, as regards different employments. Those branches of business that afford the greatest advantages to producers, can be carried on with lower profits, than those in which equal facilities are not to be had." In conformity with this principle, it is not only true, what we have just stated with regard to profits in commerce and manufactures, but it is equally true that in those countries where superior facilities exist of production from the soil, profits in all departments will generally be regulated by those in agriculture.

Every body knows how *splendidly* the manufactures and commerce of the North have been protected and fostered by the Federal Government, and as the natural consequence, what great wealth has been accumulated there from these sources. Now, notwithstanding the *material* upon which the capital in these departments has been called to operate, is the produce of Southern soil, this circumstance does not alter the principle, that where great wealth has been accumulated from commerce and manufactures, profits in these departments will regulate profits in agriculture. It is owing then to these circumstances, and *these alone*, that the capitalists of the North have been able to exert such a commanding influence over the profits of agriculture at the South. The consideration of *labour* does not enter into the case any more than all other items of economy, but as to the social relation which the labourer bears to the capitalist, it is absolutely foreign to the subject. Who can gainsay it? If the slaves in our cotton fields were hirelings instead of domestics, who will show that the commerce and manufactures of the North would ever have been one jot the less protected by government for that; or who can prove that an established principle would be completely overthrown on that account? So far from citing the commercial and manufacturing prosperity of the North as an evidence of the impoverishing effects of slavery at the South, it would be a hundred fold nearer the truth to point to the toiling slave as he gathers in the rich harvest of the South, and give him the credit of enriching the nabobs of the philanthropic North.

As proof that slavery cannot be such a draw back to the South as people would have us believe, we have merely to take up the financial and commercial history of the country; on their pages are to be found what the South *was* when it had slavery *without* a union with the North, and what the South *is* when it has slavery *with* a union with the North.

Let us now see how slave labour effects the increase of wealth so essential to the increase of population. Is it economical or is it extravagant, as circumstances control it in the Southern States? And are the health and enjoyments of our slaves equal or superior to those of other labourers in other countries? It is certain, that in every civilized country, a great proportion of the inhabitants must subsist by their daily labour. In thickly populated districts, in large towns and cities this proportion increases much more rapidly than capital can be accumulated; and as the proportion of capital to labour becomes smaller and smaller, the wages of labour must also become less and less till it is reduced to the lowest possible pitch. This principle applies, however, only in those communities where *labour is hired;* it cannot hold where labour is itself an ingredient of the capital. As a matter of course, in a community where labour is hired, when employment is scarce in proportion to the demand for it, those dispensing the favour of giving employment will take advantage of the great demand; and on the other hand, those in search of employment must necessarily yield to the pressure coming from the scarcity of it. These latter are ultimately forced to receive the smallest amount of wages that can sustain life. The constant tendency is to a reduction of wages without a corresponding reduction of labour. The war between capital and labour has for its natural object an equilibrium, *a stable equilibrium* between these opposing powers, but where one power has become so much greater than the other, no equilibrium can be established between them without the aid of an auxiliary power on the part of the weaker; this auxiliary power in the case of *labour,* is that law of nature which requires a certain amount of food to sustain life in the labourer. When, therefore, in a community where this war is raging, the triumphant party, which is always capital, has reduced its opponent to this extremity, the law of nature steps in, and the equilibrium is established, *but not till then.* Such is the state of things *inevitable at the North, impossible at the South.* Here, the very reverse is the case. If there is one item in the whole economy of the Southern States which is more invariable and unchangeable than any other, it is the wages of labour, which is but another term for the support of our slaves. Crops may vary. Prices may vary. Profits may vary. The wages of labour are still the same. Not because it is reduced to that low standard beyond which it cannot go, but because labour is at peace with capital, labour *is* capital, and therefore *cannot possibly* be depreciated without a corresponding depreciation of capital.

Moreover, there is no political or commercial revolution which does not directly effect the persons and earnings of the, so called, free labourer. If the employer finds it expedient to suspend his business, or to change his residence, his hirelings are immediately dismissed, and it is their own good luck if they soon find employment again.

In the slaveholding States a very different picture is presented. They are all essentially agricultural, their population is therefore not dense. So far from employment being in demand, it is the labourer who is in demand. And instead of the wages of labour being reduced to the lowest standard, it is rather raised to the highest. The slave feels none of the effects of financial pressure, commercial panics or any of those fluctuations which will sometimes overtake us. He is, at all times, provided with every necessary of life, and not unfrequently with many of its luxuries. If the master finds it expedient to suspend his business or change his residence he is bound, by his own interests, to find a new owner for his slave, or else to carry his slave away with him; but in no case is the negro left, as the dismissed hireling is, to seek a new employer without having the means of subsistence in the meantime. The labour to which the slave is subjected is in no respect calculated to impair the physical or mental condition of the individual; his work is comparatively light and easy to be performed. And notwithstanding all the invective that has been heaped upon the cruel slave owner, there is no master so exacting as want, no code of discipline so cruelly relentless as that of necessity. The slave has no care for to-morrow, he never knows the misery experienced by an ejected hireling. What matters it to him how the necessaries of life are selling, the fluctuations in the market do not reach him, he has a never-failing granary in his master's barn, a certain banker in his master's purse. His condition is good, his tenure certain. He enjoys this blessing, which no hireling can boast, he knows that though he may never become the possessor of wealth, neither he nor his children can ever want the necessaries of life; though he may never sway men's minds in the political arena, he nor his offspring will never be in a worse condition than at present, notwithstanding *his comforts are to be envied by perhaps half the human family.* The labourer is thus amply and certainly rewarded for his toil, and is the better enabled to preserve his energies.

In an agricultural S ate, capital is more rapidly accumulated when the profits come directly into the hands of *resident owners of large tracts of land*, than when they go to non-resident owners, or are cut up into small parcels for proprietors of limited extent. This principle operates effectually in the Southern States, the chief productions of which are cotton, rice, tobacco and sugar, and all of which are cultivated by slaves under the immediate supervision of resident owners. It has been truly observed* that "capital is accumulated on the soil more abundantly and rapidly when large money returns fall into the hands of cultivators who are owners, than when they are divided with landlords. It would, of course, be the same, should both spend alike, but the circumstance of ownership makes all the difference possible in the results. The saving from profit to add to capital, is a principle that is never weakened when the security of property is complete, and when the increased value given to capital, in whatever form that value may exist, continues with the improver instead of passing into the hands of others." Now, one of the leading peculiarities of Southern agriculture, is, that the produce of the land goes directly into the possession of the owner who is the cultivator. There are no landlords, tenants, leased lands, &c., in the South. The cultivator is almost invariably the owner; and the owner seldom fails to save from his profits to add to his capital. The chief produce of the soil is an article raised to supply the markets of the world, its price, though liable to fluctuate is always remunerating, and in proportion to the costs of production, is higher than that of most staples; and in addition to all this we have a monopoly of the trade.

There is one other consideration which must not be overlooked. When the employer pays the free labourer his wages, he takes just so much from the profits to pass entirely out of his hands, for the wages of the hireling yield no return to the capital of the employer, excepting, of course, the labour which is derived; they go to promote the comfort of himself and his family, and

* See So. Rev., 1828.

thereby, the *increase* of his family, but this increase affords no increase to the capital of the employer. But when the master supports the slave, he takes just so much from the profits *to add to the capital,* and not to pass out of his hands, for the support of the slave yields a considerable return to the master's capital, besides the labour which is derived; this support goes to promote the comfort of the slave and those of his family, and thereby the increase of the latter, *which is doubly promoted by the absence of all cares for providing,* but this increase affords a corresponding increase to the capital of the master; so that it may be said not one cent of the costs of labour in our system passes from the hands of the proprietor, whilst the labourer is nevertheless amply recompensed.

After all that has been said about the profitableness and productiveness of Northern manufactories, we believe there is no branch of industry which when properly considered, affords a greater natural increase of capital than the agriculture of the slaveholding States. We speak, of course, with reference to entire results, and not individual cases.

We have seen various estimates of the profits of slave labour, and will take this occasion to insert a few, which we believe to be as correct as estimates generally are.

In 1848, the following estimate was made of the capital invested in the culture of cotton, and the nett proceeds.* All the slaves in the cotton States who were engaged in the culture of rice, sugar, grain or any other staple than cotton, being excluded, it was believed that the number of slaves engaged in cultivating cotton was about 1,000,000. Of these, about 700,000 were workers. The following then was the table of items which go to make up the entire capital devoted to the cotton culture.

1. 1,000,000 slaves, - - - - -	at $500	$500,000,000
2. Land in cotton, 4,000,000 acres, - -	" 10	40,000,000
3. Land in provisions, 6,000,000 acres, -	" 10	60,000,000
4. Land in timber and pasture, 10,000,000 acres,	" 2	20,000,000
5. Mules and horses, 300,000, - -	" 80	24,000,000
6. Hogs and sheep, 4,200,000, - -	" 1	4,200,000
7. Cattle, 200,000, - - - -	" 5	1,000,000
8. Ploughs, 400,000, - - - - -	" 2	800,000
9. Other implements, tools, &c., &c., -	"	600,000
		$650,600,000

The interest of 650,600,000 dollars at 7 per cent. is		$45,542,000
Let us see how near the annual profits come to this. Estimating the crop at 2,000,000 bales, of 400 pounds each, we would have, at 10 cents per pound,		
1. Cotton crop 800,000,000 lbs.	10 cts.	$80,000,000
†2. The natural increase of slaves at 3 per cent., the usual average increase, would be, valuing them as above, at $500 each, - - -		$15,000,000
Making the gross proceeds amount to - - - -		$95,000,000

* In So. Rev., see Com. Rev.

† This item was not included in the original estimate, but we think it is too important to be omitted.

From which must be deducted, for overseer's wages, physicians, taxes, freight on cotton, the support of children and old negroes who do not work, about $40 per hand, which is a very liberal allowance, and we have to deduct for expenses, - - - - - - - -	40,000,000
Leaving a nett profit of - - - - - - - -	$55,000,000

Nearly 8 1-2 per cent. on the capital invested.

This estimate is made upon cotton at 10 cents, when it falls below that, the profits diminish rapidly, for the expenses continue the same, though prices diminish. And in like manner, when the price rises above 10 cts., the profits increase vastly, because the expenses remain stationary always.

"When we consider that there is an improvement in the annual value of the negroes upon every well regulated cotton farm, and that the great majority of planters raise, or support their families from what may be called the offal of a farm, that is, from what is raised on it and is scarcely missed or calculated in its products, which is always the case when the owner lives on it, then we are induced to believe there is no investment known of capital as large as 650,600,000 dollars equal in value to that in cotton."

Another estimate has been made of the profits of slave labour in Louisiana alone: "The produce of Louisiana, the average product for five years, from 1840 to 1845 inclusive, was,

1.	117,000 hhd's. sugar, - - - - -	at $60	$7,020,000
2.	5,850,000 gallons molasses. - - -	" 20 cts.	1,170,000
3.	350,000 bales cotton, - - - - -	" $30	10,500,000
	Making the gross proceeds amount to - - - - -		$18,690,000

At present the sugar crop is greatly larger, and the cotton smaller than they are here set down, though the proceeds of the crops in money are about the same. The annual expediture for machinery, engines, kettles, mules, horses, and oxen, is estimated by the chamber of commerce at $870,000; but, place it at a million, and then Louisiana draws an annual income from her slave labour of $17,690,000. Supposing the slave population of Louisiana to have been 200,000 during the five years from 1840 to 1845 inclusive, as the census in 1840 gave to her 168,452, and that statement makes the *production of each slave* in the State, man, woman and child amount to the sum of $88 45."

So much for estimates, now for facts. If hired labour was invariably cheaper than slave labour, where could we find the fact illustrated better than on the British West India Islands. There, both slave labour and "*free*" labour have been tried, in the *same pursuits* and by the *same people*. These two circumstances enable us to make the closest possible comparison, for all the circumstances of soil, climate, pursuits, production, *race*, and civilization remain the same, whilst one single social relation only has been changed.

In the "*free labour*" colonies of Great Britain, it cost, in 1847, for the *production* of every ton of sugar £20. While in slave countries it cost but £12, a little over half as much.

The following statistics show the depreciation in value of individual estates, and the consequent diminution of national weatlh, which followed the emancipation of the West India slaves. We give but a few instances. *In an article on the "West India Islands," the editor of the Commercial Review,

* See De Bow's Commercial Review of 1848.

quotes: "In 1838, the value of the estates, owing to the want of labour, had fallen from one-third to a half. The following is the account of some of the estates.

	Price in 1838.	Former Price.
Anna Catherina estate, - -	£30,000	£50,000
Providence estate, - - -	38,000	80,000
Thomas estate, - - -	20,000	40,000
In 1840, the depreciation became greater.		
Rome and Houston estate, - -	40,000	100,000
Success estate, - - - - -	30,000	55,000
Kitty estate, - - - -	26,000	60,000
William estate, - - - - -	18,000	40,000
In, and after, 1844, the depreciation was still greater.		
Groenveldt estate, - - -	£10,000	£35,000
Baillies's Hope estate, - - -	7,000	50,000
Haarlem estate, - - -	3,500	50,000

Free labour is, on these Islands, *wholesale economy* indeed, and slave labour, of course, the most headlong extravagance. In this short table, we see facts startling enough to convince the veriest *booby* in the land, which is the most economical labour, that of the slave, which enhances an estate to as much as 50,000 pounds, or that of the "*free* man," which depreciates it to 3,500, *precisely the interest of the former for one year at seven per cent.* Which was the most productive of wealth and prosperity to the nation in this case, the slave, whose labour in one year would produce a *net profit*, amounting to more than the *whole capital* upon which the "free man" operates, or the free negro, whose brutal laziness depreciates capital from 50,000 to 3,500 in a few short years.

It has been argued against agriculture that there is more waste, and a greater surplus over and above the necessary expenses of production, in proportion to the quantity produced, in agriculture than in manufactures. But we are credibly informed, and it has more than once been demonstrated that such is by no means the case. It has also been maintained, that commodities raised from the soil are not capable of regular increase from improved modes of cultivation, in the same degree as articles produced by machinery. But it has been proved, *at least with regard to America,** "that there are no just grounds for the conclusion, that improvements in cultivation are necessarily partial, and not progressive like manufactures, and that a physical law bounds human skill and invention more in that art, which provides us food (and raw material) than in the others that minister to our necessary wants. Facility of production on the land, like facility of production in manufactures, is dependent on those arrangements which best stimulate, in all departments of industry, the invention and efforts of producers, and on these alone. The price, generally, of the products of the soil, like the price of articles produced by machinery, will be governed, in the absence of all unnatural excitements, by the expense of raising that portion which is produced at the least cost."

In view then of all we have said, we have no reason to doubt that the peculiar productiveness of agriculture at the South, and the necessary demand for the products, owing to their cheapness and superior quality, and a partial monopoly, are the chief reasons why slave labour, though the mostly in other countries, is the cheapest in the Southern States. But the *chiefest* reason remains to be told. It is because *no other can be had.* Free labor has been tried, and failed.† The

* In the Southern Quarterly Review of 1828.

† In the case of the Colony of Georgia. See page 70.

experiment needs no repetition. Our fathers left us these slaves to cultivate our lands: nature smiles on our every effort, and returns an abundant harvest; our climate forbids that any other race shall cultivate our fields; our *independence* demands that we should retain our slaves, and be assured, you who doubt it, our sharpened swords will leap from their scabbards to defend *that.*

We need scarcely stop to explain why no other than slave labour can be had at the South. Every body who has ever passed a summer in any planting district of the South, already understands it; but for the benefit of those who may never have had that experience, we will insert the evidence of authentic documents.

In most highly cultivated districts in the southern country, white men are invariably the victims of a very dangerous fever, arising from malaria, but negroes almost universally escape. We have been informed by medical gentlemen, residing in such districts, that when the rare case does occur of a negro taking fever from this malaria, it is almost always of an intermittent nature, and can be more easily subdued. But in the generality of cases where the patient is white, the fever becomes remittent, and not unfrequently a congestion of the brain, or some other vital part terminates the case.

The Census of Charleston, S. C., taken in 1849, affords *the very best* information on this subject that is to be had, it is not, however, the best that could be desired, for it only has to do with the city, whereas our inquiries have a more particular relation to the planting districts of the country. We can, at any rate, gather enough from that source, to give an idea how much more fatal the climate of the South is to the white man than to the negro.

From the year 1822 to 1848 inclusive, the number of deaths in the city of Charleston *from fevers*, which are the media through which the malaria acts, were as follows:*

	Whites.	Negroes.
1. Billious Fever, - - - - -	309	144
2. Congestive " - - - - -	12	8
3. Country " - - - - -	216	37
4. Intermittent " - - - - -	44	11
5. Remittent " - - - - -	14	3
6. Yellow " - - - - -	934	14
	1529	217

In looking at this table, the following facts must be remembered:

The white population was during this whole period, on an average, about 4,000 less than the negro population.†

The whites are not half as much exposed to the injurious effects of the climate as the negroes are.

The whites resort to the city for health, whereas the negro enjoys far better health in the country than he does in the city.

Taking every thing then into consideration, we have every reason to believe that the difference between the white and the negro mortality, from the effects of climate, as expressed in these numbers, is but half what it would be if similar statistics could be collected of the South at large. Instead therefore of putting down 217 negro deaths to 1,529 white deaths, or, for the sake of brevity, 2 to 15, from the effects of climate throughout the entire planting region of the

* See tables "A" and "B," Census of Charleston for 1849.

† In the term "negro," we include all having any negro blood.

South; we will say that there are *fifteen whites* to *one* negro, who dies from the effects of the climate. But, in addition to this, it must be observed, that these fevers are with more difficulty subdued in the white than in the negro race. Where the white man will be incapacitated for a whole year, and his constitution completely ruined, the negro will take a few doses of medicine and be as well as ever.

During this period of 26 years, the average annual proportion of deaths to the population was,

Among the whites, 2.5 to every 100.
" negroes, 2.4 to every 100.

But the averange annual deaths from *fevers*, (not including yellow fever,) was,

Among the whites, 7.85 per cent of all deaths.
" negroes, 3.95 " " "

Of all the deaths among the whites, there were 685 over 70 years of age, and 3 over 100.

Of all the deaths among the negroes, there were 1,264 over 70 years of age, and 79 over 100.

The negroes then, not only escape in a great measure the diseases indigenous to our climate, but they live to a greater age than the whites. We have no doubt if a correct comparison could be instituted, it would be found that that the negroes, yes, the *slaves* of the Southern States, are the healthiest and the longest lived people of any who live in corresponding latitudes in the world, and may be, of any who live in *any* latitude in the world.

But this truth is not confined to Charleston, nor to South-Carolina. Maryland, the most northern of the slaveholding States, vouches for it with equal force. In a pamphlet published in 1827,* the mortality of Baltimore for the years 1823–'4 and '5, was given as follows: among the whites, one in every forty-four; among the *slaves*, one in every seventy-seven.

Even when compared with the negro population of the free States, we find our slaves vastly more healthy. The average mortality in Philadelphia, among the negroes, for the ten years ending with 1830, was *one* in *twenty-six*, while in Charleston, for the eight years ending with 1837, during three of which either yellow fever or cholera prevailed, it was one in *forty-four*. But even with yellow fever, cholera, climate and *slavery* all combined, how does the mortality of the negroes in Boston, who have nothing but *liberty* to contend with, compare with those of Charleston and other southern cities. *It is about three hundred per cent greater.* Where in Boston the average deaths among negroes is 1 in 15, in Charleston it is but 1 in 44. These truths speak for themselves, we leave them with the reader.

There is one consideration to which we are naturally drawn by the foregoing remarks. It is this. Whatever else may be dispensed with by the labourer, *life and health* are of the *first* importance, they are *absolutely indispensable.* It is, therefore, a primary object in the economy of labour to promote life and health to the greatest possible extent. It would then be correct to say, that, that system of labour, and those departments of industry, which, while they best promote the wealth and prosperity of a nation, detract nothing from the health and life of the labourer, are cheaper than that system and those pursuits which promote the national wealth at the expense of those who labour. The economy which this principle involves, is what we will term *the economy of life.*

In every enterprise, those who have the direction of it, make it their business to economize in the lives of those whose efforts are required to promote it. The prudent general will plan his campaign, and conduct the affairs of his army in

* By Dr. Niles, then of New-York.

such a way as to injure the enemy as much as possible, while he economizes to the greatest possible extent the lives of the soldiers under him. He that can gain a victory with the loss of but ten men, is, by just so much, a greater captain than he who, all other things being the same, gains the victory, but looses a *thousand* men. So, he is the greatest statesman who provides such laws and combines such circumstances, as will ensure the successfnl cultivation of the rich lands of his state with the least loss of human life, all other things being the same. If, therefore, it can be shown that the laws of our fathers, which regulate and perpetuate slavery, serve better than any other laws could, to promote the wealth and prosperity of our State, through the successful cultivation they insure, it follows that their councils were the best, and their economy the soundest we could desire. But we have just seen the most unmistakable evidence, that the negro race can cultivate our fields without the most trifling injury from any cause, while the white race, should they attempt to do the same, would be visited with a fearful pestilence, and, in a short time, their fields would be deserted, and their towns depopulated. Which then is the wisest and most economical measure, our slave laws, or those which northern philanthropists desire should replace them?

The fact we have cited, of the health and longevity of the negro race in our Southern States, addresses itself not only to the economist, but to the philanthropist, aye and the *abolitionist* himself, if he is not totally deranged by the frenzy of fanaticism. The negro population of Charleston, and we have no doubt the same may be said of *any southern city*, though we do not know it as a fact, shows "not only a lower ratio of mortally than any *labouring class* of any country, but a lower mortally than the *aggregate population* (including nobility and all,) of any country in Europe, except England, with which it is about at par, and would surpass even England, were the slaves taken separate from the free colored. The mortality of the aggregate colored population of Charleston now, is less than that of the aggregate of any *town* in Europe."*

"So little are they (the negroes) affected by that fell destroyer of the white race, *malaria*, which kills more than war and famine, that they suffer in the Southern States more from diseases of winter than those of summer. They are, I am informed, exempt from the violent congestive fevers of our interior districts, and other violent forms of marsh (or country) fever; and so exempt are they from yellow fever, that I am now attending my first case of this disease in a full blooded negro. In fact, it would seem that the negro blood is an antidote against yellow fever, for the smallest admixture of it with the white will protect against this disease, even though the subject come from a healthy northern latitude, in the midst of an epidemic."

The experience of every people shows that agriculture is the most healthy avocation, that is, those who occupy themselves in this department of industry enjoy more vigorous health and live to a greater average age, than those who are devoted to other pursuits. Besides that, in an agricultural country there are but few large cities, they being adverse to the genius of this pursuit. The population is spread over a large territory, with here and there a small town. Statistics have always shown, that in a large cities there is a much greater degree of mortality in proportion to population, and which we term a *waste of human life*, than is to be found in small towns and agricultural districts.

Now the South is an agricultural country, it has few large cities, and therefore is in a great measure exempt from that waste of human life which is peculiar to large cities. But if there is any one condition which is *absolutely necessary* in order that the South should be agricultural, and by that means exempt from this waste of human life, it may with truth be said, that it is to that one condition

* See an article in the Com. Review, called "Statistics of Southern slave population."

this saving of human life is to be attributed. And when that condition is *the only condition which can possibly serve this end*, it is eminently true to say, that this saving of life is to be attributed solely and wholly to that one condition. Such a condition, is that which make the negro the white man's slave. Who then will question the economy of slavery at the South? Look at the city of New-York, it is so much boasted of for its wealth and prosperity. Compare the expenditure of human life there, with that of any planting district of the same population in the world.

In the last twenty years the population of New-York has nearly doubled, *but its mortality has nearly trebled.** Can this be said of any southern community?

If it is still maintained that slave labour is not *the cheapest we could have*, why then we give up the field, we have nothing more to say; but we have this consolation, that if our slaves cost us so dearly, what is loss to us is gain to them. By as much as they cost us too much, by so much are they better off. What is lost to the wealth of the nation is gained by the humanity of it. If we are cheated, it is with our eyes open, *and no thanks to the North that we are not worse off.*

A consideration which should not be overlooked, and which is intimately connected with the economy of slavery, is the position in our States occupied by free negroes and mulatoes. At the North this class of people is a burden on the community, at the South, under existing laws, they are in no respect a disadvantage. It has been very justly remarked of these people, in the Southern Review of 1828, that they are "in a much better condition, and much less troublesome to society, in the slavehold'ng, and especially in the planting, than in the non-slaveholding States. In the first place, wages are higher, and the means of subsistance more easily attainable. In the next place, the climate is more congenial to them; and, lastly and principally, *the law coincides with public opinion* in assigning to them an inferior and servile rank. They are accustomed to their station in society, know they cannot better it, and are reconciled to it. In the States where the laws put them on an equal footing with the white population—but the opinions, or what they may justly consider the prejudices of the white portion of society, present an insuperable bar to their taking that station—their feelings are those of men who have been tantalized and deluded. They are thus rendered more discontented and disorderly, more idle, dissolute and vicious, than the corresponding class of persons amongst us. This is notoriously the case with respect to the colored population of Philadelphia.

It is not so much inferiority of *rank* that excites a feeling of contempt on one side, or of degradation on the other. A private soldier may be perfectly respectable in the station which the laws assign him, though his rank be the very lowest, and so may the peasant in Germany. To be degraded by *opinion*, is a thousand fold worse to the feelings of the individual, than to be degraded by the laws. To be despised by those with whom we conceive ourselves entitled to stand on a footing of equality, constitutes the very bitterness of degradation. Accordingly, we believe, that the free coloured persons of the South, are less contemned and more respectable than those of the North."

We must now conclude this chapter. We have seen a few of the advantages of our system of labour; we have contrasted some of our affairs with those of Northern and European States, without becoming envious of either. But we would detain the reader one moment more. Let him contrast the happy race of slaves he every day sees around him, with those poor creatures in European mines who are thus touchingly described by an American orator.†

* See "the North and the South," by Fisher.

† The late Hon. Hugh S. Legaré, of South-Carolina. See Legarés Works, page 320.

"A race, among no inconsiderable portion of whom famine and pestilence may be said to dwell continually—many of whom are without morals, without education, without a country, without a God! and may be said to know society only by the terrors of its penal code, and to live in perpetual war with it. Poor bondmen! mocked with the name of liberty, that they may be sometimes tempted to break their chains, in order that, after a few days of starvation in idleness or dissipation, they may be driven back to their prison house, to take them up again, heavier and more galling than before: severed, as it has been touchingly expressed, from nature, from the common air and the light of the sun; knowing only by hearsay that the fields are green, that the birds sing, and that there is a perfume in flowers."

CHAPTER IX.

"Look forward what's to come, and back what's past;
Thy life will be with praise and prudence graced;
What loss or gain may follow, thou mayst guess;
Thou then wilt be secure of the success."

This chapter will be devoted to the subject of cotton and the cotton trade. The culture of cotton is intimately connected with the economy of slave labour in the Southern States, and in some of them it is a prominent feature in the politics of the State. And as this department of industry *rests wholly and solely on slave labour*, we have thought it expedient to add to the preceding chapter on the *economy* of this kind of labour, a short chapter on the subject of Cotton, with which it is so intimately connected, and which has such a peculiar relation to the domestic affairs of the Southern States.

In England, France, and other European States, there has been within the last few generations a most astonishing advance in arts of every kind; labour and capital has increased apace, and so steadily have these causes been operating, that it is now acknowledged these States can with but a moiety of their labour and capital supply their respective wants; it follows then that they must look abroad for employment for the remainder of their capital and labour. For this purpose they look in those directions where their wishes are most certainly to be gratified—they invest their capital where profits are greatest—they expend their labour where wages are highest. But where must the people of Europe look with such objects? to the iceburgs of the polar regions, or to the rich valleys of the tropics; to the densely populated countries of the old world, or to the newly settled portions of the new. And what will be exchanged between these countries but their respective productions? Cotton, Tobacco, Sugar, Rice and Coffee, are five articles which, experience every day shows, render the more northern countries of the civilized world dependant, in a great degree, upon the prosperity of the more southern countries, for a corresponding increase of commerce, manufactures, navigation, wealth and power.

In the Southern States of this Union, *cotton* is the staple which serves preeminently this part. It is an article which, whether on account of its giving employment to millions in its culture—to thousands upon thousands in its transportation and shipment—to millions more in its manufacture, and as many more in its consumption; or, on account of its being the basis of the most friendly and advantageous commercial and political intercourse, between us and the leading nations of the earth; whether the crops are short, or the prices low, is like the widows cruse of oil, it never fails. It never fails in its kind offices to the millions of poor people who are connected with it, from the sowing of the seed, to the wearing of the garment of which it is made. To be sure there are oscilations in the market, daily fluctuations in the price, but the cry is still "they come."

No nation for such a series of years, with short crops and large crops, with high prices and low, and so much in its infancy as this, has ever advanced so steadily and so rapidly in its powers, both of production and consumption as the United States. For the last twenty years, the average annual increase in the production of cotton has been about 70,000 bales, and the average increase in consumption about 11,000 bales; but, during the last five years, the increase in production has averaged 80,000 bales per annum, and in consumption 15,000. Last year, France and the North of Europe consumed about 750,000 bales of the American staple, and this consumption increases about 100,000 bales every year. Great Britain consumed about 1,125,000 bales, and the United States about 545,000. The supply and consumption of the *American staples* in these countries, is always, at whatever price, certain to *equal* these amounts, and if no unnatural cause prevents, will annually increase at the rate of about *three per cent*; but *this can not be said of the staples of any other country.*

The supply from India is almost entirely dependant on the prices. The average supply received in Great Britain for the last seven years, has been about 208,000 bales per annum, and there is no regular increase.

The supply from Egypt, Brazil, and the West Indies, all put together, seldom reach 220,000 bales. It does not increase, but depends very much on prices.

So far from there being any increase in the receipts of cotton, in England, or on the Continent, there has been in late years a decided falling off. In Great Britain, she average annual imports from all other places, *except the United States*, for the last five years, have been 7,338 bales less than those of the five years ending with 1844. Whilst British imports from the United States have increased during the last five years at the average rate of 77,000 bales per annum, they have decreased at the rate of 54,000 from the East Indies.

In the infancy of British cotton manufacture, their chief supply came from the Mediterranean, especially from Smyrna and Malta. Now, neither of those places send a bag to England. In 1786, 15,000,000 pounds were exported from the West Indies to England. In 1848, only 1,300 bales, or about 4,500,000 pounds, less than a third. Since 1830, the exports of cotton from Brazil have fallen off one half. In 1845, over 80,000 bales of Egyptian cotton was imported into Great Britain, but for the last two or three years the imports have not reached 30,000 bales. In 1821, the imports of Hindostan cotton amounted to 274,000 bales, now it scarcely reaches 200,000. Depreciatlon in price is the reason of this great falling off in these countries. In some of them it is said the prices have fallen 40 per cent since 1839.* Such a depreciation, when it passes a certain point, must direct labour and capital into other channels, especially in those countries where a considerable portion of the profits are consumed in transportation. In the cotton States of America, however, there are greater facilities for transportation than most portions of the globe, hence there is no great proportion of the profits consumed in that way. The price of the raw material does not effect the consumption in the Northern States to any sensible extent. They manufacture and we help them to consume. The more they pay for the raw material, the more they may demand for the cloth, but the greater is our ability and our willingness to purchase at corresponding high prices. Besides, not only in America, but in Europé, cotton goods are the *necessaries*, not the *luxuries* of life, they

* London Economist.

must be had at any price. On the other hand, when the price is so much depreciated as to render the culture of the staple unprofitable, which can only be the case when there is a superabundance cultivated, we have simply to divert a *corresponding proportion of our labour to other pursuits*, for there will always be a certain amount of cotton absolutely indispensable to the human family, and of that amount the slaveholding States of the South, owing to their "peculiar institutions," and their peculiar facilities are destined to raise the bulk.

From a recapitulation of the history of cotton, it appears to be a fact, the Southern States constitute the only country where the growth of cotton has always been, and is now steadily increasing. But even here it does not increase more rapidly than is necessary to supply the increased consumption of it by the Northern and European manufactures. Nor can any increase in price *materially* augment the annual increase in the growth, for as much is now grown as our negroes can pick, and they increase only about three per cent annually.

But as we have such a monopoly in the growth of this important staple, let us estimate how many millions of human beings there are, whose welfare depends directly on the cotton which is cultivated by our slaves. It is stated by the highest authority,* that in England and Scotland there are over 4,000,000, whose support depends on cotton, and this does not include many of the smaller factories in those countries. Putting down 1,125,000 bales as the average amount of cotton manufactured by these 4,000,000 people, or which goes to support them.† We would have, supposing the same proportion to hold in other countries, the following table:

	Bales.		People.
In Great Britain, the manufacture of -	1,125,000	supports	4,000,000
In America, " " -	545,000	"	1,937,777
In France and the North of Europe, the manufacture of - - - - - - -	750,000	"	2,666,666
Total population supported by the manufacture of our cotton, - - - - - - - - - - -			8,604,443
Add to this the probable number of those engaged in the fields to cultivate, etc., viz: 1,000,000 slaves, and those owning the land and negroes, together with those employed to overlook and attend the negroes, those engaged in transporting, selling, shipping, etc., etc., the cotton from Southern ports, - - -			3,000,000
and we have, - - - - - - - - - - -			11,604,443

human beings, whose comfort and prosperity depends directly on the cotton raised by the slaves of the Southern States. If then we were to add the number of those employed in the culture and consumption of our other staples, it would probably astonish the most sanguine abolitionist, to see what a revolution in the affairs of the civilized world his fanatical projects aim to accomplish.

Notwithstanding, there were a variety of embarrassments attending the early cultivation of cotton, there is no one production of agriculture which has increased so rapidly, or acquired such pre-eminent influence over the affairs of mankind. During the fifty-six years, between 1787 and 1844, the cotton crop of the South increased from one million pounds to *eight hundred millions!* From 1792 to 1844, 52 years, our exports to foreign ports increased from 150,000 pounds to 600,000,000. In 1790, there were but 70 spindles in the United States, now there can not be less than two million, two or three hundred thousand. In 1803,

* London Economist.

† These 4,000,000 are composed as follows: 2,000,000 in Lancashire, 1,400,000 in the West riding of Yorkshire, and 600,000 in Lanarkshire.

the whole of Europe did not manufacture over 60,000,000 pounds, now there can not be less than 700,000,000 pounds consumed in manufacture there.

These facts surpass any thing in the annals of agriculture, and amazing as they may appear, there is another which can never be separated from them; they never could have existed without *slavery.* The fact is incontrovertible, that without the agency of slave labour, cotton for exportation never would, *never could,* have been raised in America.

But *with* the aid of slave labour, "the price of the raw material has been reduced to about one-tenth of its former value in the space of half a century; which, in conjunction with the improvement of machinery, has also reduced the price of cotton cloth in an equal ratio. Thus putting it in the power of the poor of every country to procure clothing for at least one-tenth part of the former prices. If effects could be traced to their true causes, I doubt not but that it would be discovered that the improved condition of the poorer classes in every civilized country, was as much indebted to the reduced rates in the price of clothing, as to any other one cause whatever. No physical want is so degrading to the human family as the want of clothing; nakedness and rags are the badges of poverty and degradation every where; in this condition man seems to lose all self-respect, and becomes the dependent and passive instrument of him who has courage to use him. But clothe him in comfortable and tasteful raiment, and you impart to him a new spirit; he holds up his head, looks his oppressor in the face and boldly demands his rights."*

It is by the agency of slave labour that this universal cheapening of clothes has been effected; it is by that agency that more more real benefit to our race has been accomplished, than by the agency of any one principle of modern philanthropy in the whole catalogue; it is by that agency that the North is what it now is; and it is by this agency that the South *will be* no longer the colony of the North, but a successful, independant competitor, after the bonds of our present political connection shall have been sundered forever. How *then* will the North be able to cope with the South in the cotton market; with England on one side, and the South on the other, what will become of her manufacturing supremacy, her growing commerce, her political power? Literally gone. The very fact that we have the raw material at our very doors *at prime cost,* is an advantage over all other countries, which no competition can stand. Let the Union be once dissolved, and every "Lowell" of the flourishing North will "make night hideous" with its yells of desperation. We will then have our cotton delivered at *our factories,* our "Granitevilles," for from 10 to 20 per cent less than it could be delivered at Lowell, or any other town of the North. Even if there were not other advantages, this of itself is enough to render any competition from the North, *which now requires so much protection,* signally abortive.

Cotton has all along been as much a benefit to the North as to the South, probably much more profitable; and though it has served more than any other article to advance the commercial independence of the *nation at large,* its services in this respect has, through the agency of a variety of causes, all of which spring from the union of the North and South, advanced infinitely more the wealth and prosperity of the former, than those of the latter section of the Union. We cannot deny that cotton has brought incalculable wealth to the Southern States, but it certainly has brought but a moiety of what it would have brought, were the North and South distinct confederacies.

At a convention held in Augusta, Georgia, in 1838, Mr. McDuffie, as chairman of a committee to prepare an address to the people of the South and West, submitted a report which is replete with the sternest truths. He says, speaking of

* Commercial Review.

the cotton trade among others: "Viewing the subject as one strictly of political economy—and in that light only are we now considering it—New-York, Pennsylvania, and Massachusetts are, for all such purposes, to be regarded by the staple States as foreign communities; not less so than Great Britain and France. The bonds of our political union, as confederated States, however they may bear upon other aspects of the subject, have no bearing whatever upon the question of national wealth, as it relates to the several States. The federal constitution, giving it the utmost amplitude of construction, cannot annihilate the intervening distance of a thousand miles; nor has it annihilated the separate and independent organization of the States. We cannot, therefore, regard the wealth of New-York or Pennsylvania as the wealth of South-Carolina and Georgia, or as contributing towards it, upon any other principle than that mutual dependence happily existing between commercial communities, which makes the prosperity of the one conducive to that of the other, in proportion to the extent of the exchanges of their respective productions.

"Applying these plain and obvious principles to the existing state of our commercial relations, it is apparent that the profit made by the merchants of New-York and other Northern cities, upon the exchange of our staples for foreign merchandize, is as effectually abstracted from the wealth of the staple-growing States, as if those cities belonged to a foreign jurisdiction."

Our cotton is the capital upon which four-fifths of the foreign commerce of *all the States* is based. And exactly to that extent is the *credit* obtained by *all* the States, based upon the cotton of Southern States, the produce of our slaves. But what a change must come over the spirit of their dream, when the Northern States find themselves coping with England, without the aid of *our cotton* to sustain their credit. What a change, when that *Chinese wall* springs up to sever the Union; no cotton, no slave labour, no *South*, no hobby, nothing but England! ghastly England, staring them in the face. Ruined North! when that day comes, rise up and shake your leprous carcass, cleanse it, wash it, anoint it; free it of those loathsome maggots which sap your fœtid joints, those fiendish abolitionists, which will have brought ruin down upon you. Else, you may be glad to gather crumbs where now you gather loaves and fishes.

Will there then not also be a change in the poor, contemned, despised South? Ah, her disease *is not corruption!* There is no gangrene, no soars, no loathsome harbingers of *verminous* invasion and revolting death; none of these are on the South. When that day comes, she will rise up, not to be convulsed with ruin, but to clasp her hands and rejoice on her way that *she has escaped the leper.* Where she now pours wealth into the strong chest of her Northern neighbour, she will then retain it for her own. Her commerce, now in the hands of those who would suicidally crush her through her institutions, will then, like her agriculture, be carried on by those who have an interest in her institutions, a home on her soil and a heart in her service; those who, in the case of a political convulsion, will not desert her for their Northern homes, will not seek a new country or a new destiny.

Who will undertake to estimate the value of our cotton, the value of our slaves. They are the means by which we are to ensure commercial independence *to ourselves*, political power and political independence *to ourselves.* With them we are identified with all that is majestic in the affairs of the world. We hold the Archimedean lever which can upheave a continent, convulse a world. What is an army of warriors, when compared to the potent *cotton* of our fields? Long after the din of war is hushed, when armies have met to struggle for supremacy in vain; when blood has turned the green fields red, all to no purpose; when Mars himself is dumb with disappointment; when every echo brings the plaintive cry for peace! peace! there will arise a mightier power than that of armies, a mightier cry than that for peace; it will be cotton! bread! life.

CHAPTER X.

"Poor man! I know he would not be a wolf,
But that he sees the Romans are all sheep;
He were no lion, were not Romans hinds."

Comparatively considered, slavery, so far from being a public evil, is a positive benefit to the public. It could not be otherwise, for it is in strict accordance with the economy of nature, it is at war with none of nature's laws. Chancellor Harper observes in his memoir, that "it is the order of nature and of God, that the being of superior faculties and knowledge, and therefore of superior power, should control and dispose of those who are inferior. It is as much in the order of nature, that men should enslave each other, as that other animals should prey upon each other." The only difference that we can see is, that as man is a moral being, so he is morally responsible when he enslaves his fellow man. It is the consciousness of this moral responsibility which makes the master careful how he wantonly inflicts privations and abridges the enjoyments of those in his power. But, in being the master under these obligations, there is certainly no violation of nature's laws. Where, in nature, is there a community which has not an acknowledged *master*. Every poultry yard has its *master cock*, who triumphantly lords it over all the rest. Every ant-hill has its sovereign, every bee hive its ruler. But man, more vicious than all his fellow animals, is the only one to set himself up as *masterless*, while the truth is, he has more masters, from God to Mammon, than any "kindred brute."

If domestic slavery is a system at variance with the economy of nature, it is certain there would constantly be a struggle for the supremacy between nature and this artificial economy; and there can be no doubt, that so powerful is the force of nature in the execution of all her invariable laws, she would, in such a contest, soon obtain the mastery. Her laws, her economy, can never be permanently banished from her kingdom; *they must prevail*. If then slavery is at war with the laws of nature, we may depend upon it, it is destined to disappear without the interposition of any other laws than those of nature. Abolitionists can do nothing more than retard the operations of nature, or else hasten them or too suddenly, at the expense of other laws of more fearful consequence. But, on the contrary, as slavery has existed in every age and in every climate since the world began, we find it difficult to believe that it can be such a violation of nature, as latter-day philanthropists would have it.

Viewing, in our comparison, the subject of slavery as one of political economy, we must remember not only the immediate objects, but the ultimate results. The legitimate object of life is the pursuit of *happiness;* in this pursuit, wealth is a *means*, not an end. "The *immediate* object of political economy is the accumulation, the distribution and enjoyment of national wealth or capital. The *ultimate* use of all wealth is the increase and diffusion of happiness and improvement, and the diminution of the distress and necessities of man. The ultimate and real object of *national wealth*, therefore, should be the increase and distribution of national happiness, and the relief of national want and suffering." But all wealth originates solely in labour. It is labour, and labour only, that *creates* wealth, it is economy that *accumulates* wealth; and exemption from distress, happiness, is the sole object of this accumulation.

In the Southern States, the labour which creates wealth is slave labour; in the Northern States, it is called free labour. The system of economy which accumulates wealth at the South is chiefly agricultural, that of the North chiefly commercial. It only remains for us to see whether the exemption from distress, the ultimate object of both sections, is more effectually attained in one than in the other. Without going into a lengthy discussion on the subject, let us throw together a few facts to confirm what has already been shown, that our domestic institutions will favourably compare with those of any other nation in the world.

The existence of slavery *radiates* a proper spirit of discipline and order throughout the entire community of those States in which we find it. We invite comparison. We defy any nation on the face of the earth, to exhibit a less degree of crime among its citizens; a greater degree of quietude and contentment throughout the community at large; a more sincere obedience to law and love of order; and more patient forbearance, than now characterizes the slaveholding States of America. That portion of society which, in other States, constitutes *the mob*, in ours, constitutes the industrious, frugal and orderly citizens. That portion of the population which, in other countries, consists of the pensioner, the beggar, the shop-lifter, is matched in ours by the healthy and vigorous labourer, the comfortable negro, the well-regulated slave. Whilst in Northern States we hear of theatre rows, church burnings, street fights, mobs, suicide, seduction, rape, murder, even murder *ala Webster*, and *pickling ala Colt*, pickling human flesh to ship to the South, as a moral hint of the moral evils of slavery; we hear no responsive echo from the benighted South. All is quiet there. She is transfixed with amazement at the immoral advancement of her devoted monitor, the pious North.

But it is not only the Southern States of this Union which are so secure from individual crime and social disturbance, as compared with other countries. Brazil also affords a striking evidence of the truth. In that country, where the slaves are to the free as two to one, possessed by a haughty and revengeful people, accustomed to war and fond of adventure, tranquility has reigned supreme for a quarter of a century. It is, indeed, a remarkable fact, that "Brazil and the United States, the only two nations on this continent where African slavery prevails, are the only two which have succeeded in the establishment of stable and flourishing social and political institutions. In all the Spanish American States, where the attempt has been made to introduce political equality among distinct and dissimilar races, it has been followed by incessant insurrection, anarchy, poverty, vice and barbarism."

Notwithstanding these uncontrovertable facts, slavery is denounced as the worst thing upon earth, and the Southern people the most immoral, dissolute and vicious now living. According to the fashion of the day, the Southern people are described as being without morals and without industry. A truly affecting picture is portrayed, domestic life is accurately depicted, the master is cursing, beating and wounding the crouching slave: in imitation, the young son is storming at and cursing the young slave; every household is a scene of constant tyranny; the country is like one accursed, and liberty is tottering; the intercourse between white and black is a perpetual exercise of the most boisterous passions; the most unremitting despotism on the one part, and degrading submission on the other. The people are all drunkards by common consent, no one can be a gentleman, unless he is a gambler, they know nothing but the art of flogging slaves, for science or literature they have no taste, their minds are not capable of a single idea of politeness, and women among them are little removed from slaves; their slaves of course treated much worse than brutes. Such is the most approved style of representing Southern manners and Southern institutions. Strange perversion—unaccountable ignorance. We have ourselves conversed with persons of respectable standing at the North, who were so totally misinformed on these subjects, that when told the grossest absurdities, their belief was firm and eager, but when told the plain truth, prejudice smothered the first symptoms of belief. Tell them of the most unheard of cruelty, and their avidity to hear and be persuaded is marvellous, but mention a single every-day occurrence, and they pronounce it impossible.

But the Northern people of course are all that is good, they have no evil traits, and their exalted qualities are too numerous to mention. Every body knows there is no vice in New-England, nor the semblance of it in any other Northern State. There never was a murder heard of within their limits: all those imperfect rumors about the pickling business ala Colt, and *mincing* business ala Webster must have been *a mistake*. A drunkard has never been seen north of Maryland. Gambling is quite unknown. Modern *gladiators* have never been permitted to amuse the Northern public. And reader! if you have ever heard of helpless women having their convent homes burnt over their heads, at the dead of night, on the unblemished soil of New-England; if you have ever heard of the anti-renters of New-York, the rioters of Pennsylvania, the black mobs of Ohio, the Native Americans, Agrarians, the Millerites, Dorrites, aye, and the *blue lights!* turn a deaf ear. It is not so. If you hear of divorces, *crim cons*, frauds and seductions; if you hear of jails and penitentiaries; rise in your indignation, and demand of your informant how he dares to address such notorious falsehoods to you.

If you wish evidence of what we say, take up the first New-York or Boston paper you meet with.

We have already seen how much more healthy the negroes in Southern cities are than the white inhabitants; let us now see how the mortality of the two classes compares in Northern cities. It is very much to be regretted, that authentic information as to the mortality of *whole cities* is not to be procured; but we have sufficient data, from the records of penitentiaries, prisons, etc., upon which to base a loose comparison. We will make a short table, from a condensation of the reports of the "Prison Discipline Association," for 1845, '46, and '47.* It speaks for the morals, as well as the longevity, of Northern *freemen*, of "Afric's sable hue."

IN PHILADELPHIA.

From 1821 to 1830, of all the deaths *at large* there was an average,

	Among whites.	Am'g negroes.
Annual per cent. of - -	2.42	4.75
From 1830 to 1842, " " " " in penitentiary,	2.09	6.62
" 1835 to 1845, " " " " in prison, -	1 in 46	1 in 12

" 1837 to 1847, out of 54 deaths of consumption in the county jail, 40 were negroes and 14 whites.

From March, 1841, to March, 1844, the average	Am'g whites.	Am'g negroes.
deaths in the Weathersfield Penitentiary was -	2.82	10.96 per ct.
From 1841 to 1843, in the Eastern Penitentiary, -	1.85	6.63 " "

The whole admission of convicts in the Eastern Penitentiary of Pennsylvania, from October, 1829, to December, 1845, was 2,054, of which 692, about one-third, were negroes. This frightful immorality and crime of the black population will be understood, when it is reflected how small a proportion of the population of Pennsylvania, or even of Philadelphia, it embraces. Extraordinary as it may seem, in 1840, very nearly 140 per cent. of the inmates of the same prison were coloured! "Perhaps," says Dr. Ginon, physician in charge, in his report, "the most striking feature is the great disproportion between white and coloured deaths—a disproportion that has engaged the attention and sympathy of some of our most enlightened and benevolent citizens, and given rise to various hypotheses. If my experience, etc., justify, I would say, without hesitation, it is owing entirely to their utter neglect of the necessary means of preserving health,

* An article in the Commercial Review of 1847; by the Editor.

extreme sensuality, etc. This opinion I believe myself in possession of sufficient facts to substantiate."

In 1845, Matthew L. Bevan, Esq., President of the Eastern Penitentiary of Pennsylvania, adverts again to the subject: "The increase of deaths comes from the blacks. This increase of mortality is found in the fact that those coloured inmates from the county of Philadelphia, are so constitutionally diseased, as, under any and all circumstances, to be short-lived, from their character and habits. They die of constitutional and chronic disorders, which are general among their order, *owing to the privations they undergo, and the want of proper attention in infancy, and their peculiar mode of living.*" Mr. Bevan concludes: "Indulging in the use of ardent spirits, *subjected to a prejudice, which bids defiance to any successful attempt to improve their physical or moral condition, from youth to manhood, sowing the seeds of disease in their constitutions, and at last becoming inmates of prisons.*"

These sad and mournful pictures, from a city like Philadelphia, where the blacks might be supposed to be as favourably situated as freedom could make them, are worthy of deep contemplation. If, after a period of so protracted freedom, their freedom has, so far from improving, sunk them lower and lower, beyond measure lower than in any city where slavery exists, it would seem full time for blind and raving sentimentality to come to its senses, and let alone what it is incapable of meddling with without mischief. If, however, the "*equality*" of the negroes North, South and East is the point, *degrade the Southern*, or, what is the same thing, as Philadelphia shows, *free them*, and you have the desired result.

IN NEW-YORK.

The proportion of whites to negroes, in New-York, is - -	50 to 1
In 1846, there were in the N. Y. Penitentiary 788 whites, 96 negroes, or	8 to 1
" " " " " " City Prison, - - - -	5 to 1
" " " " at Sing-Sing, 661 whites to 193 negroes, or	4½ to 1

There were 400 commitments that year for intemperance, of which 110 were negroes, *more than a fourth!*

Dr. Welch, in his report of 1844, says, "It also appears, from the records of the State Prison of Connecticut, that, since the commencement of the institution, in 1828, *half of the deaths have been among the blacks*, amounting to 5.40 per cent., (of all the blacks,) and 1.07 per cent. (of all the) whites! He also refers to the authority of Dr. Nott, of Mobile, in support of his opinion, that *the blacks of the North* "*possess less vitality than the whites.*"

We regret that our data, at this moment, are so incomplete. They, however, present some food for reflection. One might think that our *friends and fellow-citizens* at the North would have enough to do to look after the condition of their own affairs, instead of troubling themselves with ours. We do not envy them their occupation, in either case.

The task of comparing the South and North has been so ably performed by others, that but little remains for us to do but to sum up a few of the leading points which have been discussed at length by them. It will serve to show that if it is deemed expedient by the South to take a decided stand, to have no more encroachments upon her constitutional and inherent rights, or to dissolve the Union, *she can come forward boldly, and in the full confidence of success*, EVEN IF THERE BE AN APPEAL TO ARMS.

Let us first examine the wealth of the two sections. It hast been clearly demonstrated, that in no respect whatever is there any foundation for the popular belief, that the Southern States, or any of them, are, either now or heretofore, or likely to be hereafter, inferior to their Northern neighbours in wealth, but the reverse.* According to authority derived from the very best sources—official documents—it is asserted that the average property of white persons in the State of New-York is about *one-third* that of the same class in the State of Virginia. The same may be said with regard to Ohio and Kentucky. But though the *average* wealth of individuals in one State is greater than in the other, it is maintained that the *aggregate* wealth of the North is greater than that of the South. If it is so, it only goes to confirm a previous remark, that the proportion of capital to population, or of capital to labour, is less at the North than at the South.

The average wealth of each individual in the State of New-York is about 228 dollars, and of Pennsylvania $219. Of Virginia it is about $749,† and in South-Carolina, *regarding the slaves among the rest of the population, not as property*, the average wealth of each individual is $330! The States of Michigan and Aakansas were admitted into the Union, we believe, about the same time. They are both new States—both agricultural. The population of Michigan amounted, in 1847, to 370,000.‡ That of Arkansas to 152,400, *including slaves*. The whole agricultural products of Michigan amounted, in 1848, to $11,697,681. That of Arkansas, the same year, amounted to $12,304,013. Thus, in Michigan, the average production of each inhabitant was $31 50. That of Arkansas, *counting slaves*, was $80 50. Michigan produced, in 1840, 2,277,039 bushels of Indian corn. Arkansas, with not half the population, produced 4,846,632 bushels.

In the State of New-York, there is one pauper to every seventeen inhabitants. In Massachusetts, one to every twenty. In these two States—generally considered the most flourishing of the Union—pauperism is found to be advancing *ten times more rapidly than their wealth or population!* In the city of New-York, one person out of every five is, more or less, dependant on public charity. In Virginia and Kentucky, and in *every* Southern State, pauperism may be said scarcely to exist. In some of them, a genuine object of charity is rarely to be met with. In some parts of the North, pauperism is not confined to those who are *unable* to labour, but is the state in which many live who are *unwilling* to labour, or, being willing, are unable to find employment. This state of things, wherever it is found to exist, is a certain indication that the wages of labour are reduced to the cost of subsistence. The mass of the labouring people must, under these circumstances, work, not for the sake of improving their condition and accumulating capital, but merely to avoid the discipline of a poor-house. In other words, to avoid that *slavery* which stares them in the face. For what is more true, than that "the pauper in an alms-house is a slave—he works under a master and receives nothing but a subsistance." And can it be possible? We are told there are about 200,000 such slaves in Boston and Massachusetts, taken together. And, what is worse, their number increases at the enormous rate of 200 per cent. in ten years, or about ten times as rapidly as the whole population. In 1846, the net amount expended in the support of paupers, in Massachusetts, was $301,707 08, of which the State supplied $33,852.

It is also an established fact, that wealth at the South is more equally distributed than it is at the North, and, as a consequence, capital is more universally accumulated. Even throwing aside all statistics, and all documental authority, it can still be proved that the wealth of the South, in proportion to its population, must be greater than that of the North. In all well-settled countries, the price of labour indicates the proportion of capital to population, and if that price is low in any country, that proportion must be small; but we have already seen that wages are lower at the North than at the South—it follows, then, that the pro-

* "The North and South," by Elwood Fisher.

† This includes only the free population. These numbers are derived from the Post Office Report of 1847.

‡ Report of Commissioner of Patents.

portion of capital to population must be less also. As to the argument, that the North must be richer in its products than the South, because, on a given area, as, for instance, the State of Massachusetts, a much larger population is supported than on an equal area at the South, the absurdity is evident, for it is based upon the supposition that both areas are so densely populated that they can neither support one additional inhabitant, which, of course, is ridiculous. Facts authorize a very different conclusion. The produce of the North is intended chiefly for domestic consumption; that of the South principally for foreign markets. Each section supports its population and exports whatever of its produce remains. Now, because the North has a denser population than the South to support, and consequently, is obliged to cultivate more for domestic consumption, would it be proper to infer that the North is the richer for that? It would be equally wise to say of two men, each of which possessed more land than he has means to cultivate, that he who has ten children is richer than he who has five, because he manages, with a little extra labour, to feed five mouths more than the other.

A few more facts, and we are done. We have already seen how exempt negroes are from the pernicious effects of malaria in our Southern climate; let us now see how the increase and longevity of *our slaves* compare with those of the *freemen* of the North.

In 1848, the population of Charleston was composed of 14,187 whites, and 12,264 negroes, or about 7 whites to 6 blacks. The births and deaths were as follows:*

	Whites.	Negroes.	
Births,	465	540	75 more than whites.
Deaths,	303	311	8 " " "
Net increase,	162	229	67 " " "

For every 87.5 white there was an increase of one, and for every 53.5 black there was an increase of one. On the plantations, the increase among the negroes is nearly double this rate.

In Boston, the proportion of *adult* deaths in the whole population is, according to Dr. Shattuck, 43.63 per cent., and that of those over 70 years is 5.77 per cent.

In Charleston, the proportion of adult deaths to the whole population—*speaking of negroes only*—is 52.29 per cent., and that of those over 70 years is 11.25 per cent.

IN BOSTON.

Of *all ages*, the average age at death is 23 years, 4 months.
" adults, " " " " " " 44 " 8 "

IN NEW-YORK.

Of all ages, the average age at death is 21 years, 10 months.
" adults, " " " " " " 41 " 4 "

IN PHILADELPHIA.

Of all ages, the average age at death is 23 years, 4 months.
" adults, " " " " " " 46 "

IN ENGLAND.

Of all ages, the average age at death is 23 years, 5 months.

IN CHARLESTON, (among the negroes only.)

Of all ages, the average age at death is 29 years, 3 months.
" adults, " " " " " " 50 " 8 "

Here, then, is our right to claim for our institutions the superiority. Compared with the inhabitants of any country, we are prepared to pronounce *our slaves* the healthiest, happiest, and longest lived. Oh, abolitionist! what an account you

* See census of Charleston for 1849.

must render for the mischief you have done. What horror will strike your perjured soul, when, hurried into an eternal audience with your God, your groans will be swallowed up in the piercing shriek of millions, and your "*death rattles*" but the gurgling echo of a dying nation. Avaunt fiend! to the hellish manacles that enslave you; go clank them on the rocks of Plymouth, for your work is done—forever done!

In our remarks concerning the wealth of the South, we do not pretend to say that the *commercial prosperity* of the South is even on a par with that of the North. It is, on the contrary, a distressing fact, that the commercial independence of the Southern States has been completely wrested from them by the action of the federal government; but this circumstance does not affect the truth, that the South is richer than the North. It only bears on some departments of industry, not on all. But, even if it did go to confound our assertion, it the more effectually goes to assist us in our main argument; it is but another reason why the Union should be dissolved *now*, for such a measure would assuredly re-establish our commercial independence. And it is the only measure which can re-establish it, because it is the only step which the weak South can take, in opposition to the strong North.

However, if the South was poor—if it were a mere deserted wilderness—who could wonder? With the general government cruelly oppressing her, with the abolition power on one hand, and a noxious climate on the other, the only wonder is that she has been able to keep abreast with other nations. Mr. McDuffie remarks, in his report, "In addition to the ten millions of dollars yearly abstracted by the unfavourable course of our foreign trade, the action of the federal government, in the collection and disbursement of the public revenues, has operated as a burden to an equal or even greater amount. The system of raising, by duties on foreign goods, nearly the whole amount necessary to meet the wants of the government, including the discharge of an immense public debt, was, of itself, calculated to depress the industry of the cotton-growing States, which was almost exclusively employed in raising the products which were exchanged for the very articles thus enormously taxed. But when these duties were extended to an amount greatly exceeding the wants of the government, ranging from 25 to upwards of 100, and amounting, on an average, to 40 per cent., imposed for the avowed purpose of affording protection and encouragement to those, the productions of whose industry (free from all taxation) came into direct competition with the foreign goods received in exchange for our cotton, rice and tobacco; when the vast amounts thus extracted were accumulated at the North, and there expended on the army and navy, the fortifications, public buildings, pensions, and the other various objects of national expenditure—the balance being distributed in internal improvement—of which we receive but a small share, can it be a matter of wonder or surprise, that, even with the richest staples in the world, the South should exhibit the extraordinary spectacle, of a country making hardly any progress; while the more favoured, though comparatively barren, regions of the North were seen constantly advancing in wealth and prosperity? This unequal action of the federal government—as it was, in the first instance, the most prominent cause of the subversion of Southern commerce—has constantly aided in preventing its recovery, by stimulating the commercial industry of the North, and building up Northern cities at the expense of those of the South and South-West. To show the magnitude of this evil, it is only necessary to advert to the fact, that the gross amount received from customs has been estimated* at the enormous sum of nine hundred millions of dollars, nearly three-fourths of which

* It must be remembered this report was made over 14 years ago.

were levied on goods received in exchange for the productions of the South and South-West, and nine-tenths of it expended north of the Potomac."

These events, which have been growing and progressing for the last sixty years, sometimes huge in their proportions, at others trifling in their consequences, have, within the memory of many among us, reduced the South almost to the state of "colonial vassalagé," which our fathers so indignantly spurned in 1776. Look at the facts, the mortifying facts, and remember they do not spring out of our slave institutions, as Northern men maintain in their declamations, but out of the unequal action of the federal government, the loss of the balance of power essential to the harmonizing of conflicting interests.

In 1769, the value of the imports of some of the colonies was as follows:

Of Virginia,	£851,140
" all the New-England States,	561,000
" South-Carolina,	555,000
" Pennsylvania,	400,000
" New-York,	189,000
Thus Virginia and South-Carolina imported together,	1,401,140
While the Middle and Eastern States " "	1,150,000

The exports were in about the same proportion. Virginia exported nearly four times as much as New-York. South Carolina exported about twice as much as New-York and Pennsylvania put together, and five times as much as all the New-England States united.

The same relative proportion of imports was preserved, until the Union, under the present constitution, was formed. Immediately upon the formation of the Union, we see the Northern States rapidly advancing and the South falling off. As early as 1791,

New-York imported	$3,222,000
Virginia "	2,486,000
South-Carolina "	1,520,000

What a complete change, to be accomplished in 20 years!

The exports of these States amounted,

	New-York.	Virginia.	South-Carolina.
In 1821,	$23,000,000	$1,098,000	$3,000,000
" 1832,	57,000,000	550,000	1,213,000

These numbers speak for themselves. No one can shut his eyes to the inference to be drawn from them. It is as clear as the noontide sun, that, as the South has always practiced slave labour, and, prior to the formation of the present Union, was perfectly able to carry on a profitable commerce with all the world; that, as she has been deprived of this commerce by causes which are the offspring of this Union, and which never existed prior to the Union; and, as all effects must be obviated by the removal of their causes, it follows that there is no obstacle in the way of our resumption of a profitable commerce with all the world, to the same comparative extent as it formerly existed, so soon as these causes, the *offspring of this* Union, are removed; and, if they cannot be removed by other means, *their cause must be removed*—the Union must be amended, dissolved.

But, thank God, our case is not so bad as that. We do not contend for commerce; we would not dissolve the Union to retrieve the commerce which has been taken from us; we let it go; our faith has been pledged, rashly pledged, perhaps, but we are bound to let the majority rule in this respect. But is it not enough to lose our commerce? Must we lose our land, our slaves, our lives, our homes, our independence, our honour? Must we stand with our arms folded, and look on, to see *all* that we have wantonly despoiled and confiscated, because we think we ought to say we *love* the Union, *the glorious Union.* And all the while we think, we *know*, we *feel* we hate the Union, the oppressive Union, the degrading submission, the miserable vassalage the *glorious* Union imposes upon us. Shame on such hypocrisy.

In comparing the wealth, we should not forget the natural resources of the Southern States, stretching out, as they do, over so vast a territory; embracing every wholesome variety of climate, soil and production; possessing the finest harbours and noblest streams that could be desired; forests, whose timbers can never be exhausted; every grade of salubrity, from the valley of the river to the lofty mountain top; every facility for manufacture; every blessing that could be expected from a divine Benefactor. Among our people there is to be found every order of talent. There is no genius at the North but the South can eclipse it; no valour in the world but the South can equal it; no profession in science but the South can produce masters. We may cultivate the staple of any climate, or adopt the plant of any soil; commerce is invited by the beauty and safety of our harbours; our large rivers fertilize the land in all directions, and joyously bear on their exulting bosoms the richest harvests in the world; our forests can furnish navies for all futurity; and who will undertake to place a limit on our natural manufacturing advantages. Reader! if you would be convinced of the magnitude of our advantages, the immensity of our blessings, and the power we are destined to wield, if we perform our duty, you have but to lay open the map of the American continent before you, on one side, and that of the old world on the other. From them you may learn that "had it been left to man to plan the form of a basin for commerce, on a large scale—a basin for the waters of our rivers and the products of our lands—he could not have drawn the figure of one better adapted for it than that of the Gulf of Mexico, nor placed it in a position half so admirable."* "Rightly to perceive how admirably located and arranged for the purposes of commerce, are the Gulf and Caribean Sea, and duly to appreciate the advantages arising therefrom, let us, before comparing the river basins of America with those of Europe and Asia, or before tracing further the effects which the course of the rivers of a country has upon its commerce, take a glance at the geographical position of this our central sea."

Curtained, on the east, by a chain of fruitful islands, stretching from Trinidad to Cuba, it is, on the north and the south and the west, land-locked by the continent, which has bent and twisted around this sea, so as to fold it within its bosom, and hold it mid-way between the two semi-continents of the new world.

In this favoured position, it receives, on one side, the mountain streamlets of a sea of islands; on another, all the great rivers of North America; and, on the others, the intertropical drainage of the entire continent.

The Atlantic Ocean circulates through this our Mediterranean. Its office in the economy of the world is most important. It not only affords an outlet for the great American rivers, but it makes their basins habitable, by giving them drainage, and sending off, far away into the ocean, the drift and the over-heated waters which the rivers bring down. It also, through its system of cold and warm currents, makes its own shores habitable to man, tempers the climate of Europe, and, by its genial warmth, makes productive the soil there.

The Amazon, rising in the Andes, and emptying in the ocean under the line, also finds its way through the magnificent llanos and pampas of the tropics down to the margin of this sea.

In consequence of the Gulf Stream the mouth of the Mississippi is really in the Florida pass. The waters of the Amazon flow through the same channel. The great equatorial current of the Atlantic sweeps across the mouth of this river, and carries its waters into the Caribbean Sea: from the Caribbean Sea they

* We quote from an article of Lieut. Maury, U. S. Navy, lately re-published in the Commercial Review.

flow into the Gulf of Mexico, and thence, by the Gulf Stream, back into the Atlantic. Such is the channel through which the waters of the Atlantic complete their circuit, and are borne back into the ocean again. The distance, in a straight line, from the mouth of the Amazon to the Florida pass, is only twenty-four hundred miles. Therefore, the Amazon may be very properly regarded as one of the tributaries, and its basin as a part of the back country, to this, our noble sea.

The connection is even more close ; for one mouth of the Amazon is that of the Orinoco, which empties directly into the Caribbean Sea. These two streams present the anomaly of two great rivers having sources that are common. A person sailing up the Amazon, may cross over into the Orinoco, and re-enter the sea through that river, without having once set his foot on shore. The Rio Negro, by its branches, serves as a canal to connect the two.

The Mississippi and the Amazon are the two great commercial arteries of the continent, and this sea is like a heart to the ocean. Its two divisions of sea and gulf perform the office of ventricles in the system of ocean circulation. Floating bodies, from the region of Cape Horn, from the coast of Africa and the shores of Europe, are conveyed into the Caribbean Sea, and thence into the Gulf of Mexico, whence its waters are again sent forth over the broad bosom of the Atlantic. Upon summing up all the river basins of this gulf and sea, they are found to cover *more than four times* the area of those which are drained by the streams emptying into the Mediterranean.

The history of the world shows that the greatest commercial cities are those which are most advantageously situated with regard to the outlets, natural or artificial, of great river basins and producing regions. All of these advantages are pre-eminently possessed by the cities on our gulf coast, and in addition to this, the Gulf presents greater facilities for *navigation*, than any similar sea in the world.

The shores of the Mediterranean are indented by deep bays and projecting points of land, which greatly lengthen the sailing distance from port to port. The sinuosities of shore lines add to the expenses of commercial intercourse. By *land*, the distance from Genoa to Venice is that only of a few hours travel; but by *water*, they are more than a thousand miles apart. There are no such interruptions to navigation in the Gulf of Mexico. The *shortest* distance from port to port there, as from New-Orleans to the ports of Texas and Mexico, to Pensacola, Havana and the like, *is by water.* From the ports of the Levant and Black Sea to the ocean, a vessel, under canvass, requires a month or more; but from any point on the coast of this central sea of America, a vessel may be put out upon the broad ocean in a few days. Winds and currents, with all the adjuvants of navigation, are here much more propitious to the mariner, than they are in any other part of the world.

The windings of the Mediterranean shore line, exclusive of its islands, measure 12,000 miles; whereas, those of the Gulf and Caribbean Sea do not measure half that distance.

The area of all the valleys which are drained by the rivers of Europe, which empty into the Atlantic, of all the valleys which are drained by the rivers of Asia, which empty into the Indian ocean, and of all the valleys that are drained by the rivers of Africa and Europe, which empty into the Mediterranean, does not cover an extent of territory as great as that included in the valleys drained by the *American rivers alone, which discharge themselves into our central sea.* Never was there such a concentration upon any sea, of commercial resources. Never was there a sea known with such a back country tributary to it.

From the ports of Europe to those of India, the distance is from 15 to 20,000 miles, and a voyage each way often occupies 200 days. The distance from the Balize to the Orinoco or Amazon, may be accomplished in 20 or 30 days. One ship, therefore, trading between our system of river basins, may fetch and carry, in the course of one year, as many cargoes as ten ships can, in the same time, convey between the remote basins of the system in the old world. Thus, in our favoured position, we have, at the distance of only a few days sail, an extent of fruitful basins for commercial intercourse, which they of the old world have to compass sea and land and sail around the world to reach.

From 50° north to 20° south, the Mississippi and the Amazon take their rise. A straight line from the head waters of the one to those of the other, measures a quadrant of the globe. They afford outlets to all the producing climates of the earth. Upon this gulf and sea, perpetual summer reigns; and upon their shores, climate is piled upon climate, production upon production, in such luxuriance and profusion, that man, without changing his latitude, may, in one day, ascend from summer's heat to winter's cold, gathering, as he goes, the fruits of every clime, the staples of every country.

Invaluable as this gulf *naturally* is, what will it not become when man shall have joined the great oceans of the earth in eternal wedlock, when Europe and Asia will make it their common highway, and the commerce of the world attest the truth that it is the heart of the *ocean system.* Then, indeed, will the Gulf of Mexico be the water to which all eyes are turned; her coasts must become the home of commerce, the seat of wealth. But that coast is already half encompassed by the Southern slaveholding, cotton-growing States. Where then must the South look for commercial independence; which is her proper front? Must she forever cling to that *glorious* phantom, the Union! that her life blood may be abstracted by vile leeches. Or must she turn her face to the South, the Gulf! the highway of nations, the heart of navigation, the centre of commerce. What then is to prevent the South fromattaining to the h ghest commercial independence, if, in her present desperate degradation, she throws off the yoke she has unfortunately too long borne.

With respect to our military resources, we will speak more at length in another chapter. For the present it will be sufficient to remark, that during the revolutionary war, the Southern States furnished men and money, even beyond their quota. It is true—and we would not detract a single iota from Northern valor—the North also furnished her quota, but there was this difference: the men furnished by the North, fought chiefly on their own soil; those furnished by the South, were transported far away from their homes, to assist in the defence of the North, which was, for a long time, the principal theatre of action. It has been estimated by a writer of those times,* that, in one aggregate view, the debt and expenses incurred by one of the *smallest* of the Southern States,† during this war, exclusive of the blood of its citizens, amounted to upwards of *thirteen millions of dollars.* In the late war with Mexico, *two-thirds* of the volunteers mustered into service, were citizens of slaveholding States. As to the *conduct* of the Southern volunteers, it was certainly as good as that of the Northern. Besides furnishing this majority of troops, the revenue by which this and other wars have been supported, the public debt paid,‡ and the price for the territory furnished, has been raised chiefly by duties which have notoriously operated, designedly and incidentally, to promote the industry and capital of the North, and to oppress those of the South.

The resources of genius and intellect at the South will, in no way, suffer by being contrasted with those of the North. While we do not deny that both sections possess great worth in this department, it is nevertheless true, that "the North has never produced a statesman, who has durably stamped the impress of his mind upon the legislature of the country, and made his thought, the thought,

* Winterbotham. † South-Carolina. ‡ The North and South, by Fisher.

of his own generation, and of posterity.* There is no great measure of public policy, which was originated by a Northern lawgiver. Not even such men as Adams, or Webster, have been able to associate their names with the authorship or development of any far-reaching, abiding acts of legislation. The union of wisdom, in the highest scripture sense, with moral and physical boldness, with firmness and prudence, which made Washington the leader of our revolutionary armies, and the appropriate guardian of our infant federation, was eminently characteristic of the *Southerner* and the *slaveholder;* it was the *degree* only, not the *kind*, that was miraculous. Such were the chief leaders of the convention, the men to whose suggestion the constitution owes its essential features—Madison and Mason, Randolph and Pinckney, all of the South. The founders of the two great parties were neither from the North; Hamilton was a West Indian, and Jefferson, who breathed his soul into the republican party, and Madison, who gave it shape, were both Virginians. In the war of 1812, two Virginians, Scott and Harrison, drove back our foes in the North, while, a South-Carolinian led the Southern rifles to victory at New-Orleans. All the great measures which have agitated the present generation, the Bank, and the Independent Treasury, the Internal Improvement system, the American system, and free trade, have been brought forth or shaped by the mind of a Calhoun or a Clay, or carried into practice by the iron will of a Jackson. The only Northern Presidents we have ever tried *have been failures.* The elder Adams, who came into power on the popularity of Washington, in two years broke down, and every vestige of his administration was swept away by the popular voice. His son fared no better, and Van Buren, who mistook cunning for wisdom, was a *politician* instead of a *statesman.* The prestige of Jackson's favour could elect him, *but nothing could save him after a single trial.*

Whatever of greatness our country has attained, has been chiefly due to the administrative talent of Southern men, and above all, to the Southern vote, which, while it was yet strong enough to be heard, restrained the disposition of the North to convert this federal Union into a grand consolidated State, *on the French model*, where the numerical majority might have absolute sway. If the free States were to form a separate confederacy, it would soon assume this character. The measures which, as a section, they have advocated in the present Union, all have that tendency. The forms of their State governments—their political theories—all conspire to make such a result certain. The small States would be deprived of their equal vote in the Senate, and speedily absorbed by their more powerful neighbours. All the proper work of the several State legislatures, as well as of private enterprise, would be thrown on the central government; the States would become mere provinces, and Congress a National Assembly. In such a state there would be no safety for property. The number of those who want property is always greater than that of those who have it—the poor more numerous than the rich; and they will certainly use their acknowledged sovereign right, as a majority, to gratify that want, and take what they please. The Northern plan of meeting this danger, has always been to create a strong moneyed interest by class legislation, by large government expenditures, and by patronage. Northern statesmen know that the aristocracy of birth is impossible; they hope to substitute the aristocracy of money, by means of the funding and paper system, and by the yet more potent empire of the manufacturing system. In other words, the plan is to govern the masses by the power of money and corruption. The evil day may be thus delayed, but the remedy increases the inequality of fortunes and the difficulties of the labouring poor. Their sufferings are aggravated, and their character degraded; and when the

* See "the Union," by a "Virginian."

outbreak comes—as come it ultimately must, with the accumulated force of pent-up waters—*it is the outbreak, not of men, but of demons.*"

While we freely admit that the whole Union is well stocked with the resources of intellect, it is nevertheless beyond dispute, that people of a Southern climate attain to maturity at an earlier age, as well in mind as in body, than do those of more Northern latitudes; they possess natural genius, spirit and acuteness, at least equal to their neighbours of the North. And whatever may be said of the mental and social qualities of the people of the Northern States, *as instilled into them by their everlasting principles of liberty, equality, free soil, &c.*, it is certain, "that for a warm heart and open hand, for sympathy of feeling, fidelity of friendship, and high sense of honour; for knowledge of the sublime mechanism of man, and reason and eloquence to delight, to instruct and to direct him, the South is superior; and when the North comes into action with the South, *man to man*, in council or in the field, the genius of the South has prevailed, from the days of Jefferson to Calhoun, from Washington to Taylor. And it is to the solitude which the rural life of the South affords, so favourable to reflection; and it is to the elevated rural society of the South, so favourable to the study of human nature, that we must ascribe those qualities of persuasion and self-command, by which her statesmen and captains have moved the public councils, and won so many a field."

There is another contrast to be made. It is in relation to what we may term the *foreign resources* of the South and North in case of their separation. What would be the effect of that measure upon their intercourse with foreign nations, and with each other? Would the South loose, or be benefitted by such a step?

In obtaining the friendship of foreign powers, the paramount objects are friendly intercourse and commercial exchange. If this Union were at an end, the Southern States would have precisely the same commodities to exchange that they now have. The question now comes up, would these commodities, after such an event, be received and exchanged for others in the *same markets* as at present? As for European markets, we answer *assuredly;* as for Northern markets, we answer *necessarily they must.*

First, for foreign markets. The popular belief is, and it may be correct, that if the South and North dissolve their Union, whatever may be the *modus operandi* of the dissolution, a war between them will inevitably follow. There are then two views to be taken of the foreign markets, one where there is no war, one where there *is* war. If there is no war, there will be no probable change in the conduct of foreign nations, either towards the Southern or Northern States.

The ministers, consuls, etc. of the present Republic, would probably vacate their positions in foreign courts with the best grace they can, for the very obvious reason that the government which they represent has *itself been vacated.* There would be a thorough renewal of diplomatic intercourse between these foreign nations and the Southern and Northern States respectively. Nothing that we know of would prevent such renewal on the part of the South. Every foreign relation would therefore remain friendly, and the South would in that respect be just where it is now. Hence, if there is no war, there will be no loss of foreign friends, no loss of foreign intercourse, foreign commerce, foreign influence.

Now, if there is a war. In the first place, it will not be a *civil war*, as the common cry now has it, it will be a war between the North and South, then become two foreign powers; it will be a foreign war. As much a foreign war in point of fact, as the wars of '76 or of 1812. Like all other nations at war, they would each try to injure the other as much as possible. The commerce of both belligerants would be *both equally crippled;* the more the commerce of one is interrupted, just so much more will that of the other be. It is a happy circumstance for both parties, that for every wound it inflicts upon the commerce of the other, it inflicts one also upon itself; but it will be a long time before they will be convinced of this. Immediately upon the breaking out of the war, all shipment of cotton to the North, will, of course, be stopped. The cotton factories there will be closed as soon as the stock on hand is consumed. This circumstance, taken as an isolated fact, will have a worse effect upon the North than the South, because there will be a *total* cessation of the cotton trade at the former, whereas there will be but a *partial* cessation at the latter, and this falling off would be under any circumstance occasioned by a corresponding falling off in cultivation. This partial cessation at the South will then be no essential inconvenience. Moreover, this universal stillness of Northern spindles, as it suspends the operations of England's only formidable rival, will throw the monopoly of the manufacturing trade into her lap—it will leave the prices at her disposal—the carrying trade at her command. So long as this continues, England and the other European consumers, can have no earthly objection to the longest possible continuance of the war. Fortunately, however, the efforts of the belligerants to injure each other, would soon render such a state of things impossible. The whole coast, from Maine to the Rio Grande, would be under a state of nominal blockade, each party will *declare* the coast of the other to be blockaded. As long as the war goes on without any material interference with the British cotton trade, England must, through policy and interest, be a neutral in the strictest sense of the word; for being a neutral, she will be able to carry the cotton and other produce, both from the South and the North, excepting only such articles as are declared by the law of nations to be *contraband of war*. England will, therefore, adhere strictly to the law of nations, because her true policy will dictate such a course. But the law of nations, as it regards blockades, is one of those laws which are no longer binding than physical force renders them so. The law of blockades is of such a nature in its operation, that in order to apply it, the fact of the actual blockade must be established by clear and unequivocal evidence. "The squadron allotted for the purposes of its execution, must be competent to cut off all communication with the interdicted place or port." "A blockade must be existing in *point of fact*; and, in order to constitute that existence, *there must be a power present to enforce it*." "All decrees and orders declaring extensive coasts and whole countries in a state of blockade, without the presence of an adequate naval force to support it, are manifestly illegal and void, and have no sanction in public law."* The definition of a blockade given by a Convention of the Baltic powers in 1780 and in 1801, and by the United States in 1781, required that "there should be actually a number of vessels stationed near enough to the port to make the entry *apparently* dangerous." Now when the North attempts to blockade the Southern ports from the Potomac to the Rio Grande, it will manifestly be *unable to enforce* the blockade, or it will be *able* to enforce it. If it is unable to do so, we have just seen it would be no violation of law or custom, for English ships to enter those ports with foreign produce, and to carry away our domestic produce. But if the North *is able* to enforce the blockade, then British ships will be *unable* to carry away our cotton. The consequence will be, the greater proportion of the English manufacturers will be forced to suspend business. Over *four millions* of the inhabitants of Great Britain will be left without the means of support, they consequently will revert to the care of governmental charity. The same will be the case with about three million on the continent. Can it be supposed that a nation like Great Britain, knowing her own interest and her true policy by the saddest experience, and backed as she will be by the continental powers, will allow such a state of things to continue? The North and the South may be very good matches for each other, but it would be hard for either of them

* See Kent's Commentaries.

to contend with Europe in addition to the other. As far as England is concerned, it is too clear to be disputed, the law of nations would conflict with the law of self preservation, *nature's first law.* We need not question which law of these will prevail. England will preserve herself from the ruin thus thrown upon her. What will she do? Why, inasmuch as it was the *blockade* which brought her to this distress, it is the blockade which she must remove. Inasmuch as it is cotton she wants, it is cotton she must have. But how can she remove the blockade without coming in direct collision with the power that blockades—the North. And after—how can she get the cotton without being at peace with the power that makes the cotton—the South—the *slave power.* She will, therefore, reason thus: As long as the carrying trade was left open to me by the absence of blockades, I was in no respect injured, rather benefitted. Now, however, that the Southern ports are blockaded, I not only loose the carrying trade, but I loose the manufacture of *two millions bags of cotton!* I loose the means of supporting *four millions of my people!* This cotton, this means of support, *all* comes from the South. My cotemporaries on the continent tell me they suffer in like manner, they are forced to come into my views, they get their cotton from the South also, they will support me in the eyes of the wide world, I ask no more, the blockade *must be raised or England fall!!* To think, in this emergency, will be to act; and long before the retreating northern hosts shall have turned their spears to pruning hooks, our cotton will be turned to gold—our war to peace—our colonial vassalage, our tame submission, to sovereign independence.

With regard to the Northern States, a few words will suffice to show that they must import from us. It is a common remark, "how dependent the South is upon the North." But when the crisis comes, when the last convulsive throe is over, what a change will there be. Commercial and manufacturing interests are by far the leading interests of the North, its agriculture is supported only for these interests. All the cotton, rice, sugar and tobacco that she imports, manufactures, consumes or exports, comes from the South. But the importers, manufacturers, consumers and exporters of these four staples, constitute the great mass of her people, and possess the bulk of her capital. It may, therefore, be said that the great mass of her people depend for employment, and the bulk of her capital depends for accumulation, upon the supply of these four staples of Southern States. The South then stimulates, or rather sustains the commerce and manufactures of the North. But that which thus sustains the industry of a people, and yields an increase of capital to one class, and employment to another, must be an indispensable resource to that people. Nobody can deny that these four staples of the South perform this office for the people of the North. It therefore follows that the produce of the South is indispensable to the commercial and manufacturing interest, and *through these*, to the bulk of the people of the North. Or, in fewer words, the produce of the South is the great means by which the prosperity of the North is sustained. If then the North consumes by its factories, domestic use, or otherwise derives profit from, a given number of bales of cotton, barrels of rice, hogsheads of sugar and tobacco, in its present state of prosperity, it follows that any material diminution in the supply of these commodities, will be followed by a corresponding diminution in the prosperity of the people, whose livelihood depends on it; and if the Northern markets were, on account of a dissolution of the Union, closed against southern produce, the prosperity of that country would be doomed.

In view of these facts, we adopt the opinion, that if the Union were dissolved, the South would not lose *one dollar*, either from a diminution of its foreign commerce, or its commerce with the North. Neither will it retrograde one jot from that eminent degree of foreign influence which it now possesses, but which it is forced to share with its domestic enemy, the Northern States.

It may here be said that the same argument applies to the North, but we deny it. If the North uses cotton at all, *she is compelled* to use ours; for the reason that she can get it no where else. The same applies in a less degree to other products. But there is no product, of national importance, raised or manufactured at the North, which the South is *necessarily* compelled to use. The South when she becomes a separate nation from the North, will be able to manufacture every thing for herself which the North now manufactures for her. There is nothing manufactured in the free States, which can not be manufactured elsewhere. But there is that extensively produced in the slaveholding States which can not be produced *or replaced* elsewhere at remuneration prices, and probably, at *any price.* Thus the North has competition to contend with, whilst the South has a natural monopoly to rely on. This monopoly judiciously controled can never be a *disadvantage.*

We would not be understood to argue, that after dissolution the South should not continue to import from the North; that would depend on circumstances as they may then exist. We simply mean to say that *if she does,* she does it *not through necessity,* but through choice. And as the doctrines of "free trade and low duties," seem to be becoming more and more in vogue, we think it a nice question, whether, upon the whole a dissolution of the Union would not prove a decided advantage to the South, in a commercial point of view, at least.

CHAPTER XI.

"Grim visaged war has smoothed his wrinkled front."

As regards the relative strength in population of the two sections, we of course, must acknowledge the North to have a great advantage *in numbers.* The free population of the North was, according to the census of 1840, 9,803,273, and that of the South 4,733,703.* But this circumstance can have no bearing on the point in view, unless the two sections in dissolving their political connection, come to open war. Let us then see how the matter stands in this respect.

At the last presidential election there were 2,043,528 votes polled in the free States,† and 832,593 in the slaveholding States.‡ Now if this is a fair exponent of the number of effective citizens in the two sections, or of *the ratio of those numbers,* we may without any material error take it as a basis upon which to rest our conjectures; and, by a reference to statistics, it will be found that this proportion has been kept up, more or less exactly, for the last fifteen years, to wit: the votes at Presidential elections in the free States, have been to those in the slave States as 2½ to 1; and, since the election of 1836, there has been, during every period of four years, an average increase at the North of 320,244½ votes, and at the South 138,834½ votes. Taking this ratio to be as correct as any which can be derived from authentic sources, there will not probably be any practical error in adopting it as the ratio of the number of effective fighting men residing in these respective sections. All other considerations being for the present thrown out of view, it may then be said, that, *merely with respect to numbers,* where the South possesses a force of 100,000 men, the North possesses 250,000.

* The District of Columbia not included.

† See American Almanac.

‡ In this the vote of South-Carolina is not included, the electors being elected by the Legislature.

This difference is not of primary importance, for in modern warfare numbers are not a deciderātum. The battle is not always to the strong, nor the race to the swift. It remains for us to see whether the two sections could *bring into the field* armies whose numbers bear that ratio; and, if they could, whether the *military qualifications* of the opposing forces would be equally good or not; and, if not, on whose side the advantage in this material respect would rest. It is also to be seen which section could with least inconvenience bear the enormous expense of such a war; for of all public expenditures, those of war are the greatest and most ruinous, to the party defeated. The American Revolution cost Great Britain $680,000,000. The French Revolution of nine years, cost $2,320,000,000. The wars with Napoleon, during twelve years, cost $5,795,000,000—*more than a million a day!* The wars that raged in Europe from 1793 to 1815, *only twenty-two* years, cost $15,000,000,000. The French war with Algiers, for sixteen years, cost $320,000,000, or $20,000,000 per annum. The Florida war cost $42,000,000.

We will not here undertake to give an opinion on these matters, for it is more than probable the question could never be decided, except by actual experiment; and it is possible there may never be any necessity for a decision upon it. It will, therefore, be sufficient for our purpose, to lay open such facts and considerations as we are cognizant of, and leave the reader to form his own opinion on the subject, entreating him always to remember, what a vast difference there is between *voting* and *fighting*, between voting down the South and fighting down the South. The only analogy between the ballot and the rifle is, that each can be aimed by but one man at a time. One superior bayonet may transfix a dozen voters. In the first place, then, as to MILITARY FIXTURES. There are 8 arsenals and 26 military posts belonging to the Federal Government in the free States; there are 9 arsenals and 33 military posts in the slave States.* It is believed that though the South has the greater number, the defences of the North are in several instances superior to those of the South. The partiality of the Federal Government in making appropriations for the defences of the Northern Atlantic coast, can not have failed to render them so. The South, however, has some of its chief stratagetic points well defended. The harbour of Pensacola was, in 1846, regarded as "the only harbour in the United States where the system for its defence, *by sea and by land*, was complete." But there are other points of no less importance wholly undefended. The dry Tortugas, Key West, and Key Biscayne, have been pronounced, by the most competent judges, to be "the great stratagetic points on the Southern frontier," yet they are not defended. Their defence, however, has been strongly urged, and an estimate of the costs has been made by officers of the scientific engineers. The result of their calculation is, that for about one-sixth the value of the annual exports of Mobile, or *one-twentieth* of those of New-Orleans, for the sum of $3,000,000 to $3,500,000, the military defences of the Gulf coast could not only be completed, but that the Tortugas could be rendered "impregnable to assault, and nearly impracticable of blockade;" and, in an emergency, a well appointed garrison "would be able to dictate the terms of peace from the Fortress of the Tortugas," to the strongest foe.

As to the MILITARY HISTORY of the people of the two sections, we have but imperfect data upon which to base an opinion. It is true, we have on record the valorous deeds of our ancestors in the Revolution of '76. We have faithful accounts of their vigilance, privations and endurance, in their early struggles with the Indians. We have living heroes of more recent occasions, but we have no positive evidence as to what should be expected in the event of a war between the South and the North. We know, from good authority, the Secretary of war in

* See American Almanac and Army Register.

1790,* and give it for what it is worth, that in the revolutionary campaign of 1776, the five Southern States furnished 22,013 militia men for the common defence, and the eight Northern States furnished 67,638. Of those from the North, 8,000 enlisted for but *four* months, whilst 7,000 from the Carolinas *alone*, averaged 6 and 8 months.

In 1777, the South furnished 24,032 men, and the North furnished 44,688. The shortest enlistments were from New-England, over 6,000 enlisting for but *two* months, and the longest from New-York and South-Carolina, the men from the latter serving eight months.

In 1778, the South furnished 20,033 men, and the North 31,019. Here, we again find the greatest number of shortest enlistments from New-England, and the greatest number of longest enlistments from Southern States. Georgia furnished 2,000 men for six months, *four times as many men*, to serve *three times as long* as those from New-Hampshire.

In 1779, the South furnished 20,679 men, and the North but 20,905. In this campaign the longest enlistments were from Virginia, North and South-Carolina, being respectively 6, 8 and 9 months.

In 1780, the *unfortunate* and *imbecile* South, notwithstanding the *unpardonable sin* of holding upwards of 500,000 Africans in bondage, furnished 26,187 men, whilst the North furnished but 16,639—less than was ever furnished by the South, even when the war was altogether at the North. From this year to the close of the war, the South furnished more than half of those who fought, and the Southern troops invariably enlisted for a longer period than the Northern. Now if any thing is to be deducted from these facts, we may safely infer, from the length of their enlistments, that the Southern militia endured more of the hardships, and suffered more of the privations of war than their Northern co-patriots. We will, however, leave these facts with the reader for his consideration, and will bid adieu to the venerated efforts of our revolutionary sires, after inserting this remark. "Supposing the average period of enlistment for all the years to be about the same, North and South, (which will be favouring the North,) it will be seen that in the first years of the revolution, when the war was chiefly at the North, the Southern States supplied, each year, about one-third of the whole number of enlistments; as soon, however, as the war extended southward, and became general, the Southern States rapidly advance, supplying one half, and for 1780, '81 and '82, more than one half of all the enlistments."

Let us now see how the monied contributions compare:†

Virginia contributed to the expense of the war, - - - -	$9,085,982
New-York " " " - - - -	7,179,983
South-Carolina " (according to this writer,) - - - -	11,523,229
(But, according to Winterbotham, over $13,000,000.)	
The seven free States united,‡ contributed - - - - -	$61,971,170
The six slave States " " - - - - -	52,438,123

We will not detain the reader, to tell him how the North has feasted on revolutionary *pensions since the war.* We will merely assure him that the State of New-York has received *in pensions to its citizens* nearly 700,000 dollars *more than it contributed* during the whole war.

The part taken in the revolution by the different States, affords, however, but little ground upon which any surmise can be made at the present day. The Mexican war being a recent one, as well as a foreign war, will perhaps be a better guide. The following facts in relation to it are authentic. During this war, which, being a foreign war, it was not in the power of the President to *order* out the militia, and therefore no citizen need take part in it, except it be his voluntary

* See Commercial Review, 1848. † "The Union," by a Virginian.
‡ Calling Delaware a slave State.

act—the State of New-York, with its *two million six hundred thousand* FREEMEN, (in 1845,) furnished but 1,690 men; while the State of Louisiana, with but 352,411 inhabitants, (in 1840,) of which 168,450, nearly half were slaves, furnished 7,041 men; of which one particular corps—a battery of light artillery—was pronounced equally as efficient as any in the regular army. Now allowing a greater increase in five years than previous increments would warrant, in the population of Louisiana, there could not not have been more than 230,000 free inhabitants in the State in 1845. Then taking the population in 1845 as the surest basis for comparison, we say that in order for New-York to be on a par with Louisiana, in the voluntary contribution by her citizens of their lives and services, for the vindication of their countries honor in a foreign land, she should have sent at least, 79,593 men. For, as 230,000 (inhabitants of Louisiana,) is to 2,600,000 (inhabitants of New-York,) so is 7,041 (volunteers from Louisiana,) to 79,593 (volunteers due from New-York—*more than forty-seven times* as many as were actually sent.

The six New-England States, wherein the sublime spirit of liberty is totally uncontaminated by the *debasing influence* of slavery. These six States, whose yearning after universal freedom and equality, excites the admiration of the world. These six States, whose chivalrous emulation of the South ennobles their every act. These six States, with a population (in 1840,) of 2,234,812 inhabitants, *free as air*, sent the *enormous force of* NINE HUNDRED AND THIRTY MEN! While the six States of Georgia, Alabama, Mississippi, Louisiana, Tennessee and Missouri, with a population (in 1840,) of 2,063,684 free inhabitants, owing we suppose to their miserable degradation in holding at that very time no less than 1,139,438 Africans in slavery, owing also perhaps to the imbecility, laziness and effeminacy of southern men, were so lukewarm to their countries appeal, as to send the small force of but *twenty-six thousand and eighty-five men.* Then taking the population of 1840 as a basis of comparison, we state the proportion, as 2,083,684, (population of these six Southern States,) is to 2,234,812, (population of New England,) so is 26,085, (volunteers from the six Southern States,) to 28,248, (volunteers that should have been sent by New-England,) more than thirty times as many as were actually sent. If the population of 1840 should be objected to as a basis of comparison, let us suppose that the population of the six Southern States had increased in so much greater a proportion than that of the New-England States, as to be equal to the latter; it will still be found that the six Southern States furnished more than twenty-eight times as many as New-England; and, if desired, we will add the slaves to the free population, and even counting them among the citizens, the proportion will still be about *eighteen times* in favour of the Southern States.

All the free States together, sent - - - - - -	22,136 men
" slaves States, " " - - - - -	43,213 "
The population of the free States, was (in 1840,) - - -	9,803,273
" " slave States, " " - - -	4,733,707

Then as 4,733,707 is to 9,803,273, so is 43,213 to 89,491, the number of volunteers that should have been sent by the North, in order to have contributed as many as the South, and which is *four times as many* as were actually sent.* Each of the fourteen slaveholding States contributed men to conduct the war. But out of the sixteen non-slaveholding States, there were *six* from which *not one man was sent*, nor a dollar contributed.

The first regiment of Tennessee volunteers numbered 1,000 when it went to Mexico; when it returned, it numbered 350, an average loss of 50 men per month. The North-Carolina regiment was reduced one fifth in two months. The

* All these numbers are derived from *northern authority.*

Mississippi regiment had some companies reduced from 90 to 30 in a few weeks. Out of 400 men, in a battalion from Georgia, there were, at one time, only 40 fit for duty, the rest being sick or wounded, in the hospitals. The South-Carolins regiment, of 1,100, had, at the end of nine months, only 80 or 90 remaining to enter with Scott the city of Mexico. "The destruction of life in Napoleon's march to Moscow did not equal this." Can such troops be conquered? Can such people be subdued? Have not the veterans of Waterloo, the troops of Wellington, been conquered by Southern rifles, lead by Southern generals? Of a truth, such men may be outwitted in politics, they may be defeated in *civil wars of words*, but once rouse them, once place them on the tented field, and victory is perched upon their brow, or death is seated on their lips. They never can be conquered, for they never will submit. Their spirit is indomitable, their cause good, their hope eternal.

As to the natural *military spirit* and predilection of the two people, we belive there can be but little difficulty in reaching a definite conclusion. A strict obedience to the laws of discipline is the first requisite of the modern soldier, and we have already observed that this very institution of slavery carries with it a *radiating* power, one that is calculated to create in the breast of the master as well as the slave, the mere resident as well as the slaveholder, a just appreciation of the great virtues of discipline. Wherever a people is noted for love of order and obedience to law, it is from among them we must procure troops, if we would have such as can be relied on in the most desperate emergency. From a people who are given to disorder, riots and rebellion, soldiers can only be had while the *sun shines* and the *pay lasts*. But when we add to the good discipline of our citizens, the peculiar nature of our laws arising out of our domestic institutions, and the familiarity of almost every Southern man, from early childhood, with the use of weapons and the vicissitudes of his forest sports, we cannot but endorse the remark that, "our laws and habits tend to make almost every individual a disciplined and effective soldier. A large number, and indeed, most of the inhabitants of the South and West are trained from their earliest youth to the use of arms. Their pursuits and mode of life render them skilful in manly exercises and capable of enduring fatigue. These qualities joined to their proverbial love of country, create a spirit within them, which, once aroused, never could be conquered."* This opinion is confirmed in every quarter, and by the statistics of the country. The South, with a free population of *less* than half that of the North, and a community of electors *two and a half* times less than the North, has at this moment a militia organization by *far more than half* as numerous as that of the North. There are 1,151,756 men in the militia of the free States, and 762,445 in that of the slave States.† A proportion of about 7 South to 11 North, whereas, to be comparatively equal, the North should have at least 15 to every 7 of the South. Compare, now, the following number of free inhabitants. electors and citizen soldiers in the two sections respectively.

	Population, (1840.)	Electors at last Election.	Militia force.
The North,	9,803,273	2,043,528, about twice the	1,151,756
The South,	4,733,707	832,593, little more than	762,345

Compare these numbers as you please, it speaks well for the South, and we will soon take occasion to show why it is our militia is comparatively so much more numerous.

* Com. Rev. 1846.

† American Almanac.

A good test of the spirit of any community in any one department of life, is the desire of individuals for advancement in that department. In accordance with this principle, if we find the high affices in the military department in greater demand in one country than in another, *especially when the organization in the two is regulated by the same laws*, we must conclude that there is more military spirit in that country where the officers are in greatest demand. We have already seen how the rank and file of the militia compares; let us now compare the number of commissioned officers. In the slaveholding States there are 38,845, in the free States there are only 30,658; but to bear the same comparison to the rank and file as the Southern officers do, there should be over 76,000 commissioned officers in the Northern militia. Upon investigation it is found that one great reason for this discrepancy exists in the fact that at the North the "*staff offices*," are many of them vacant, and others so little in demand as to be with difficulty filled; whereas, at the South, they are in such estimation that they are no sooner vacated than they are occupied again. Nor can it be said that there is too great a proportion of officers to men in the Southern militia, for when it is remembered that a considerable number of these are staff officers, and the country in profound peace, it will be conceded that the " officers of the line" are in very just proportion to the rank and file. On the contrary, it must be admitted by the North that there is a great deficiency in her ranks. But if more conclusive evidence is desired of the superior military spirit of the South, we have simply to be reminded of the fact, that there are three flourishing State Military Academies at the South, at which about 300 cadets are annually engaged, whilst *there is not one institution* of the kind at the North.*

Now, when we consider that war is no longer a trial of physical strength, but is reduced to a contest of scientific skill. When it is known that every year about seventy young men are graduated by these schools *exclusively for the South,* and that the number is annually increasing,† we think the Southern States may feel satisfied with their resources in this respect, and need not shrink from a comparison, or a contest whenever necessary, of their citizen soldiery with the Northern hosts. There is one portion of the North, whose history has *a peculiarly peaceful cast,* and whose citizen soldiery, since the days of the revolution, seems to have fallen into a *Vanwinklean* slumber, only to be aroused on such occasions as a "*review*" by General Jackson and "*Major* DOWNING, of the DOWNINGVILLE MILITIA, 2d *Brigade*." The people of New-England are not a warlike people, they are a pious people; a good people; a thrifty people; a smart people; a free people; a charitable, a business people; a rich people; a sagacious people; a tolerating people; an orderly people; a prosperous people; a happy people; a virtuous people; a patriotic people; a voting people; a powerful people; but they are not a fighting people, not a warlike people; for these latter they have neither taste nor predilection. Single out the wealthy State of Massachusetts, the soul of New-England, the pride of the Republic. Pass in review some of her military exploits *since the Revolution*—for we would not class Massachusetts *then,* with Massachusetts *since*—where was the spirit of Bunker Hill in 1812? Massachusetts, who owned one third of all the navigation, and furnished one half of all the seamen in the Union. Massachusetts, whose sons were forcibly drafted into the service of her avowed enemy; Massachusetts, who so proudly took the lead against this same enemy but a span before. Where was she now? "*With*

* The Military Academy at West Point is a National School, it belongs neither to the North nor the South,

† One in Virginia, one in South-Carolina, one in Kentucky.

one eye upon Bunker's Hill, and the other upon Yorktown, she LAUDED KING GEORGE, THE THIRD, AND CALUMNIATED MADISON; *and when she found that her efforts to arrest the war proved abortive, she sent one portion of her children to* PLOT *a dissolution of the Union,* and another to her waterfalls to supplant her beloved* FRIEND *in manufactures.*" Massachusetts, by a solemn act of her legislature, condemned the war of 1812, and when, on the 13th of June, 1813, a proposition was introduced before her Senate approving the noble conduct of one of her own sons—the brave commander of the "HORNET," in the destruction of the British ship "PEACOCK,"†—she refused to act on the proposition, because the good people of that Commonwealth considered the war an *unjust*, *unnecessary* and *iniquitous* war. The Senate of Massachusetts resolved, "*that in a war like the present, waged without justifiable cause, and prosecuted in a manner which indicates that conquest and ambition are its real motives, it is not becoming a moral and religious people to express any approbation of military or naval exploits, which are not immediately connected with our sea coast and soil.*" This is a specimen of New-England's *martial demeanor* in the war of 1812. What was it in the Mexican war?

The Legislature of Massachusetts, in a series of resolutions, declares the war with Mexico to be "hateful in its objects, wanton, unjust, and unconstitutional." "A war against freedom, humanity, and justice, against the Union, the Constitution, and against the free States." That all good citizens should endeavour "to correct this gigantic crime, by withholding supplies, or other voluntary contribution for its further prosecution, by calling for the withdrawal of *our army*, &c., &c. What absurdity. OUR ARMY! Massachusetts have an army? Her army? Was the army that won the day at Buena Vista, and scattered the Mexican troops to the four winds of the earth, indebted to *Massachusetts* for a single man, a single dollar? If it was, the more shame on Massachusetts, for her ungrateful course, when a member from Boston offered resolutions of thanks to the General, and the officers and soldiers under him, for such unparalleled success. Shame on her, for her Senate *rejected* the resolutions which passed the house only after much wrangling and dispute. These were resolutions; here is one of the acts of Massachusetts in relation to *our* army. When one of her patriotic citizens had, after much exertion organized a regiment of volunteers in her own limits for the Mexican war—said to be the *first* that State ever sent forth from her own borders to meet the enemies of her country—and a slight and temporary assistance was solicited from this wealthy State, until the regiment could be mustered into service; she, true to her resolutions, refused to grant a cent and was deaf to the indignant cry of patriotism and honour, even when it arose within her own contracted limits. So much for Massachusetts, the same for the other States of New-England. Is it not amazing that these States which prize the Union so much, that they denounce the consultation of Southern States to be a plot for disunion, still, some of them have never struck a willing blow in *defence* of the Union. It is because of these facts that we say the people of New-England are not a warlike people.

A few words on the *means of supporting a war*. Not all the ingenuity of man has ever yet been able to make war a cheap business. None of the multifareous inventions of our Northern inventors have ever served to eliminate the expenses of war. If then a war is destined to arise between the South and the North, both parties must expect to pay well for their materials. We have only to see which of the two can be the highest bidder.

* The famous Hartford Convention.

† Captain James Lawrence.

In such a war, the productive industry of the South would not be called upon in any new capacity, it would still be productive. At the North, the productive industry would not only cease to be productive, but would be changed into consuming industry. Our cotton would still grow, her spindles would cease to revolve. Our slaves would still produce, her operatives would only consume. Our income would still support us, her income would be wrested from her. While our fields are cultivated, her ships would be dismantled in her ports. Our credit would be high, hers would be prostrated. If we incur a debt we would soon pay it, as experience shows, if she incurs one it would not only be a large one, for the reasons above set forth, but she will be a *great deal* longer paying it. With us the stake would be victory or death, inevitable death; with her it would be victory or defeat, disgrace. We will be united in a common cause, she would be disunited, New-England would certainly derange her harmony. Our cause would be sacred, hers infamous. We would have the sympathy of enlightened nations, she their contempt. We would be the defender, she the aggressor. And what is more certain, we would be the Victors *in the end,* she the bankrupt. In the first scramble for spoils we would assuredly get all posts and arsenals *in our limits,* she those in hers. In the breaking up of the army of the United States, our chances are as good as hers, the same for the navy: the officers in these branches of service, are gentlemen of high toned honor, they are contaminated with none of the sectional prejudices of civil life, they have no sympathy with abolitionism. They will each act, in such an event, on their individual responsibilty, they will either side with that section which has justice on its side, or they will go to their homes to defend the soil of their birth and of their father's ashes. Out of our 762,000 militia we could spare *three* or *four hundred thousand,* without cultivating a bag of cotton the less for it; out of her 1,151,000 militia the North could not take 100,000 without diminishing her productive industry. But we would not require more than 100,000, the North could not well support a larger force. When men are fighting for their homes, their lives, their honour, their wives, their children, and *their slaves,* they require but little pay, they will fight for a tenth of the wages of those who fight merely because they hear their political leaders say they *ought to fight.* We would be such men as the former, the North would send such men as the latter; we would be content with victory, they must have an *inducement.* Such a war would perhaps be a long one, the longer it continued the greater would be the loss of the North. We, with absolute certainty, could "muster into the field an army five times as large as Bonaparte conquered half of Europe with, five times as large as Alexander conquered the world with, and larger than any nation upon the face of the globe ever carried to the field, save one; and that one was whipped by a little band, no larger than the Texas Rangers." It would be folly for the North to presume on her numbers, a few words will show it. If she attempts to invade us, she will be compelled to have an enormous force in her service, she will not only have an army of invasion in one quarter, or another in another, but she must have her ports defended and her Southern frontier towns garrisoned; her operations must be divided into two grand departments, those on the Atlantic slope and those in the Mississippi valley, and the operations of these two armies will necessarily be in a great measure independent of each other. To supply these armies, and to defend their base lines will require not less than 100,000 men, for with less than that their campaign would be child's play. What then would this force cost? At the *lowest possible* calculation, placing every expenditure lower than any previous war would authorize. To organize and equip such a force would consume $1,000,000 per day. The first two months would be consumed in collecting and drilling recruits, arranging outfits, and such other preliminary business, the next two would elapse before a shot cold be fired to any effect. These four months, at the lowest estimate of outlay in arms, accourtrements, waggons, horses, &c., &c., besides the pay of the troops, the ordnance expenses, &c., would cost $200,000,000. The rest of the campaign would complete the total amount of 365,000,000 of dollars. But it could not be expected that we would be conquered in one campaign. And as we were not conquered in that one, with 100,000 men, perhaps the next year there would be 150,000 against us. They would cost, at the same low rate, 547,500,000 dollars. If by good luck we should escape subjugation that year, the next would be like unto it, viz: $547,500,000, and no conquest. Thus, in three years the North will have assumed a debt of $1,460,000,000. If she could not at the end of these three years whip us back into the *glorious* Union, depend upon it, she will not be able to do it in the next three. She must then either give up the chase, or commence another three years seige. But by this time her expenses will have augmented in proportion to her forces, the price of supplies will have risen as they invariably do under like circumstances, these three years will then cost her about $2,000,000,000, which being added to the costs of the first three years, makes the neat little sum of $4,460,000,00! *And the South not whipt yet!!* Where under heavens will the North get the money to pay this debt? California, to be sure, is a land of gold, but the North will learn by sad experience that California gold will find its way to other countries than those embroiled in wars. The North will evidently not have the means of supporting such an army, and as the South is equally able to support an army *within this limit* as the North, it follows that it is folly for the North to presume on its superior numbers. We will always be able to meet her man for man, dollar for dollar, however long the war may last. But, it will be urged, the Southern ports will be blockaded and no cotton will be shipped; that matter admits of no doubt, we have discussed it already a few pages back. Then comes up the old cry of "our internal foes," insurrections, rebellions, treasons, stratagems and spoils. But it is a last lingering hope. It is absurd. "No people profoundly ignorant of government, with no settled rights of property, with no means of defence, with no means of subsistence, with no confidence of security, could gain or hope to gain any thing by flinging off their vassalage. Negroes know this, or what is the same thing, instinct teaches it to them." Now comes the "dernier resort," the slave would be emancipated and won over to the North. This supposition is more childish than the other. The Northern troops would perhaps carry off some, but they would soon be tired of the game. And even admitting, for the sake of argument, that they persisted in the scheme. How many slaves is it supposed will be annually abducted. Perhaps the most invéterate abolitionist would be satisfied to get 50,000 a year, well we will double it; we will suppose 100,000 were annually carried off. Then supposing the yankees foolish enough to keep up the war six years, they would at the end of that time have stolen 600,000. We now have over 3,000,000 slaves, after these 600,000 were taken, we would have 2,400,000 left. Almost exactly the number we had in 1840. The natural increase during these six years would replace at least 300,000, we would then have a total sum of 2,700,000. The number we had in 1843. The effect of the war then would be to put us back to where we were in 1843, except, that instead of having to assist in the support of the North, we would be a distinct nation, with a remodeled government and no more *compromises* on the public mind. We would have a public debt to be sure, but before the North will have paid the interest of hers, ours will be entirely cancelled.

CHAPTER XII.

> "When devils will their blackest sins put on,
> They do suggest at first with heavenly shows."

It seems to be impossible for man to preserve either mediocrity or moderation in any thing to which he sets his hands. From his primitive state, down to his present overstrained degree of nice refinement, he is constantly plunging headlong into some extremity, or wantonly falling into some futile hallucination. Having always to reproach himself for his own sin and folly, he expiates his crimes by ascribing to his neighbour those of a more heinous nature. If, by any possibility, he becomes convinced of his error, he can readily account for it in the conduct of his neighbour. If he is accidentally rescued from the ridiculous fantasies of one extreme, reaction hurries him into the grosser absurdities of another. There is no falsehood so gross that he will not believe it; no truth so clear that he will not doubt it; no bigotry which cannot enslave his intellect; no subterfuge to which he cannot descend; no meanness of which he is not capable. There is no trust he will not abuse; no confidence he will not betray; no truth he will not pervert, no virtue he will not disgrace. In the conduct and language, the theory and object of abolitionists, both in England and America, these truths are forcibly confirmed. Whilst, in America, the abolition of African slavery is yet unaccomplished, in the British realm the accomplishment of it is complete; and a summary of the measures adopted and principles involved in that transaction affords food for reflection to every Southern man.

In America, African slavery originated in precisely the same way as it originated in all the British colonies—it has ever been practised on the same fundamental principles as in the British colonies, and, *if it is ever abolished by the decree of government, it will be done in a similar manner, and it will arise from similar causes, to those which we have witnessed in the British government.* It may, then, be interesting and instructive to review the chief proceedings of the abolition party in that government, and see what bearing they have on the present position of affairs in ours. On this subject we had intended to devote three chapters, under the three heads of the abolition of the right of property in slaves in England, the abolition of the slave trade, and the abolition of slavery in the British colonies. But, as we have already trespassed so much on the reader's time and patience, we will abridge our remarks, and condense them into one chapter.

We know with what avidity the most trifling affairs of domestic economy, and even the ordinary matters of national policy, are commingled with doctrines of the Christian Church, by busy-body, gossiping church-women, and priest-ridden church-men. We know, too, that to every action of man his Divine Author is privy, and that it is contrary to the requirement of that universal Author, that every matter of politics should be mixed up and confounded with religion. And we also know that no subject is better calculated to excite men's minds than religious controversy; no conviction so immutable as religious conviction; no bigotry so unconquerable as church bigotry; no animosity *so cordial* as church animosity. There is, consequently, no instrument in the hands of a political fanatic so powerful as religion, which he can so easily distort. It can, then, be matter of little surprise, to find that, whenever a question of *political* expediency can, by any possibility, be in any way whatever linked together, confounded with, or distorted into a question of *religious* expediency, it is invariably done. It is in keeping with these truths, that abolitionists are everywhere found to be the weak dupes of religious bigotry, the ignorant victims of prejudiced education, the mean-souled sharper, who, feeling envy to be the cause, ascribes humanity as the motive of his creed, or else the crazy enthusiast, whose empty ravings are repulsive to every ear. It was from such as these that the world was taught, a hundred years ago, that slavery was a sin, and, being such, should be abolished in every christian land. All the invective of christian Europe having been exhausted, the streams of church controversy having run dry, the numberless victims of religious persecution, arising out of the reformation, having been exterminated, and every possible mode of testifying by their actions the working of the spirit among them being tried, the good people of England tasked their ingenuity to find an object of solicitude and pious care, upon which to lavish their christian counsels and admonition. They were not long in finding the object of their search. It was a darling morsel, an English article, the produce of English skill and ingenuity, a specimen of English manufacture—it was African slavery. It was forthwith discovered to be a sin, from beginning to end, and all true-hearted Englishmen must needs set about to expiate the crime of their fathers, who introduced the system. How this was done, we are informed from a variety of sources.

It has already been shown that Great Britain, at the time when the slave trade flourished most, was by far the greatest importer of slaves from Africa, consequently, the greatest promoter of the slave trade in the world. Now, we have no room to doubt that this trade was the subject of the most cruel abuses, and, had it not been made the pretext to European adventurers, for every kind of piracy and wrong in Africa, it is probable it would be an approved traffic to this day. Be this, however, as it may, it is certain it was the first department of the system which was attacked by abolitionists, as a combined party.

Anterior to the year 1670, African slavery seems never to have received the direct attention of abolitionists; but between that year and 1680 there seems to have been a few individuals disposed to notice the subject. The first publication in relation to the subject, which ever appeared in England, was a treatise, written by a clergyman of the Church of England, called "The Negroes' and Indians' Advocate." This drew out another, from a non-conformist clergyman, called the "Christian Directory." And these were followed by others. They afford evidence that the abuses of the slave trade began to be talked of, among the *clergy*, at any rate. But the first glimmering of the light of abolitionism seems to have fallen on the society of Friends or Quakers. This society seems evidently entitled to the claim of having conceived, and duly brought forth, the idea of *sin in slavery*. About the time the abovementioned publications were coming before the English public, the Quaker people, in some of the West India Islands, began to prate so freely with the negroes, about their peculiar notions of equality, etc., that these uninformed creatures were seduced from the path of duty, and had to be punished. The cause of their misconduct was, however, traced to the teachings of the Quakers. So that, in 1676, an act was passed in Barbadoes, entitled "An Act, to prevent the people called Quakers from bringing their negroes into their meetings." In 1680, it became necessary for the governor of the island to "prohibit all meetings of this society." On the island of Nevis, as early as 1661, a law was passed, prohibiting Quakers from coming on shore, and, in 1677, another act was passed, laying a heavy penalty on every master of a vessel who should even bring a Quaker to the island. In Antigua and Bermuda similar laws were established.*

In the year 1688, a collection of Quakers assembled together in Pennsylvania, and, without being informed by what succession of inspired thought, or what process of profound reasoning they obtained the knowledge, yet we do know that

* See Clarkson on slavery.

these very Quakers, having gravely assembled and met together, did seriously consider, and, with one accord, demurely agree upon urging among their fellow Quakers "the inconsistency of buying, selling and holding men in slavery, with the principles of the christian religion." In 1696, the same collection again met together, and again urged the same inconsistency, and, in addition thereunto, they did meekly exhort all true and faithful Friends and Quakers, from that day forth, even unto all futurity, piously to refrain from ever purchasing an African slave, and, over and above all other virtues, it was devoutly suggested—not to liberate those in bondage—"but to treat with *great humanity* those already in their possession." In 1754, about 58 years after the last mentioned gathering, by which time they could easily dispense with the few old negroes still surviving in their possession, they issued a most *powerful* appeal, to christians of all denominations, entreating them, "*in the bowels of Gospel love*, seriously to weigh the cause of detaining them (their slaves) in bondage." In 1776, it was enacted, "that the owners of slaves, who refused to execute proper instruments for giving them their freedom, were to be disowned." In 1778, it was enacted by the same meeting, "that the children of those who had been set free by members *should be tenderly advised and have a suitable education given them.*" We have not been credibly informed whether those children, thus *tenderly advised and suitably educated*, were the ancestors of the present generation of sable brothers in Philadelphia or not. In 1774, a society was formed, called "The Pennsylvania Society, for promoting the abolition of slavery, and the relief of free negroes unlawfully held in bondage." In 1787, this society was considerably enlarged, and its influence greatly increased. In 1789, "The Providence Society, for promoting the abolition of slavery, for the relief of persons unlawfully held in bondage, and for improving the condition of the African race," was established, and was incorporated the following year. It originally consisted of one hundred and fifty members, among whom were several *humane gentlemen* from Massachusetts. In the city of New-York, about the year 1790, "The Society for the manumission of slaves, and protecting such of them as have been, or may be, liberated" was eitablished; and had stated quarterly meetings.

In the year 1727, the whole society of Quakers held a meeting in London, and passed a general resolution, "That the importation of negroes from their native country, by Quakers, is not a commendable nor allowed practice, and is therefore censured by this meeting." Sundry other meetings were held, and a great variety of resolutions and addresses, aimed at the entire system of slavery, but chiefly the slave trade, were the result. These proceedings, as yet, had no visible effect. The slave trade was carried on as extensively as ever; but, when the American Revolution broke out it was considerably decreased. British ships, transporting slaves, were exposed to the attacks of American vessels, and American ships were otherwise employed. American and British merchants had other interests to protect, and, owing to the general state of affairs, the demand for slaves was less than ordinary. This trade, therefore, in common with others, experienced a considerable decline. After the termination of the war, however, the traffic was revived, though it has never been carried to its former extent, by British or American ships.

Previous to the year 1729, all the functions of slavery were exercised, without dispute; but, during that year, an idea originated—we cannot tell where—that all persons who were baptised in the Church of England, whatever may have been their previous condition, became free. Another followed, that, as there was *no definite law* authorizing a citizen of Great Britain to hold a man *as property*, any person landing on the shores of that free island became himself free, whatever may have been his previous condition or obligations. A case arose, to determine which the solicitor general of the district was called upon for a correct version of the law. The reply was, "We are of opinion, that a slave, by coming from the West Indies into Great Britain or Ireland, either with or without his master, does not become free, and that his master's right and property in him is not thereby determined or varied, and that baptism doth not bestow freedom on him, nor make any alteration in his temporal condition, in these kingdoms. We are also of opinion, that the master may legally compel him to return again to the plantations."

In the year 1765, the question was again agitated in the abolition circles; but this opinion was confirmed by several eminent jurists of the day, among whom was the celebrated Judge Blackstone. Some years after this, however, a case was brought before an English court, involving the question, and it was decided that the laws of England admitted of no slave property. In 1772, another case* terminated in the opinion, that, on any slave coming into Great Britain, he became free. Thus ended slavery—*or rather its name*—in England. After the lapse of about forty years, the first great step towards abolition was accomplished. And there is no doubt that, at the time of its accomplishment, the parties engaged in it had no intention to push measures any farther. Why should they? British subjects unquestionably had a right to enjoy all the privileges appertaining to their rank, and, if the laws of England did not permit slavery *in England*, surely no slave could lawfully be held there. But there, we would suppose, the matter should have ended; on the contrary, however, it was there the matter *began.* It was *there* a struggle commenced, which was destined to last nearly three-quarters of a century. It was there abolition was first secreted in the womb of fanaticism, and hope first breathed into the nostrils of the *fœtus.* It was there our present ruptured condition dates its origin.

This decision gave an impetus to the Quaker doctrines, it opened a new field for demagogues, a new road for frenzy. The slave trade was talked of, slavery discussed, and *the rights of man* decided on. A short time was sufficient to bring together a few zealots in search of excitement. All that was wanted was a theme. A committee of abolitionists was formed, plans devised, and objects discussed. In a short time, it was settled among them, that to succeed in abolishing slavery, not only in Great Britain, but in all her colonies, they would be crowned with unprecedented glory. They determined upon their course. And, as Clarkson tells us—for he was one of the committee—they settled upon two evils from which to save their country. Their *ultimute* object was to abolish slavery, their *avowed* object *only to suppress the trade.* The two evils mentioned by Clarkson were, first, "the slave trade, in consequence of which many thousand persons were every year fraudulently and forcibly taken from their country." "The second was the evil of slavery itself, in consequence of which the same persons were forced into a situation, where they were deprived of the rights of men." "It appeared soon," says Mr. Clarkson, "to be the sense of the committee, that to aim at the removal of both, would be to aim at too much, and that by doing this we might lose all." The question then was, which they should take as their *avowed* object. Like sensible men they took that which was most likely to succeed. They soon perceived that to abolish the slave trade, *the abuses of which* were every where known and condemned, would be a matter more easily accomplished than the abolition of slavery, which was but little abused, and the right to interfere with which was exceedingly questionable. Upon a further discussion of the subject, they perceived, according to Clarkson, that "by aiming at the abolition of the slave trade, they were laying the axe at the very root. By doing this, and this only, they would not incur the objection, that they

* The case of *James Somerset*, a fugitive slave. See Clarkson's Slavery, vol. i., page 65, also Copley's History of Slavery.

were meddling with the *property* of the planters." "By asking the government to do this, and this only, they were asking what it could really enforce." They knew that if the slave trade* was once abolished, the same jargon which justified *it*, would also tend to justify the abolition of slavery, which *came out of it*, and would be fortified by the *precedents which would be established in the course of abolishing the trade.* "Impressed by these arguments," says the humane but misguided Clarkson, "the committee were clearly of opinion, that they should define their object to be the abolition of the slave trade, and *not of the slavery which sprung from it.* Thus, at the very outset, they took a ground which was forever tenable. Thus they were enabled also to answer the objection, which was afterwards so constantly and so industriously circulated against them, that *they were going to emancipate the slaves.* And I have no doubt that this *wise* decision contributed greatly to their success; for I am persuaded that, if they had adopted the other object, they could not, for years to come, if ever, have succeeded in their attempt." This unveils the hypocrisy of the abolitionists of that day, intent on one object, they avow another. Think you reader, the abolitionists, free soilers, or whatever else they may be termed, of the *present* day, are any more candid?

Not very long after the decision above mentioned, when a bill for "further regulating the African trade," was pending in the House of Commons, the Quakers presented a petition, praying for legislative interposition on behalf of Africans, and the slave trade, &c. This is said to have been the first *petition* ever presented for the abolition of the slave trade. The press, also, at this time, began to contribute its quota of abolition doctrines. The public was frequently entertained with all sorts of remarkable publications. At this time, July, 1783, the first abolition society in England convened to determine what steps should be taken "for the relief and liberation of the negro slaves in the West Indies, and for the discourgement of the slave trade on the coast of Africa. It was then scarcely known that such an association existed.

The first formal and official procedure for the abolition of the slave trade, took place in 1785. It was a petition duly drawn up by the Mayor and council of the town of Bridgewater, addressed to Parliament, and praying for the abolition of the slave trade. It was little regarded, however, for it was merely read and ordered to lie on the table, and was never afterwards disturbed. In a discussion on the subject in the House of Commons, during this session, one of the members objected to the measure in these words.* "I object to the abolition of the slave trade for twenty reasons: the first is, *it is* IMPOSSIBLE, the rest I need not give." This one potent objection has never been removed, as we will soon see. It *is* impossible. Early in 1788, the attention of the British government seems to have been brought to the subject; for the King, by an order of council, directed that a committee of his privy council should convene as a board of trade "to take into their consideration the present state of the African trade; particularly, as far as related to the manner of purchasing or obtaining slaves on the coast of Africa, and the importation and sale thereof, either in the British colonies and settlements, or in the foreign colonies and settlements in America or the West Indies; and also, as far as related to the effects and consequences of the trade both in Africa and the said colonies and settlements, and to the general commerce of this kingdom; and that they should report to him in council the result of their inquiries, with such observations as they might have to offer thereupon." This committee was a long time in existence, and will be again referred to.

Abolitionists now began to extend their operations beyond their own country;

* We speak of the *trade*, NOT ITS ABUSES. † Mr. Grosvenor.

corresponding agencies and similar societies were established in Scotland, Ireland, Germany, America and other countries. It is said that an abolition fraternity was established in Paris, having among its members, "*several ladies of the highest rank and intellect.*" Up to this time, however, the British Parliament would have no part in the matter. Some petitions had been presented, it is true, and one or two measures proposed, but immediately rejected.

In 1791, Parliament sanctioned the establishment of the Sierra Leone Company, the object of which, was "to colonize a small portion of Africa, as an asylum for negro slaves obtaining their freedom by coming to England, and yet who were destitute of maintenance." The *humane* principles of this company, as well as the *bland honesty* of its purpose, would appear from the following circumstances. We have, in a preceding chapter, stated how many slaves were stolen from some of the Southern States, by the British, during the American Revolution; and that about two thousand were carried to Nova Scotia. These two thousand negroes seem to have been the spoil of the Sierra Leone Company. The precise method by which these two thousand escaped being sold along with thousands of their fellow slaves sent to the West Indies, we have not been informed of. However, these *chosen few* remained for a time in Nova Scotia, but after a few years residence there they began to be burdensome to the public, and were with difficulty sustained. Some departed this life from the injurious effects of the severe climate; the chilly blasts of which, their half clad limbs were unaccustomed to. Some made their escape from the warm embrace of their kind benefactors, and returned to the hardships of their former condition, many finding their way even as far as Carolina. The rest remained with their white *supporters* like sensible negroes. They had nothing to do, but to feast on the folly of the white simpletons who carried them to the land of liberty, why should they not remain content. These considerations, *together with other humane motives*, induced the company to transport as many as could be prevailed upon *to indulge in further travel*, to the embryo colony of Sierra Leone. Accordingly, the company, out of deference to the distinguished services of the well known Thomas Clarkson, appointed his junior brother, Lieut. Clarkson of the British Navy, to "undertake the conduct of this business." The latter gentleman visited Nova Scotia, with a view of carrying out the designs of the company. After the most indefatigable exertions, a little more than half the negroes were induced, under one pretext or another, to *extend their travels* across the Atlantic, and return to the land of their *injured sires*. Transports were provided for about eleven hundred negroes, and they, under the younger Clarkson, embarked for Africa. Having arrived at their new home, we are told that Mr. Clarkson, as a reward for his services, had honours heaped upon him, and was crowned with the imposing dignity of *governor*. "The first governor of the new colony!" *The mighty governor of* 1,100 *runaway negroes!* Thus was that illustrious empire, the shining light of Africa, first populated by the stolen slaves of Southern planters. Previous to this, however—in the year 1786—an attempt was made to establish this colony, under the direction of Captain Tomson of the British Navy, "who took with him *four hundred distressed negroes* from London, with about sixty whites, to prepare and cultivate that portion of the country which was ceded by King Tom for the purpose of colonization." This, in a short time, proved a failure, and the scheme was abandoned, to be revived five years after by the company in 1791. We need not say this last enterprise met with as signal a failure as the former.

At this time, another very *plausible idea* was gayly passed around to all the abolition gossips, old and young, high and low. It was proposed that all persons opposed to slavery in the colonies, should religiously abstain from consuming any article produced by slave labour, *but especially sugar and rum.* If, said they, *if* universal concurrence *could only be obtained*, the consumption of West India produce would cease, and of course the West India planters *would fail*, and immediate abolition ensue. Thus their darling object would be accomplished, all by means of a little self-denial. It was a very *fine idea*, but we must say it was hardly practicable. Some few were foolish enough to try the experiment. They practised a little self-denial, but soon were convinced of the error of their way, and returned to the path of *rectitude, sugar and rum.*

In 1793, a motion was made in the House of Commons, "for leave to bring in a bill to abolish that part of the slave trade, by which British merchants supplied foreigners with slaves;" but it was rejected. In 1799, the motion was again made, but with like success. In 1804 and 1805, the same thing took place. After the failure of the motion in 1799, a bill was introduced to confine the slave trade within certain limits. The direct object of this measnre, was the safety and prosperity of the colony at Sierra Leone. This measure was also defeated. The abolition party in Parliament was, at this time, considerably reinforced by the union with Ireland; the majority of the Irish members being in favour of the measure. It was about this time that the most ridiculous, if not the most infamous, of all the schemes of abolitionists was planned. But, owing to the better judgment of some of those in authority, it was frustrated. The scheme was to *buy up African men* to recruit the black regiments of the British army.* The abettors of this scheme argued that the situation of the negroes, as *soldiers*, would be, beyond comparison, preferable to that of plantation slaves. This project was *ridiculous*, because *if it is true*, that it is better to take a man *who is a slave*, from the cultivation of fields and those comforts and enjoyments which belong only to peace, and put him in the ranks of the army to kill, or to be killed, and to subject him to the severest discipline in the world; it is *also true*, that the pursuits and accidents of war, are to be preferred to the pursuits and accidents of peace; or war is to be preferred to peace, which is obviously absurd.

It was *infamous*, because, to buy a slave expressly to place him in an army, *not because the service of the slave is wanted there, to defend the country*, but because by putting him there, one slave less remains on the plantations; by replacing him, when he is killed, with another slave, there will be two less on the plantations, &c., is a scheme which, in order to abolish slavery, would slaughter the slaves. It was, therefore, infamous, and does no credit to the humanity and philanthrophy of the abolitionist. But strange to say, it was objected to *on none of these grounds.* Mr. Wilberforce, in whose character, philanthropy was as prominent as statesmanship and economy were wanting, objected to it on very different grounds. "How," says he to Mr. Pitt, "can we justify buying slaves for that desirable and *even humane* purpose, when we reflect that the increased demand will produce a proportionately increased supply, and consequently as many more marauding expeditions, acts of individual rapire, injustice, witchcraft and condemnations, &c., as are necessary for obtaining the requisite number of negroes.

"It has occurred to me as extremely probable, that Buonaparte will resort to this mode of obtaining a black army for the reduction of St. Domingo, and I should be sorry that we should set him the example." The project was abandoned.

In the year 1807, the contest was permanently decided. After a series of efforts—some successful, some abortive—which continued nearly eighty years, it was enacted by Parliament, "that no ship should clear out for slaves, from any port within the British dominions, after the 1st of May, 1807, and that no slave should be landed in the colonies after March 1st, 1808." This bill has been *poetically styled* the "Magna Charta for Africa in Britain."

* See Wilberforce's Correspondence, vol. i, page 240.

And what has been the result of this Magna Charta? The trade has not been stopped, it has not even been diminished. Notwithstanding the solemn sentence of condemnation which was pronounced against the slave trade, by the assembled powers of Europe, at Vienna and Aix-la-Chapelle, it is still carried on without the least diminution, and that too by several of the powers which joined in the condemnation of it.* So far from decreasing, the trade has increased to at least twenty per cent. more, in the number and value of the slaves, than it was ever known to be when it was not prohibited by law. This "Magna Charta" humane and proper as it may have been, was not *the rightful remedy*, as experience shows, for it has proved an utter failure. Fifteen years ago, according to *English authority*,† it was thought that England was forever done with slavery and the slave trade. After an expenditure, estimated at one hundred and forty millions of pounds; after all the efforts of hundreds of associations, thousands of committees, public speeches, sermons, prayers, missions, tracts and pamphlets, to abolish them, they both exist in complete vigour. The only effect of all this commotion has been to increase the value of slave labour, to enrich the slaveholders of other countries, and to impoverish the richest colonies of England. The experience of these fifteen years teaches the world, that England can abolish neither slavery nor the slave trade. The English people, by their way of getting rid of slavery, made slaves more valuable, and the trade more profitable than it ever was before. They seem to have expected other people to follow their example, notwithstanding *they made it the interest of those people not to do so.* They forgot how slavery was abolished in the Scottish coal mines. Not by speeches, neither by acts of Parliament, nor yet by compensation, *but by free labour becoming cheaper.* Even now, at this late day, there are thousands yet to learn that slavery can only be abolished by being under-sold. The moment free labour becomes cheapest in any country, slavery is there already at an end. Six of the leading nations of the earth have entered into a league to suppress the slave trade by ARMED PREVENTION,‡ and the result of their efforts we will now proceed to consider. In the first place, the expenditure of life and treasure involved in this policy is obvious, and needs no argument to show the peculiar difficulties attendant on it. It costs Great Britain *alone*, half a million of pounds sterling, per annum.§ But this policy involves the "right of search," and that is very liable to be abused. It is *defective;* for it does not accomplish all that was anticipated from it, and from its very nature, it is actually unsuited to cope with the evil it pretends to remove. It not only fails to accomplish its end, but it aggravates the miseries of the negro in the clandestine passage across the sea. Let us refer to documents. In 1848, it was reported to the House of Commons, by "the select commitee on the slave trade," that during the year, ending in November, 1847, the number of slaves landed in Brazil from the coast of Africa, "was not less than 60,000, and not exceeding, perhaps, 65,000, *landed alive.*" And to secure that number of living subjects in Brazil, there must have been originally taken from the coast of Africa, that year, at least 100,000; the remaining 35,000 being taken by English cruisers, or dying from various causes on the passage. Thus, notwithstanding the African blockade, and all this formidable armed prevention, it is now demonstrated beyond doubt, that "*while in the year* 1794, *when there existed no obstruction to the traffic, the whole demand for African slaves, throughout the markets of the world, was adequately met by an annual abstraction of negroes from that country, to the extent of* 80,000*; in the year* 1847, *when the greatest naval powers are actively employing the most powerful of all obstructions to its preven-*

* See Wilberforce's Cor., vol. ii, p. 265. † Westminster Review, 1849.
‡ England, United States, France, Spain, Portugal and Brazil.
§ See North British Review, 1849.

tion, the demand for slaves in the market of BRAZIL *alone, requires, in order to meet it, a yearly drainage from Africa of* 100,000 *negroes*."

As confirmatory evidence that the trade has not been lessened, but has only changed its channels, and that the supply and the demand bear about the same relation as they did before the prohibition, consider one circumstance in the Brazilian market. In 1790, when slaves were imported into Brazil without hindrance, their average price was £54 sterling each; in 1847, in spite of armed prevention, their number being over 60,000, they sold at an average of £50. This goes forcibly to corroborate the statement in the report of the select committee.

A plain matter-of-fact view of the "whys and wherefores" of this subject will bring us to the correct conclusion. The object of all police systems in custom-houses, as well as revenue vessels, is to prevent smuggling and all illicit traffic. And it must be conceded that this police system is as complete as it can well be, and *its jurisdiction as unlimited* as, in the nature of things, it can be. Yet it is well known that the commodities of other nations are smuggled, *even in* ENGLAND, where the obstacles in the way of the smuggler would appear almost insurmountable. Here, then, with the best system of prevention, and with powers the most commanding, England has failed to *completely* suppress smuggling in her ports; and so has America, to a far greater extent. Add to this the fact, that the smuggling of these commodities, at the most exorbitant estimate, cannot ensure over 100 per cent. profits, and that the field of operations is very limited. Now, the object of placing cruizers on the coast of Africa, frem Senegal to Benguela, is to prevent the *exportation* of slaves. This system of prevention must necessarily differ from that to prevent the *importation* of commodities. It is defective, and *never can be half so complete* as the Custom House system. And, which is greater than every other consideration, the field of operations for the slave trader is almost unlimited, and his traffic ensures him *the enormous profit of at least* 800 *per cent.**. On account of this, there can be no surprise at the failure of the armed prevention. For, when we see the completest system, with unlimited powers and universal co-operation, fail to suppress the illicit traffic in commodities of comparatively small profit, and holding out limited inducements, with great fears of detection, to the smuggler, we have no reason to expect that we can, with a defective system, limited powers, and little or no co-operation, suppress the illicit traffic in a commodity of immense profit, and offering great inducements, with few fears of detection, to the sea-faring adventurer. On the subject of the slave trade, then,—and slavery also—as with many other things, we think nature will not bend her views, nor alter the course of her operations, to suit the requirements of human law, neither to yield to the entreaties of mercy. In order to obviate any effect, the most direct process would be to remove or extinguish the cause. And, until armed prevention, and the league of six nations, can remove the *cause* of slavery, and the slave trade, we look to find them in existence. There can be no doubt that when the slave trade ceases to be profitable it will cease to exist. When *free labour*, so called, becomes cheaper than slave labour, the latter will assuredly be abandoned, As a closing remark, it should be stated that, notwithstanding the government of six leading nations, and the public opinion of the people, prohibit and condemn the slave trade, it is nevertheless true, that citizens and vessels of those nations are busily employed

* For $30 the African chief will sell a slave; and, for the expense and risk of transporting him to Brazil, the planter there will give $400 for him. This is a gross profit of 1333 per cent. After making the liberal deduction of 533 per cent., for expenses, risks and losses, either by death or re-capture, there remains the net profit of 800 pér cent. Thus, by the outlay of about $600, for twenty negroes, the trader is enabled to realize the net sum of $4,800.

in conducting it. From the highest authority in this country,* we learn that "this trade is still, in part, carried on by means of vessels built in the United States, and owned or navigated by some of our citizens." Were these vessels built in the *free* States? Are these citizens Northern or Southern men?

The holding of slaves within Great Britain having been pronounced illegal, and the importation of them into any of the British colonies having been prohibited by law, one would suppose the abolitionists must feel themselves satisfied at the *good works* they had done, and would be willing to rest from their labours and be content. No one would suppose that their christian consciences would ever have pricked them on to do any thing further in the great cause of humanity. And it may well be asked, what more was to be done? If slavery was unlawful in England, the law had been executed, and slavery had disappeared. If the slave trade proper, and the man-stealing connected with it, which British subjects carried on, were wrong, a law had been passed, prohibiting it for the future. No one entertained a doubt that, if the law was violated, the culprit would meet his reward.

Abolitionists, however, were not permitted to stop here. Their enlightened minds conceived the great justice of an *ex post facto* law; and, if they could, they would have, immediately after the abolition of the slave trade, enacted a law to liberate every slave in the British colonies, by way of punishing slaveholders for importing and purchasing slaves, *when there was no law which in any way prohibited their doing so.* It is true, this was not done immediately; but the sequel will show how soon the ex post facto principle of abolition doctrines was successfully applied. British abolitionists, actuated by that misguided zeal which belongs to every fanatic, either political or religious, were impatient to rush headlong into the most wicked and preposterous extremes; but they have those cooler heads and more pious souls to thank, who kept them from accomplishing their nefarious designs. In abolishing the trade, they had established the precedents upon which their future operations were to be based, and they were restless till they could be busied in the final work. It is true, after the abolition of the trade, in 1807, the party was materially diminished. All had been accomplished which had been *avowed as their object,* and those who knew nothing further than the *avowal* were content, and seemed disposed to let the matter rest. But not so with all. There were a considerable number who still felt envy and bore malice, and an equal number of bigots, whose reasoning faculties had long been lost, and who lived for phrenzy and excitement. These composed the bulk of the abolition party at that time. And, for the succeeding sixteen years the slave and the master had each of them a little quiet rest and contentment. During this period, slavery in the British colonies was vastly improved. The interest, both of master and slave, invariably tends to improvement, provided they are not compelled or tempted—the one to exercise too much severity and vigilance, or the other to be insolent and vicious—by the stealthy intrigues of foreign abolitionists. The government of the colonies was constantly projecting new improvements, to the advantage of all concerned. The negro population increased naturally, the condition of society was bettered, agriculture and commerce flourished, and the whole population was gradually settling down to that state of equilibrium which will invariably be attained when a community is left quietly to pursue the arts of peace. It is true, there may still have been many abuses existing, many crimes committed, and many instances of cruelty exposed; but where is a community to be found free of these imperfections?

It was not destined that this state of things should last forever. The abolitionist, true to the principles of his creed, could not endure to look on and see,

* See President's Message, March 4th, 1849.

with eyes of envy, the flourishing condition of the slaveholding colonies. He could put up with the rags, beggary and vice all around him—he was accustomed to them, and besides, these people were white, *free*, they could take care of themselves, *their* misery did not cause a single pang in his *humane* breast; but every lash that was inflicted on an Ethiopian hide, in a colony with which he had nothing to do, in a community to which he was a perfect stranger, and at a distance of three thousand miles, pierced him to the very inmost recesses of his christian soul. Strange inconsistency! Anomalous charity! Most dubious piety!

In the year 1823, after a short rest, the press was again put into requisition, meetings were again held, societies again formed, and another "Magna Charta" again planned out. A society was formed, "for the mitigation and gradual abolition of slavery throughout the British Dominions." Among the members of this society we find the names of many who were actively engaged in all the proceedings just recorded. One of the chief arguments used by Mr. Clarkson, the leading man of the association, to strengthen the society and stir up a new excitement, was the *flourishing* condition of Sierra Leone, colonized by a *multitude of negroes*, who joined the British in the Revolution, *panting for liberty*, and eager for *self-government:* to wit, eleven hundred vagabonds, whom the people of Nova Scotia were glad to get rid of, under any terms. On this occasion, every religious hallucination was brought to bear upon the one isolated question, of policy involved in the relations of slavery. This society succeeded in bringing the matter before Parliament, on the 15th May, 1823; for, on that day a petition was presented, and a motion made *by one of its members*, to the effect, that slavery was irreconcilable with the principles of the British constitution and the christian religion, and "that it ought to be gradually abolished throughout the British dominions, with as much expedition as may be consistent with a due regard to the well-being of all the parties concerned." This resolution, with some amendment, was finally adopted by both houses of Parliament.

On the 25th of May, 1829, the subject of slave evidence was introduced before Parliament. It was urged that this description of evidence should be eligible in all cases where that of any other person would be admitted. And it was agreed that, during the next session, a bill should be brought forward, for the reform of the colonial judicature, in which provision should be made for the admission of this species of evidence.

The abolition bill was next presented, and, after going through the regular ordeals, was finally passed. It provides for the entire extinction of slavery in the British colonies, on the 1st of August, 1834. All field labourers, above the age of six years, were to pass into the state of apprenticed labourers, for six years, to terminate on the 1st of August, 1840. All domestic slaves to pass into the state of apprenticeship for four years, to terminate on 1st of August, 1838. All children, under six years of age, on the 1st of August, 1834, were exempted from the necessity of becoming apprentices, under certain conditions. And all born on or after the 1st of August, 1834, were to be considered free. Thus was the law abolishing the *name* of slavery in the British colonies permanently established, only twelve years ago. From beginning to end, it was the work of more than one hundred and ten years.

This was in 1834. The very next year shows the effect of the measure. The Jamaica Assembly, in a document addressed to the Governor of that Island, in August, 1835, exhibits the state of the colonies, after the lapse of a twelvemonth. "Seeing," says the Assembly, "large portions of our neglected cane fields becoming overrun with weeds, and a still larger portion of our pasture lands returning to a state of nature—seeing, in fact, desolation already overspreading the face of the land—it is impossible for us, without abandoning the evidence of our own senses, to entertain favourable anticipations, or to divest ourselves of the painful conviction, that progressive and rapid deterioration of property will continue to keep pace with the apprenticeship, and that *its* termination must, unless strong preventive measures be applied, complete the ruin of the colony." How true these early convictions were will appear from the following table, which we take from a carefully compiled article in the Commercial Review, of 1848. The exports of sugar, rum and coffee from Jamaica were, on an average,

	Hhds sugar, at £20.	Pun's rum, at £[illegible]0.	Lbs coffee, at 60s. pr. cwt.	Annual value.
For the 5 years, ending 1807, the last of the *slave trade*,	131,962	50,462	23,625,377	£3,852,621
For the 5 years, ending 1815, the year of the Registry act,	118,490	48,726	24,394,790	3,588,903
For the 5 years, ending 1823, the year of Canning's resolut's,	110,924	41,046	18,792,909	3,192,637
For the 5 years, ending 1833, THE LAST OF SLAVE LABOUR,	95,353	35,505	17,645,602	2,791,478
For the 5 years, ending 1843, THE FIRST 5 OF FREE LABOUR,	42,453	14,185	7,412,498	1,213,284

Up to 1807, the exports of Jamaica progressively rose, as cultivation was extended. But from that date it commenced gradually to decline. From the last two periods in the table, it appears that, by abolishing slavery, the annual value of these three principle staples was, in ten years, reduced from £2,791,478 to £1,213,284, which, at five per cent, is equal to annihilating an investment of about thirty-two millions of pounds. "We believe," says the writer, "the history of the world would be searched in vain for any parallel case of oppression, perpetrated by a civilized government, upon any section of its own subjects." We could give other evidence of the monstrous results of England's folly on this occasion; but will refrain, as they are too generally known to require repetition here.

A very short time after slavery was abolished in the British colonies, it became evident that the British government not only *expected* others to do likewise, but actually hoped *either to force or induce them to do so.* This was the greatest folly of the whole catalogue of follies. And we have every reason to believe that this hope has since been abandoned, at least as far as it concerns us.

Mr. Calhoun, writing from the "Department of State," in 1844, says, "that its ultimate abolition throughout the entire continent is an object ardently desired by her, (*England*) we have decisive proof in the declaration of the Earl of Aberdeen, delivered to this department, and of which you will find a copy among the documents transmitted to Congress with the Texan treaty. That she desires its abolition in Texas, and has used her influence and diplomacy to effect it there, the same document, with the correspondence of this department with Mr. Pakenham, also to be found among the documents, furnishes proof not less conclusive. That one of the objects of abolishing it there, is to facilitate its abolition in the United States, and throughout the continent, is manifest from the declaratien of the abolition party and societies, both in this country and in England. In fact, there is good reason to believe that the scheme of abolishing it in Texas, with the view to its abolition in the United States and over the continent, originated with the prominent members of the party in the United States; and was first broached by them in the (so called) World's Convention, held in London, in the year 1840, and through its agency brought to the notice of the British Government."

The experience of ten years has, however, wrought a great change in England on the subject. The ardour of the English people has cooled amazingly since the conviction has forced itself upon them through the medium of their pockets, that *their* experiment has failed, and that other nations are determined to benefit by their error.

"This experiment," says Mr. Calhoun, "has turned out to be a costly one. She has expended nearly one hundred millions of dollars in indemnifying the owners of the emancipated slaves. It has been estimated that the increased price paid since, by the people of Great Britain, for sugar and other tropical productions, in consequence of the measure, is equal to half that sum; and that twice that amount has been expended in the suppression of the slave trade—making together, two hundred and fifty millions of dollars as the expense of the experiment. Instead of realizing her hope, the result has been a sad disappointment. Her tropical products have fallen off to a vast amount. Instead of supplying her own wants and those of nearly all Europe, with them, as formerly, she has now, in some of the most important articles, scarcely enough to supply her own. What is worse, her own colonies are actually consuming sugar produced by slave labour, brought direct to England, or refined in bond, and exported and sold in her colonies as cheap, or cheaper, than they can be produced there; while the slave trade, instead of diminishing, has, in fact, been carried on to a greater extent than ever. So disastrous has been the result, that her fixed capital vested in tropical possessions, estimated at the value of near five hundred millions of dollars, is said to stand on the brink of ruin.

"But this is not the worst. While this costly scheme has had such ruinous effects upon the tropical productions of Great Britain, it has given a powerful stimulous, followed by a corresponding increase of products, o those countries which have had the good sense to shun her example. There has been, it is estimated by them, invested in the production of tropical products, since 1808, in fixed capital, nearly four thousand millions of dollars, wholly dependent on slave labour. In the same period, the value of their products is estimated to have risen from about $72,000,000 annually, to nearly $220,000,000, while the whole of the fixed capital of Great Britain vested in cultivating tropical products, both in the East and the West Indies, is estimated at only about $830,000,000, and the value of the products annually, at about $50,000,000. To present a still more striking view: of three articles of tropical products—sugar, coffee, and cotton—the British possessions, including the West and East Indies, and Mauritius, produced, in 1842, of sugar, only 3,993,771 pounds, while Cuba, Brazil, and the United States, excluding other countries having tropical possessions, produced 9,600,000 pounds; of coffee, the British possessions produced only 27,293,003 pounds, while Cuba and Brazil produced 201,595,125 pounds, and of cotton, the British possessions, including shipments to China, only 137,444,446 pounds, while the United States alone produced 790,479,275 pounds."

"It is little short of mockery to talk of philanthropy, with the examples before us of the effects of abolishing negro slavery in her own colonies, in St. Domingo, and the Northern States of our Union, where statistical facts, not to be shaken, prove that the freed negro, after the experience of sixty years, is in a far worse condition than in the other States, where he has been left in his former condition. No, the effect of what is called abolition, where the number is few, is not to raise the inferior race to the condition of freemen, but to deprive the negro of the guardian care of his owner, subject to all the depression and oppression belonging to his inferior condition. But, on the other hand, where the number is great, and bears a large proportion to the whole population, it would be still worse. It would be to substitute for the existing relation a deadly strife between the two races, to end in the subjection, expulsion or extirpation of one or the other; and such would be the case over the greater part of this continent where negro slavery exists."

All the legal enactments requisite for the consummation of their designs, having now been completed, it would be reasonable to suppose, the English abolitionists would have found no further matter for their pious concern. But when will that day come? So far from being satisfied with the results they had just brought about, they redoubled their infernal efforts. Having transformed the slave into the apprentice, it now became their avowed object, to release the apprentice, before his term of service, distinctly designated by law, had expired; and this too, without any compensation to the master. It was a striking feature in the abolition philosophy of the times, to mistrust the efficacy of their own measures, and abolitionists knowing themselves to be hypocrits *at heart,* were exceedingly slow in confiding to others. The very *crazyest* of the creed, were afraid to trust the execution of the apprentice laws and the darling interests of the apprentice, in the hands of the colonists. They were like men frightened at their own shadows. They believed the very concurrence of the colonies in the measure to be portentous. They made themselves even more busy in framing excuses for the failure of their visionary theories, than they had previously been in heaping calumny on the slaveholder. A year had scarcely elapsed before the London Anti-Slavery Societies resumed their accustomed *duties,* which were, presenting memorials, pointing out grievances, and praying for redress, whether the parties agrieved would have it or not. In 1836, a select committee was appointed by the House of Commons to examine into the state of things in the colonies, *but especially* JAMAICA. The report of this committee caused some sensation in abolition circles; and in a review of the report, published in 1837, the insanity and absurdity of abolition doctrines is clearly set forth in these words, "*we say, therefore, boldly, that we will not trust any government, to whatever party in politics it may belong, with the interests of the negroes.*" Here is the *broad principle of justice* which has, in every instance been the basis of abolition. Governments can be trusted with the interests of the white man, but the negro is a creature whose interests are too sacred to be entrusted to the care of human governments. The interests of the starving Irish, the Chinese, the East Indians, and all the world beside, may be trusted to the care of the British Government; but the African is above government, *he* can be cared for by no others than *the people of Enland.* How far this principle obtains in America is every day more apparent.

If there is one fact more forcibly exhibited than any other, in the abolition of slavery in the British colonies, it is this. In a population composed of white men and negroes, the condition, both moral and physical, of the latter, is far better in a state of involuntary servitude to the former, than in any other state they have heretofore been placed. It is admitted by the most sanguine abolitionists, and for the very good reason that it cannot be denied; that the negroes condition was worse under the ambiguous name of apprenticeship, than under the name of slavery. This fact is clearly established by official documents and actual observation. We need not cite instances. And how could it be otherwise? During slavery, when the mother and her offspring were the property of their master, common interest, *if no other motive,* would induce such treatment as was essential to the health, comfort and preservation of both. But when slavery ended, this common interest also ended. Under the hireling or under the apprentice system, this treatment was not to be expected, *except as charity.* Under the apprentice system—which professed improvement in all things—infants being no longer the property of the master, elicited no care or kindness from him, and perhaps were even regarded as *burdens.* For instead of increasing the property of the master, and thus involuntarily rendering a return for its support; it interrupted the labour, and consequently lessened the value of the mother. Similar remarks might be made with regard to other accidents and conditions of the two systems. But let it not be said we take too mercinary, or too degrading a view of the case. If we do, it is because human nature is too mercinary or too degrading. Ours is the most practical way of accounting for the miserable condition of the negroes after emancipation, even if there was no positive authority for the assertion. People talk of PHILANTHROPY! They imagine the most visionary conditions of society, and pursuade themselves into the absurdity of expecting divine attributes in man's imperfect nature. But we are content to limit our cogitations to *facts as they exist* in this sublunar world, our ideas are entirely of a *mundane* nature. We cannot fail to believe that interest is a much more powerful incentive than charity or philanthropy; nor do we recollect ever having met with a man who would not prefer receiving a debt of gold to a debt of gratitude; who would not consider a thousand guineas a far more substantial return than "*a thousand thanks.*"

Early in 1837, there was some dissention in abolition circles. All abolitionists agreed in the opinion that the apprentice system was no improvement on slavery. Some wished to moralize in public, on the reformation of abuses, to protect the rights of the poor apprentice, by stepping in, in the place of the law, between him and his master, and *compelling* the latter to do *their* will in his domestic affairs. Others were of opinion that past experience pointed to a different course. They thought the only christian way of proceeding would be to *abolish apprenticeship.* They piously urged that, slavery was wrong, because it grew out of the slave trade; so apprenticeship was wrong, because *it* grew out of *slavery, which* was wrong. The first mentioned class refrained from any efforts to cut short the period of apprenticeship. They regarded the bill, creating apprenticeship, as the creature of their own hands. They were sensible enough to refrain from the glaring inconsistency which the others were eager to persist in. Moreover, they very well knew that the British Government was not apt, *wantonly,* to violate a compact of its own choice and making, when the ink was scarcely dry with which it was written. These, together with other differences, which must inevitably spring up among frenzied zealots, lead to the formation of "the Central Negro Emancipation Committee."

This committee was not slow in enlisting the services of the pulpit, it addressed circulars to "ministers of every denomination throughout the kingdom, calling their attention to the state of the apprenticed negroes, and inviting their co-operation in seeking, at the hands of Parliament, the immediate repeal of the system." The press was also brought into action. The favourite plan of distributing tracts, pamphlets, and all manner of impositions was resorted to with redoubled energy. And on the 22d of January, 1838, the subject was brought before Parliament, in the form, not of the "Wilmot Proviso," but of the Wilmot *Repeal;* for it was on that day that "Sir Eardly Wilmot gave notice of his intention to move for a bill for the immediate repeal of the apprenticeship clause in the abolition act."

Just about this time, a petition from "the Town Council of Liverpool," was presented, praying for the immediate abolition of the apprentice system. The effort, however, was unavailing. And it soon became known that government was resolved to carry out the provisions of the law, and to preserve the system to the latest period of its legal existence. If, then, the system was abolished before the time appointed, it must be by the colonists themselves. On this account, the foolish clatter of abolitionists was partially hushed. But it received an essential *quietus,* when Sir Wilmot's motion, after having passed the House of Commons by a majority of THREE, was, by a subsequent manœuvre of ministerial policy, virtually cancelled and set aside.

These dying embers serve forcibly to show the spirit of fanaticism, which gives life to the doctrine of abolition. First, to abolish slavery and create apprenticeship, then because apprenticeship did not come up to the paradise it was conceived to be, to attempt to abolish *it* also, though it was the institution of *their own creation.* They serve to illustrate their impertinent officiousness, in constantly interfering where they have no interest, with the execution of laws which appertain in no way to them. But the virtuous consistency of the British people, and abolitionists in general, is exhibited by the following circumstance, to greater advantage than we have ever yet seen it, We would be inclined to doubt the truth of it, but for the very general knowledge of the fact. At this very time, when English philanthropists were so busy in their endeavours to abridge the African's apprenticeship, a new slave trade was in actual existence. By an order in council,* which had passed some months previous, there was a palpable encouragement held out for a species of slave trade, very much resembling that of Sir John Hawkins, under Queen Elilzabeth, three centuries ago. British laws having forbidden the African trade actually sanctioned a new slave trade, bearing a different but specious name. We refer to the regular importation of Coolies. By the 6th of March, 1838, this trade began to be conducted to such an extent that " Lord Brougham brought forward a motion on the subject of the importation of hill Coolies of Calcutta, into British Guinea."

British abolition was now nearly at an end, there was but little left for it to prey upon. The subject having been finally dismissed from Parliament, it only remained for the " *outsiders*" to amuse the public with a few entertaining exhibitions. Of all these amusing evening entertainments there were perhaps none so well got up as the grand public meeting at Exeter Hall, on the 4th of April, 1838. The meeting was numerously attended, and is said to have been *deeply interesting.* Many new fabrications were brought to the notice of the enquiring public, and abolitionists cajoled each other in a most ludicrous manner. Before the *sages* separated they issued a circular, recommending the prompt and general adoption of the following measures :—Petitions to Parliament, praying for immediate, entire, and *uncompensated* abolition of apprenticeship. This was unkind; uncompensated abolition was *too* unkind. It was the greatest as well as the last improvement in abolition doctrines. When the " abolition act" was passed, an appropriation of money was made to serve as a recompense to owners for the loss of their property; but on this occasion it was proposed to withhold all pecuniary remuneration. Now, surely, if a price was to be paid for the slave, the right of property in whom *was questioned*; it was far more proper that a price should be paid for the apprentice, the right to the services of whom, *was solemnly recognized*, *granted*, *created by law.* This was the last gasp, and most ridiculous giration of the abolitionists as a political party in England. Their spirit has been wafted across the Atlantic, to find a resting place in the crumbling capital of a disunited Union, a distracted country. They need no further existence, for there are no more *African martyrs* in the realm, wherewith to feed their hungry bowels. The frantic vomitings of a century have disgorged them of their loathsome spleen. The *glorious* result of their labours is their best epitaph ; it is recorded in the islands of West India.

* Copley's Hist. of Slavery. Appendix.

CHAPTER XIII.

"'Scaped from the ravage of the Turk and Goth,
Thy country sends a spoiler worse than both."

We need not offer an apology for citing the facts we have in relation to the British colonies; nor do we think it can be looked upon as a digression. For we hold that, if slavery is ever abolished, or in any way embarrassed, against the desire of the shaveholding States, it will be owing to the application of the same principles, and the result of the same causes, as those which accomplished the measure in the British colonies. But, independent of this, the genius of our people assimilates with that of the English people. Our language is the same as theirs, and the force of this circumstance alone, is incalculable. Besides that, the spirit of our laws is caught from theirs in many respects. Though the reports of cases determined in English courts are not precedent in ours, yet *they are authority.* They have great weight, and though they are open to observation, animadversion, and contradiction, yet they are generally decisive. We are unquestionably the offspring of Great Britain; and if we inherit some of the infirmities of our parent State, do we not also owe it to ourselves to be benefitted by her experience, as well as to take advantage of the many favours nature has heaped upon us?

But sixty years ago, men were wont to indulge in the pleasing reflection, that the similarity of the people in every respect and in all directions of the country, must unavoidably perpetuate the then really glorious Union. As all the great empires of preceding ages were formed by the conquest of kingdoms, different in arts, manners, language, temper, and religion, from the conquerers; so that the Union, though in some cases very strong, was never the real and intimate connection of the same people; and this circumstance principally accelerated their ruin, and was the absolute cause of it in some. And our Union having been formed by very different means, and the population, generally, speaking the same language, the people were supposed to be one and the same in every interest; the same in religion, in laws, manners, tempers and pursuits; it was eagerly believed that *time* could do no more than strengthen every tie; and that every increase in States, would be an additional bond of harmony. But could this pleasant reflection find an echo now? Do the same state of things exist now, that existed sixty years ago? Do the same *men* exist? Do the two great sections, the South and the North, maintain the same relations they did then? In short, if the same religion and the same laws regulated the society of both sections then, do they continue to do so now? By no means.

It is very true, the advantages enjoyed by this nation are immense; the astonishing increase in its population, wealth and resources, is the natural effect of plenty of land, a good climate, and a benificent government, in which corruption and tyranny *were once* unknown: but that time has forever gone. The great Roman Empire perished by the hands of northern barbarians, whom the masters of the world disdained to conquer; but this can never be the case with our Union. Our people inhabit every desirable portion of the Northern continent, and, if our Union should be preserved sufficiently long, they will, doubtless, possess it altogether. From what quarter then would our Goths and Vandals come. No dominion can ever be extended over us by the *Southern* continent; for among a thousand other reasons, the greater portion of that country lies in the torrid none, a region that has never yet sent forth nations of conquerors. Being thus exempt from invasion, from any quarter of the Globe, where can our end originate but with ourselves. Being beyond the reach of all external foes, what can ever terminate our *Union* but *a disease within.* Our federal constitution is based upon principles of justice, and was created in the spirit of compromise. Our laws undertake to ensure to every *citizen* his *inprescriptible political rights*, and guarantee *security both of person and property; resistance against oppression*, a voice in the formation of laws, and an equal chance of arriving at places of honor, reward, or *employment*, according to his virtues or talents. "These are the principles of our constitution, and laws grafted upon these simple, but substantial principles, and a system of legal jurisprudence, organized and acting accordingly, form the essence of our government; and *if ever the government swerves materially from these fundamental principles*, THE COMPACT IS DISSOLVED, *and things revert to a co-equal.*"

That the government *has swerved*, or that it will *swerve*, because owing to the nature of things it must swerve, is a truth which no longer admits of a doubt. A retrospective glance at the history of affairs will convince any sane mind.

Our system of government rests on "*the broad basis of the people;*" like a pyramid, it narrows as it ascends; its powers gradually rise, while they are confined in proportion as they rise. Every "course" in the structure is cemented to that immediately beneath, and finds its real support in the broad foundation course of all—*the voice of the people, the spirit of their laws, and the genius of their pursuits.* Let *these* be homogenious, *homogenious throughout*, and the fabric can never fall. But, as the unequal settling in the foundations of the grandest edifice, will inevitably weaken and distort the strongest walls of the superstructure, and ensure their final downfall; so, the heterogenious matter in the broad basis of our political structure, faithfully promises the most serious distortions and enduring ruptures. The basis is the people, the people are not homogenious, they do not assimilate, they are opposed in interests, at variance in opinions, *they are at war*, inevitable, unavoidable war. The basis is convulsed, the superstructure must totter. The basis is corrupt, the structure is contaminated. The basis is decayed, the structure must fall. The cement is broken, the house is divided against itself. IT MUST FALL. Is proof wanted, it is at hand.

Are the religion, laws, manners, tempers and pursuits of the people of this union, so similar as to ensure perpetual union? Is the foundation of the Republic composed of homogenious or heterogeneous matter? First, in relation to religion.

Has any schism of a sectional nature taken place in any religious denomination, calculated to weaken the political bond of any two sections of the Union. We have already shown at how early a period slavery was denounced by the "Society of Friends;" and that slavery is believed to be a sin by every conforming Quaker of the present day, we have no reason to doubt. This denomination of christians resides, we believe, almost exclusively in the free States. It is a small denomination, and any schism in it would have a proportionately small effect upon the politics of the country.

The largest, and one of the most influential denomination of christians in the United States is the Methodist Church. The chief branch of this Church, is the "Methodist Episcopal Church," which numbers, according to the best information we have been able to procure,* at least 1,112,756 communicants, and 5,042 ministers—making an aggregate of 1,117,798 *members.* In this church, the subject of slavery has ever been one of no small consideration. The subject has been one of primary importance in the temporal affairs of the church ever since its first establishment in America; and in spite of every possible effort to perpetuate harmony, this unpropitious connection of slavery with the church has been

* American Almanac.

productive of results, the end of which are yet to appear. But let us turn to the unvarnished evidence of documents; there we will see the inevitable discord resulting from discussions, even among the clergy, of the vexed question, which is so foreign, both to the business of the church and of the government.

At the General Conference of the Church in 1836, the question of slavery was warmly discussed, and the evils flowing from such discussions became quite apparent to many; so much so, in fact, that when the Conference convened in 1840, it was urged by the Bishops, in their address, as the solemn conviction of their minds, that no ecclesiastical legislation on the subject of slavery, would at that time have a tendency to the accomplishment of any desirable object.* As an evidence of the irresistible power of fascinating, which the subject seems to possess over the minds of the northern conferences of this church, it is sufficient to state, that, notwithstanding it was the declared opinion of the majority of the conference of 1836, based upon the most careful examination of the whole ground, and aided by the light of past experience, that "the interests of religion would not be advanced by any additional enactments in regard to slavery;" notwithstanding the whole body of communicants was solemnly admonished, by the heads of the church, to abstain from all abolition movements, and from agitating the exciting subject in the church; yet, in some of the Northern States, in spite of this pastoral counsel, the subject was agitated in such forms, and in such a spirit, as to disturb the peace of the church, and was made the absorbing business of numerous "self-created bodies." Notwithstanding it was strenuously urged by the wisest and best men, that neither individual members, nor official bodies in the church, should employ terms, and pass resolutions of censure, or condemnation, on any member, or public officer, or official bodies, *over whose actions they had no legal jurisdiction;* notwithstanding it was clearly demonstrated that such a course of conduct, in so large and influential a church, would materially effect the union of the States, the perpetuity of the national confederation, the reciprocal confidence of the different members of the great civil compact; in a word, the welfare of the entire community: notwithstanding, ever since the year 1792, the "general rules of the united societies" expressly prohibited "the buying and selling of men, women and children, with an intention to enslave them: notwithstanding, the diversity of the institutions of the different States is such as to render it impossible to suit all the incidental circumstances of *church economy* to the views of every individual: notwithstanding, it had been a well settled and long established principle in the polity of the church, never to insist upon the emancipation of slaves in contravention of civil authority, it being always considered unjust and unreasonable to hold individuals responsible for the destiny of circumstances over which they have no control; in spite of the exertions of the most liberal minds, the subject of slavery was called up before the General Conference of 1840, no less than *ninety-one times*, by delegates from Northern States, in the form of petitions and memorials *alone.*

Geographical dissentions had attained a startling attitude when this conference adjourned. But if there was any thing to awaken the apprehensions of the most timid *then*, what must we not expect at the succeeding Conference in 1844. The spark had been kindled. The subject had a firm foothold in the minds of those who were capable of fanning it to flame; but it is a source of no little pride to us, as a Southern man, to review the conduct of those firm and truly pious men, who represented the South at this Conference; when they—a small minority—vindicated the honor of the South, on the purest principles of charity, humanity and justice. The manly conduct of these good men on this occasion, affords no contemptible example for Southern statesmen at the present time.

* See Appendix to Journal of Conference, 1840.

At this Conference (1844,) there seems to have been a fixed determination on the part of Northern men, to keep the subject in agitation as much as possible, for by a reference to the Journal of the Conference, it will be found that in the short space of eighteen days, there were no less than *two hundred and seventy-four* memorials and petitions on the slavery question, presented by *nine northern* Conferences, and many from northern people in their private capacity, there being as many as ten thousand signatures attached. It was only on the 14th day of the Conference, when the evils of the agitation had assumed so palpable a form, that, as a last effort towards conciliation and compromise, and in view of the distracting controversies which had been so long existing, and the unpleasant position in which most of the delegates found themselves placed, it was resolved "that a committee of six be appointed,* to confer with the Bishops and report within two days, as to the possibility of adopting some plan for the permanent pacification of the church." But after a calm and deliberate investigation of the subject, the committee reported that they were "unable to agree upon any plan of compromise to reconcile the views of the Northern and Southern Conferences." Every effort to *compromise* having proved abortive, a series of resolutions were next presented, and referred to a select committee, providing for the amicable *dissolution of the Church Union*, if we may be permitted to use the expression; the line separating the two proposed branches being that which separates the slaveholding from the non-slaveholding States. Pending the consideration of this measure by the committee, a declaration signed by *fifty-one* delegates from the South, was presented and referred to the same committee. In this it was set forth "that the continued agitation on the subject of slavery and abolition in a portion of the church—the frequent action on that subject in the General Conference, and especially the extra judicial proceedings against Bishop Andrews, which resulted on Saturday last, in the virtual suspension of him from his office as superintendent, must produce a state of things in the South, which renders a continuance of the jurisdiction of this General Conference over these Conferences, viz: those represented by the signers—inconsistent with the success of the ministry in the slaveholding States." This committee was again instructed to devise, if possible, a constitutional plan for a mutual and friendly division of the church. During the consideration of this, a formal protest of the minority of the Conference, against the proceedings in the case of Bishop Andrews, was presented and laid on the table, and a committee appointed to inquire into the merits of the case. In this protest, made in behalf of thirteen Southern Annual Conferences, and portions of several others, embracing nearly 5,000 ministers and 500,000 communicants, it was clearly set forth that the entire proceedings were contrary to law and informal; were in violation of the fundamental law, usually known as the *compromise law* of the church on the subject of slavery.† That on this occasion a precedent was established, subversive of the union and stability of the church. That precisely in accordance with the state of feeling in the general population of the North and South, the church itself had been divided in opinion on the subject of slavery, ever since its organization in 1784; two separate and distinct parties had always existed; and nothing could ensure harmony, but a pious observance of that virtual, though informal, contract of mutual concession and forbearance between the North and South, upon which the compromise law of the church on the subject of slavery was originally founded. That whenever this law, the only bond of connection, is rendered null, no matter in what form, or by what means, the church was to every practical purpose already divided, without the intervention of any other agency. That the North had always found its security in-

* Three from the South and three from the North. See page 43 of Journal of Conference

† This compromise is not unlike the Missouri compromise in spirit and in principle.

numbers, and the untrammelled right of suffrage; and that no concession, beyond peaceable submission to the right of suffrage, would ever be submitted to by the South. That from *the compromise basis* of union in the church the South had never swerved; but that it had been abandoned by the North; and that principles and purposes were entertained there driving the South to extreme action, in defence both of her rights and her reputation. That as soon as the compromise was abandoned, the law of union, the principle of gravitation binding the two sections together became dissolved, and the general superintendency of the church was no more, the absolute necessity of division was already dated.

On the 8th of June, the select committee (of nine) made its report, which was amended and adopted. It provides for the division of the church, points out the dividing line, permits ministers to remain in the church South, without any blame being attached to them for so doing. Thus was accomplished the geographical division of the *then* largest church in the Union, *not on doctrinal grounds*, but because of an attempt of northern people to overrule the civil laws of the South, through the action of their ecclesiastical laws upon the individuals of their church, and thereby to force southern men to be doubly recreant in their duties, first as christians, then as citizens. The dissolution of this church is pregnant with the most salutary truths. It instances the most admirable rectitude, the most manly independence, the soundest appreciation of rights on the part of those staunch representatives of the South, who, headed by a *Bascom*, dared to maintain the dignity of their calling, at the same time that they vindicated the justice of the principles they defended. When we see venerable men, whose piety we cannot mistake, and whose virtues are on every lip; when we see such men after mature deliberation, openly avow by their most solemn declarations, that on the score of Northern interference with Southern slavery, *even in the church*, there is a point beyond which forbearance ceases to be a virtue, and submission becomes a crime; must we not feel sad at the tamer course which certain Southern Congressmen, in all the majesty of their wisdom, are base enough to pursue. Oh that the purity, determination and independence of those unpresuming patriots, had ere this been imparted to the degraded politicians, who in the time of need have the cowardice and treachery to desert the people who made them what they are, and reposed in them their dearest interests.

Another denomination of christians which is openly divided on the question of slavery is the Baptist Church. This denomination numbers 953,693 communicants, besides 8,673 ministers,* making altogether 961,366 members. These two churches alone comprise an aggregate of 2,218,642, nearly half the entire number of professing christians in the country, there being but 4,544,841 in all. Besides these open ruptures, there are other denominations which in principle are equally divided. We have read sermons from the Presbyterian pulpit of the North, which could better have been called free soil stump speeches than sermons. There are frequent conventions of churches in the Northern States—as for instance, the one in Cincinnati last April—the avowed object of which are to denounce the religion of the South, and to encourage the expulsion of slaveholders from the communion table. The ratio of communicants to population in all denominations, taken collectively, is about one to five. If to the Methodists and Baptists, we add the odd portions of other denominations, chiefly in New-England, New-York and Ohio, known to be opposed in their ideas about slavery, we will have a sum of at least 2,500,000, Now according to the ratio just mentioned, this about one-fifth of the population, which is related or connected to these communicants; and although they do not *belong* to the church *proper*, yet they are so related to those who do belong to the church, that they must inevita-

* American Almanac.

bly take part with the one side or the other. Taking all these together, we would have no less than 12,500,000 people ready to be arrayed against each other whenever the 2,500,000 are disposed to make the issue, and of these latter, every body knows how small a proportion were the originators of their schisms. It cannot then be said that the religion of the people of this glorious union is so harmonizing in its offices as to render the union *forever glorious.* No: the raving fanatic does not confine his frenzy to the things which concern the order of society, or the government of a people; he has not been content to defile the things of this world with his loathsome touch, but he has mounted up on high to cast back into the teeth of Moses the sinfulness of his dispensation, and to stamp IMMORALITY upon the brow of Jehovah. It has been reserved for *him*, to storm the precincts of Heaven, and in the rage of his indignation, to hurl down the escutcheon of "*Faith, Hope* and *Charity*," that it might he replaced by the modern dogma—"*Liberty, Democracy, Equality.*" He is not only empowered to level all distinction in the rights and suffrages of man whilst in this mortal coil; but he has reserved for himself the discretionary power of casting off those who have not the wedding garment from the table of the eternal supper.

Abolitionists, not satisfied to confine their strictures with regard to the *irreligion* of slavery, to the christian faith, attempt to bring the evidence of Mahometan laws to show how irreconcilable such a custom is with the principles even of that surreptitious faith. If *Mahometans* discountenance slavery, they exclaim in the depth of their indignation, how much more should christians abolish the infamous practice! But in this, as in most other respects, the abolitionist is wrong, wholly wrong. Wrong in the premises, wrong in the conclusion. If Mahometans *did* forbid slavery, it does not follow that christians should do likewise. But it is a mistake. The faith, the text book, the Koran itself, does not discountenance slavery any more than our own Bible does. The whole orgin of the error, which is so greedily snatched up by rabid dreamers, is briefly as follows:—After the arch imposter had made sufficient advancement in his projects, to discover that he was likely to succeed, he began to operate upon the minds of those around him. "Encouraged by so good a beginning," says Lane, from whose translation we quote—"he, that is Mohammad, resolved to proceed, and to try for some time, what he could do by private persuasion, not daring to hazard the whole affair by exposing it too suddenly to the public. He soon made proselytes of those under his own roof, namely: *his wife*, Khadeejeh, *his slave*, Zeyd Ibn-Háritheh, to whom he gave his freedom* on that occasion,† *and his cousin and pupil* 'Alee, *then very young.*" This is the whole origin of the delusion. The imposter in order to gain a follower, liberated a slave. What a powerful argument for modern abolitionists! Who that aspires to the eminence of a God, would not discharge a slave that he may gain an apostle? The example of the so called prophet was imitated to a limited extent, until the "faith" had been permanently established. The policy dictating the measure is of course obvious.

So far from slavery being contrary to the spirit or intention of the "faith," it is actually enjoined and provided for in certain cases, similar to the Jewish provisions on the subject. The prophet declared and openly proclaimed that he had received God's permission to attack and dertroy his idolatrous enemies, if they would not atone for their injurious conduct by embracing El-Islám, excepting the women and children, whom, if they remained obstinate, he was *commanded* to make slaves. "It has been said even by some of their leading doctors, that the

* For he was *his purchased slave*, as Abu-l-Fida expressly tells us; and not his cousin-German, as M. de Boulainville asserts, (vic de Mah. p. 273.)

† Sale here adds, "which afterwards became a rule to his followers;" but the conversion of a person after he has been made a slave, does not entitle him to, and seldom obtains for him his freedom. (See Lane's Chap. on "*the establishment of El-Islám,*" p. 61.)

Muslims are commanded to put to death all idolators who refuse to embrace El-Islâm, excepting women and children, whom they are to make slaves; but the precepts on which this assertion is founded relate to the Pagan Arabs, who had violated their oaths, and long persevered in their hostility to Mohammad and his followers. According to the decisions of the most reasonable doctors, the laws respecting other idolators, as well as Christians and Jews, who have drawn upon themselves the hostility of the Muslims, are different. Of such enemies, if reduced by force of arms, refusing to capitulate, or to surrender themselves, the men may be put to death, or be made slaves; and the women and children, also, under the same circumstances, may be made slaves."

CHAPTER XIV.

"* * * * * * Romans now
Have thewes and limbs like to their ancestors;
But, wo the while! our father's minds are dead,
And we are governed by our mother's spirits;
Our yoke and sufferance show us womanish."

As to the manners, customs, and pursuits of the people, do they serve to cement the union of the States? Look for a moment behind the mere gloss of polite society, it will be found that even in these respects there is a marked geographical distinction. Where is that lauded bond of *sympathy and interest* which was to bind the Union eternally? Where is it, but under the mouldering tomb with those who endeavoured to create it. Is it between the cotton grower of Mississippi and the coal monger of Pennsylvania? Is it between the sugar planter of Louisiana and the lumber merchant of Maine? Is it between the Carolina rice planter and the Massachusetts whale-fisher? Is it between the land owner of Georgia and the pork merchant of Ohio? Is it between the slaveholder of the South and the abolitionist or free-soiler of the North? Is it between the black slave of the South and the white pauper of the North? Is it even between the church of the South and the church of the North? Between the judicature of the South and the judicature of the North? If this fellow sympathy and common interest ever did exist, why does it not exist now? Is it because slaves are held at the South now? Then why did it ever exist. Slavery has ever been in practice at the South. Is it because Southern men love Cæsar less and Rome more, or because Northern men love Rome less and Cæsar more. There is no such sympathy. This union can never more rely on fellow feeling for its endurance. There is no common interest which can perpetuate the union of these States one moment longer than it continues to possess its *original value.* There is no identity of manners, interests or pursuits between the people of the South and those of the North, of such value, as to compensate for the slightest depreciation in the original value of the union. This union is a species of property among the States, the value of which does not admit of the slightest fluctuation. No one, nor no set of these *thirty* CO-PARTNERS, can better test the binding force of their compact, or the value of their *stock in trade,* than by attempting at the present time to appropriate to themselves more than their acknowledged dues, on the ground of *common interest* or *fellow feeling.* Whatever *armed forces* or *degrading submission* may preserve the *name of the Union,* it is certain sympathy and interest never will.

There is an undying hatred, a sovereign contempt in the breast of every man, for the neighbour who would, under the name of *humanity*, pilfer the property of another; or under the protection of *Constitutions* and *laws*, would wantonly, without cause and without provocation, trample on the rights, and impose upon the confidence of a weaker party. It is on account of this unconquerable feeling in the heart of man, that we believe the strong North is unalterably hated by the weak South, which is also, in this case, the injured party. Now that the property of the South is pilfered by the North; her rights trampled under foot, her independence shaken, her sovereignty well nigh gone, her remonstrance ridiculed, her protest scoffed into silence; her existence has indeed become a *boon* from the mighty North. Soon all friendships will be swallowed up in national animosity; the greatness of the past in the infamy of the present; for the Union is now but a shorter word for submission, and submission but another for infamy, shame, degradation—must we say *cowardice?*

It was upon the similitude of the *laws* of the different States that great hopes rested for the perpetuity of the Union. But, are those laws a pledge of Union? Less than a century ago slavery was universally allowed by law. But during the early period of our national existence, several of the States thought proper to enact laws prohibiting slavery in their limits. Being urged by too fervent a zeal on behalf of the negro, the Northern people, in the exercise of their prerogative, rendered it necessary in the eyes of Southern statesmen to take some legislative steps to counteract the obvious effects of their proceedings; and none of these effects were regarded more obnoxious than the tide of emancipated slaves from the North, which would inevitably flow all over the South, if not positively prohibited in the first instance. It was therefore, prohibited in many, if not all, of the Southern States,* that any negro coming from a non-slaveholding State, should be permitted to enter the State. This law has often been executed, and the constitutionality of it is unquestionable. But what is the result of it? A vessel sails from Boston, for example, with a cargo to be delivered at Charleston. The commerce between the States being regulated by the general government, every encouragement is held out for free intercourse between them. But this vessel, being owned in Massachusets, is navigated by the citizens of Massachusetts, and some of these *citizens* thus navigating the vessel happen to be negroes. Now these negroes are the acknowledged citizens of a sovereign State, and very properly deem themselves entitled to all the considerations appertaining to other citizens of their State, among which, the right to go into *any other State* in pursuit of business or pleasure is one. Much to their surprise, however, on entering Charleston harbour, their vessel is boarded by a public officer, and the negroes are informed that, notwithstanding they are citizens of Massachusetts, they are not looked upon as such in South-Carolina; and in obedience to the laws of the State, they will not be permitted to remain at large within her limits. On the landing of the vessel, these negro citizens of Massachusetts are marched up to the district jail of South-Carolina, and there retained until the vessel has unloaded, taken in a cargo, and is ready to sail; when they are re-conducted to their vessel and permitted to depart. The question then comes up, is this proceeding constitutional? Is it constitutional for South-Carolina to confine within the limits of a jail-yard any negro citizen of a non-slaveholding State, who comes within her limits? It is answered that *such citizens* must either keep themselves out of the State, or must be amenable to the law if they come in it. In the slaveholding States the presumption is, that all negroes are slaves; in the free-States the presumption is, that all negroes are free. The Southern man thinks his fugitive slave

* In Maryland. Virginia, South-Carolina, Georgia, Mississippi, Louisiana, and we believe many others.

ought to be delivered up to him by the people of the North; and the Northern man thinks his fellow-citizens, though they be negroes, ought to be permitted to go at large as other people at the South. The Northern man says:* "If the Constitution gives the Southern planter a right to seize his slave in New-York or Massachusetts, equally explicit is the grant to citizens of those States to enjoy all the rights of citizenship in South-Carolina. Yet if certain of our citizens, *freeholders and electors at home*, think proper to visit that State, a prison is the only dwelling they are permitted to occupy; and should the State to which they belong, send an agent to enquire why they are immured in a jail, and to bring their case before the Supreme Court of the United States, he is compelled to flee at the hazard of his life." The Southern man says, if the people of the North had never harbored abolition societies among them, whose sole object can be no other than the instigation of our slaves to disobedience and desertion, such laws would never have been called into existence. The State of Massachusetts, feeling bound to defend the rights of her citizens on board her ships in the port of another State. Being on these occasions more tenacious of her people's rights than she was when the British were impressing her seamen in 1812. And, feeling agrieved at what she deems both a violation of the Constitution, and of the law of nations; sends a formal AMBASSADOR to remonstrate against the proceeding, and for other purposes. This not being altogether an admissible thing, according to the notions of propriety entertained by citizens of South-Carolina, the *extraordinary envoy* is induced *informally* to re-embark, without having had more than sufficient time to make known the *dignity of his mission.* Diplomatic intercourse is thus cruelly cut short, between two loving sisters of this most loving and most glorious Union. The *envoy*, being nothing loath, is further induced to present his credentials in the State of Louisiana. But there, alas, he finds his mission is a mockery, and is forced to return with a melancholy brow to recount the *dangers of the South*, in the midst of admiring New-England patriots, and inwardly exult in the delightful consciousness of being "the noblest Roman of them all."

The most fruitful source of discord between the States, arising out of conflicting laws, is the general practice in the Northern States, with regard to the delivery of fugitive or stolen slaves. The provision of the Constitution on this subject, according to decisions of the Supreme Court, leaves it in the power of the owner to recover his slave without obstruction, in any State or Territory belonging to the Government. This is the spirit and intention of the Constitution. It is the law of the land, but it is one of those laws which do not carry the executive principle along with them. However clear this law may appear, it is in practice *null*, effectually *nullified*, for, in a community where every body is opposed to the law, it can easily be conceived how difficult it would be for a hated slaveholder to capture his slave without the assistance of the proper officers of the State. Thus the provision of the Constitution is rendered subservient to the laws or caprices of the State or the *mob.* Unless, then, the free States co-operate with the Constitution in this particular, or at least allow its officers and police to do so, the protection of the rights of the slaveholder, guaranteed by the Constitution, is absolutely denied him by the free States. To such an extent, is this the case, that most of the Northern States have passed laws, preventing State officers and tribunals from interposing *for* the arrest or delivery of fugitive slaves.

It is somewhat remarkable that the very States which are now most earnest in their opposition to this clause of the Constitution, are the very States with whom the idea first originated. *The Veritable New-England States!* Mr. Webster, their greatest man, says so. New-England, says he, "it is well known, is the chosen seat of the Abolition presses and the Abolition societies. Here it is, prin-

*See Judge Jay's letter to Hon. Wm. Nelson, M. C., from New-York.

cipally, that the former cheer the morning by full columns of lamentations over the fate of human beings, free by nature, and by a law above the Constitution; but sent back, nevertheless, chained and manacled, to slavery and to stripes. And the latter refresh themselves from daily toil, by orgies of the night, devoted to the same outpourings of philanthropy; mingling, all the while, their anathemas at what they call "man catching," with the most horrid and profane objurgations of the Christian Sabbath, and, indeed, of the whole of Divine Revelation. They sanctify their philanthropy by irreligion and profanity; they manifest their charity by contempt of God and his commandments."

Yes, the same New-England whose proceedings against the Quakers we have mentioned in another place, is the source of this very clause. In the eighth article of confederation of the old "New England Confederacy," framed in 1643, it is agreed, says Mr. Webster, "that if any servant run away from his master into any other of these confederated jurisdictions, that, in such cases, upon the certificate of one magistrate in the jurisdiction out of which the said servant fled, or upon other due proof, the said servant shall be delivered, either to his master or any other that pursues and brings such certificate or proof." In the "articles of agreement," of 1650, between that confederacy and the Governor of New Netherlands—now New-York—it was stipulated "that the same way and course concerning fugitives should be observed between the English colonies and New Netherland, as had been established in the articles of Confederation between the English colonies themselves." These were the precedents, the unquestionable authority upon which Mr. Nathan Dane, of Massachusetts, based his provision in relation to the subject in the celebrated ordinance of 1787, which was drawn up by him. And it was from that ordinance that the provision in the present Constitution was in substance borrowed. No body objected to the clause *then* as the awful violation of *rights* which it is *now* pretended to be esteemed. Not one of the men of Massachusetts herself—the very *cradle of human rights*—not even her Hancock or her Adams, nor even her Rufus King objected to it then. But now the far-seeing eyes of greater intellects discern the unrighteousness of it. *Now* we must have a jury, a jury to try not a *criminal*, but a runaway servant. Next perhaps we will have a jury to try a truant school boy. Then a jury to try an unruly son. Then a jury to try a pugnacious wife. And then, who knows, a jury to try ones own mortal self; a jury to try this mortal *clay* so sunk from immortality. Ah, that report of *the* THIRTEEN was famous indeed. It learns us divers lessons, but this lesson on the "jury trial" of runaway slaves is *peculiar in the extreme.* We can imagine the sage composer wrapt up in the deep folds of his originality as the idea first flashed across his mind; there must have been something awful in the scene; how like another "wonder of the world" he must have paused in his reflections that, other men might know he had caught an idea which as "*grand, gloomy, and peculiar.*"

This "jury" part of the report gives us an opportunity to call up the analogy between the British abolition agitation and ours. The *first cause* of British legislation on the subject of slavery is, generally speaking, very much overlooked on account of its apparent insignificance. No positive action towards abolition was ever dreamed of in Great Britain, even in private circles of society, until the question of *right of property in a runaway slave* was discussed in the Court of the King's Bench. And the principles involved in that case* are precisely the same as those which would be involved in our Courts, if the system of jury trials recommended in the report of the committee is ever adopted. The first circumstance which produced any visible effect in England, was the case of a slave belonging to a West India planter, who escaped from his master while in England,

* The case of James Somerset, already mentioned.

The slave, after running away, had been recaptured and returned to the master, and by him was conducted to a vessel in which he was about to embark. The slave was taken away from the vessel by an officer of the law, and the question raised whether the planter had the *right* to take his slave. The case resulted in the opinion that when the negro landed in England he became free. He was therefore liberated, because there was no positive law in England which authorized slavery. Heretofore, abolition was confined chiefly to Quakers, and their influence in society amounted to nothing, till the efforts of a single individual made an issue which resulted in the overthrow of a whole system. That *issue* was the question of the *right of property.*

Now, suppose this "jury" system of the Committee of Thirteen were to be adopted, and the runaway or abducted slave were to be empowered with the right of claiming a *jury* to decide whether he is a slave or not. It matters not so much, in point of principle, where the jury sits, whether it be in Philadelphia or Charleston, in Boston or New Orleans, *who is in reality to be tried?* Is it the *slave,* or is it *the master?* Is it to test the claims of the slave or those of the master? Who is willing, who is prepared, to have his right of property in his slave disputed, and perhaps, owing to some technicality or local prejudice, annulled, because the abolitionist of the North has succeeded in engrafting such a clause in the law of the land? Where is the spirit of a freeman when his constitutional rights are to be made *questionable* by the whims or disaffection of his ungrateful slave? Could any Southern man make up his mind to sit on a jury to try the validity of his neighbours claim to the services of his slave, which claim, be it remembered, has never been disputed since that slave was born, but is *now* made questionable because some abolition pamphlet has poisoned the affections and deranged the mind of that slave to such an extent as to induce disobedience and desertion? Is there one man in the whole South who is prepared to see the slave, whenever he may think proper to elope into another State, hurl defiance into his master's teeth, dispute his authority, and actually appeal to the laws *made by Northern abolitionists,* by calling a jury of citizens to forsake their business and come to deliberate over his dogged impudence? The text of the Constitution upon which this part of the "report" is based, requires that fugitive slaves "shall be delivered up on the claim of the party to whom such service or labour may be due." It is admitted in the report, that "in all cases of the arrest within a State of persons charges with offences; in all cases of pursuit of fugitives from justice from one State to another State; in all cases of extradition provided for by treaties between foreign powers, *the proceeding uniformly is summary. It has never been thought necessary to apply, in cases of that kind, the forms and ceremonies of a final trial.*" The summary proceeding here refers to the *capture* or *delivery* of the FUGITIVE; the final trial which awaits the return of the fugitive to his own State refers to the CRIMINAL. The final trial is not to decide whether the individual is a *fugitive,* but whether he is a *criminal,* or a violator of the law. But the trial recommended in the report is quite different from either "the summary proceeding" or "the final trial." It is meant, not to decide whether the individual is a fugitive, but whether he is a *slave.* Thus, the free citizen who flies from the yoke of the law which he has violated, is to be delivered up by a summary proceeding, without any conditions being imposed upon the pursuing party; whilst the slave, who flies from the yoke of his lawful master, whenever the freak may enter his brain, is to be delivered up only on condition that the "claimant" or master shall return the fugitive "to that county in the State from which he fled, and there *take him before a competent tribunal,* (viz. a jury,) *and allow him to assert and establish his freedom if he can,* AFFORDING TO HIM FOR THAT PURPOSE, *all needful facilities.*" In other words, whenever a negro, either through his own designs, or those of some contemptible abolitionist, thinks proper to escape into a neighbouring State, his master is not only to incur the expense of travelling perhaps a long distance, employing agents of the law, besides being put to numerous other inconveniences, in order to regain his property; but on returning home, instead of putting the negro to work as he has been accustomed, he is *at the request of the negro*, to surrender him up, to wait like *a gentleman* till the sitting of the court, when he will summon a jury on the vaguest pretensions to freedom. In this way the citizen's right is to be tampered with by his own slave; and the slaves rebellion or the abolitionists treason is to be made matter of grave discussion in the presence of the outraged master, *and at his expense*. We say at his expense, for the costs of every kind will eventually fall upon him. ALL THIS, too, is to be done, according to the report, "IN DEFERENCE TO THE FEELINGS AND PREJUDICES WHICH PREVAIL IN THE NON-SLAVEHOLDING STATES." Now, any body knows, who has ever read the Constitution, that it requires fugitive slaves to be delivered up to their owners. And every body knows, who has taken the trouble to enquire, that the laws of the several States award freedom to any negro *who is free*, even though he be claimed as a slave. Then, since the fugitives must be delivered up, and since free negroes *do* enjoy the protection of law against a deprivation of their freedom, why should Congress enact this new *jury law?* The report truly says, it should be done "in deference to the feelings and prejudices which prevail in the non-slaveholding States." Here, then, is that spirit of *compromise* and *mutual concession* existing between the South and North, elegantly illustrated. The South has both master and slave to protect; the North, both "feeling and prejudice" to gratify. The South, in order to protect master and slave, or, in other words, to preserve its political existence, must so far gratify the feelings and prejudices of the North, as to allow the Federal Government to step in between master and slave, and fix conditions to the ownership of the one, and give incompatible rights to the other. This is compromise! this is concession. But such as can only end by placing both master and slave at the South, to dance attendance on the whims and fancies, the "feelings and prejudices" of the LORDLY NORTH. Trial by jury! why that is the peculiar boon of liberty. When the day arrives, on which a slave is to usurp his master's rule, and openly appeal to a jury to sustain him, whatever may be the voice of the jury, a precedent will have been established, by means of which, the doom of the South will be sealed; abolition already accomplished. When that day comes, as come it surely will, if this Union lasts a few years more, the exhausted South, in the agony of despair, will remember, when it is too late, what

> "You and I have heard our fathers say,
> There was a Brutus once, that would have brook'd
> The eternal devil to keep his state in Rome."

The question may well be asked what bond of union is there between these States. What is law in one is not law in another. Public opinion in one is opposed to public opinion in another. What is respectable in one is debasing in another. The Federal Government acknowledges that man to be a citizen in one State, which in another it calls a slave and denies the right of citizenship. The unfortunate negro gentleman at the North is bandied about between government and society, law and public opinion, always basking in a full blaze of hideous mockery. A citizen here, a slave there. Where the law of one State will arrest and imprison, or banish, the law of another confers citizenship and equality. Where the laws of one State prohibit and denounce one practice, those of another command and encourage it. What is openly professed and esteemed essential in one quarter, is abjured and considered crime in another. Even in the *once* dignified Senate, the incongruity finds a cheering echo. The intercourse between the sovereign States is in some instances of such a nature as would ensure open hostilities between foreign powers. Not only are citizens of one section denied entrance into another. Not only is the property of one section openly stolen by citizens of another with impunity. Not only is disobedience to law in one quarter carefully instigated by citizens of another. But the very legislative and executive departments of almost every State are already in a menacing attitude. When the government of one State transmits to the government of another, a correspondence of such a nature as to be deemed insulting, and to be returned with contempt to its authors, there can be but little friendship between them. Union between *them* finds no stability in intercourse, but is rather shaken by that contempt which too much familiarity breeds. And this is not confined to two States only, it is sown broadcast throughout 20,000,000 inhabitants of thirty States. Can any one be acquainted with the transactions of these thirty States for the last few years and think them thirty SISTERS? We see some States declaring the extension of slavery to be a policy they *will not sanction;* whilst we see others no less fixed in their determination not to submit to any restrictions. We see gentlemen sent to Congress by some States to oppose, under all circumstances, the very measures which are to be unflinchingly supported by gentlemen from others. We see the comparatively harmless controversies of political parties rapidly sinking behind the huge giant of Geographical animosity. Where the great ruling majority of either of the leading political parties was once distributed in every State, we now find the galloping approach of a geographical concentration of a majority. Is the Union, then, in a wholesome state—is it in a *peaceful* state? Are the people literally at peace, or are they not at war, the worst of wars, a war of words, a war in the dark, at war with swords sheathed, hands tied, and only able to buffit and butt about in the utmost profoundity of darkness and corruption? It matters not *now* where the fault lies, the time to discuss *that* has long since passed. We speak of *facts as they exist.* Nothing but an *issue* is wanted to develope their far-reaching influence. There was a time when the South could condescend to argue for her rights and discuss the merits of her cause; but that time has passed. Her great misfortune is, that she has too long submitted to the bandying of words, too long in argueing, too slow in acting. We cannot think, after what has been seen, that the religion, laws, customs, manners and pursuits, taken collectively, of the people of this Union, indicate a long duration of our present Republic.

It has been said, in many quarters, that all the people of the South are not slaveholders, but that a considerable number have no connection whatever with slavery; that is true in the sense in which it is meant, but it is equally true that all the people at the North are not abolitionists. Indeed we know a vast number of them have no sympathy with abolitionists. But this does not alter the facts we refer to. The GENIUS of the North is unquestionably adverse to slavery, while the GENIUS of the South is inseparable from slavery.

"The people of the North want simply to know if they can do anything for the abolition of slavery, without violating their constitutional faith. For this alternative they are not prepared, (as I admit they ought to be, if they had ever pledged themselves to the support of slavery,) but they are prepared for almost anything short of that. At any rate, they are prepared to stand by the constitution, if it supports liberty. If it be said that they are not, the speediest process by which to bring them to that state of preparation, is to prove to them that slavery is unconstitutional, and thus present to them the alternative of overthrowing the constitution for the support of slavery, or of standing by it in support of freedom.

In a speech at Charleston, on the 9th of March, 1847, Mr. Calhoun gave the following estimate of popular feeling at the North, on the subject of slavery:

He said, "They, (the people of the North,) may, in reference to the subject under consideration, be divided into four classes. Of these, the abolitionists proper—the rabid fanatics, who regard slavery as a sin, and thus regarding it, deem it their highest duty to destroy it, even should it involve the destruction of the Constitution and the Union—constitute one class. It is a small one, not probably exceeding *five per cent.* of the population of those States. They voted, if I recollect correctly, about fifteen thousand, or, at most, twenty thousand votes in the last test of their strength, in the State of New York, out of about four hundred thousand votes, which would give about five per cent. Their strength in that State, I would suppose, was fully equal to their average strength in the non-slaveholding States generally.

"Another class consists of the great body of the citizens of those States, constituting at least *seven-tenths* of the whole, who, while they regard slavery as an evil, and as such, are disposed to aid in restricting and extirpating it, when it can be done consistently with the constitution, and without endangering the peace and prosperity of the country, do not regard it as a sin to be put down by all and every means.

"Of the two others, one is a small class, perhaps not exceeding five per cent. of the whole, who view slavery as we do, more as an institution, and the only one, by which two races, so dissimilar as those inhabiting the slaveholding States, can live together in equal numbers, in peace and prosperity, and that its abolition would end in the expatriation of one or the other race. If they regard it as an evil, it is in the abstract, just as government and all its burdens, labour with all its toils, punishment with all its inflictions, and thousands of other things, are evils, when viewed in the abstract, but far otherwise when viewed in the concrete, because they prevent a greater amount of evil than what they inflict, as is the case with slavery as it exists with us.

"The remaining class is much larger, but still relatively a small one, less, perhaps, than twenty per cent. of the whole, but possessing great activity and political influence in proportion to its numbers. It consists of the political leaders of the respective parties, and their partisans and followers. They, for the most part, are perfectly indifferent about abolition, and are ready to take either side, for or against, according to the calculation of the political chances, their great and leading object being to carry the elections, especially the presidential, and thereby receive the honours and emolument, incident to power, both in the Federal and State government."

This estimate is allowed to be correct by Northern writers; it is probably sufficiently accurate for all practical purposes. Adopting it as correct, it shows that *five per cent*, only of the North sympathize with the South; that the other *ninety-five per cent.* (seventy-five per cent. acting from principle, and twenty per cent. for spoils,) "are disposed to aid in restricting and extirpating slavery, when it can be done consistently with the constitution, and without endangering the peace and prosperity of the country."

Mr. Webster says: "It is my firm opinion, this day, that within the *last twenty years* as much money has been collected and paid to the abolition societies, abolition presses, and abolition lecturers, as would purchase the freedom of every slave, man, woman and child, in the State of Maryland, and send them all to Liberia."

The total number of slaves in Maryland, says Mr. Horace Mann in reply, according to the last census, amounted to 89,405. At $250 apiece—which is but about half the value commonly assigned to Southern slaves by Southern men—this would be $22,273,750. Allowing $30 each for transportation to Liberia, without any provision for them after their arrival there, the whole sum would be $25,058.600—in round numbers twenty-five millions of dollars!—more than a million and a quarter in each year, and about thirty-five hundred dollars per day. "I had not supposed the abolitionists had such resources at their command."

Now, with such authoirty as Calhoun and Webster, not to mention the distinguished and rising Mr. Mann of Massachusetts, no one can accuse us of error. Putting down the population of the North at the very low estimate of 12,000,000, the abolitionists proper "*the rabid fanatics*," as Mr. Calhoun calls them, being *five per cent.* of this number, would amount to 600,000. Now we are certain this number is not more than *two-thirds* of all the abolitionists, *at the present day*, but for the sake of preventing any possible objection, on the score of the number being too large, we will take the 600,000 as the average number of abolition population, men and women and their children. Mr. Webster says that these 600,000 have spent as much money in furtherance of their schemes as would buy up every negro in Maryland and transport them to Liberia. Mr. Mann denies it, and to support his denial, shows that the negroes in Maryland would cost $25,000,000, to be carried to Liberia. But we, in our turn, *deny* Mr. Mann and *confirm* Mr. Webster, by bringing Mr. Calhoun to witness that these $25,000,000 were the contributions of a population of 600,000, in *twenty years*, as Mr. Webster says. According to these numbers, each individual would average $41.66 for his twenty years contribution, or $2.08 for his annual offering on the altar of LIBERTY! This is surely not much. Why, Mr. Mann might double the expense of the measure and it would still be but $4.16 for each philanthropist. Whereas we are sure they each go as high as $5.00 for their African divinities.

But we return to the analysis of the Northern population. We see that, in 1847, ninety-five out of every hundred at the North, was, through principle or motives of interest, opposed to slavery. We cannot doubt that a similar investigation of the feelings of the Southern people would result in finding at least ninety-five out of every hundred, including slaves in the number, in favour of slavery, either through motives of interest or from principle. But these immense majorities of the people in the two sections are not in that state of indifference they were in a few years ago; the Northern people do not ponder so much on the constitution as they were wont to do; they have learnt a *higher law* than the constitution; the Southern people do not sleep so soundly; they do not kiss so sweetly the rod that smites them as they were wont to do; they have learnt a higher theme than submission, a dearer name than Union. These great masses of people *are not friends!* To say the least, they only await the issue which must soon envelope them. Let the *issue* be made, let the two sections once be called up to the mark, to say shall *this* or *that* be, and the most sanguine adorer of the Union would be convinced that, where a man's treasure is, there also will his heart be. Whether he be no slaveholder or no abolotionist, the man would do violence to his impulses and his interests who would not identify his actions with those of the section to which he belongs.

In an attempt at ridicule, the Northern press, and no small portion of the Southern people, have pointed to South-Carolina nullification, and scoffed the idea of Southern unanimity and Southern resistance; but it would be well for such persons to hush their taunts, and behave with the gravity which becomes the present crisis. That same affair of nullification, from beginning to end, whatever may be said with regard to the expediency of it, affords the most valuable instruction in the present state of affairs. It is, however, totally inapplicable to the case in point, and, whenever it is held up as evidence of Southern politics, on the question now before the country, we cannot but think it is done in a spirit of childish ignorance and timid incredulity. That question involved principles quite distinct from those in the present controversy. Nullification sprang out of circumstances too distinct from the slavery question ever to be confounded with it.

The history of the affair, as well as a conjecture as to its effects, were briefly summed up in these words, more than twenty years ago. "In an evil hour, they (the Northern people) not satisfied with the domestic market, which was fairly open to them, required a monopoly at home, making all interests tributary to to their speculations, as a means of enabling them to contend with other nations, in foreign markets. Politicians seized upon this excited spirit as a means to promote their personal views. The peace of the country has been shaken. It is now no longer a question of political economy, but a contest upon higher principles; and hostility and sectional feelings have been created, that may act injuriously, not only to this interest, (the manufacturing interest,) but on the Union itself, for a longer period than the superficial will readily imagine."

We will perhaps be pardoned for alluding to this subject, which has so long been buried in the past. When we see our native State, the land of our birth and most endearing associations, pointed out as all that is vile and imbecile, we cannot refrain from expressions of contempt for her revilers, and admiration for her independence. It is unfortunate for the South that such a spirit has been fostered against her, on account of nullification, as exists in many parts of the Union. The wily politician of the North, and the political traitor of the South, are not slow in taking advantage of this contracted spirit, to turn the noble little State into ridicule. But these efforts are futile. So far from being derogatory, they are in fact complimentary, for, as things now stand, they show how early she discerned the darkened brow of battle lower. They show that she was prompt to burnish her armour, gird up her loins, and set her lance in rest. Without regard to the conduct of her neighbours, her banner has been unfurled, and she is to be seen in her true colours. Her crest has waved high enough to be seen, and to be felt; and, but little doubt remains, that if every Southern State had but acted as she did, *in the early stages* of that controversy, the Union would not be the tottering cripple it now is.

It is indeed strange, aye, *passing strange*, that the indignation of the whole Union should fall upon *poor* CAROLINA, for nullifying a measure which the world must pronounce *oppressive*. Yet every State at the North can pass laws which positively and most effectually *nullify the constitution itself,* in that clause, for instance, relating to fugitive slaves. When South-Carolina *nullifies the tariff acts*—acts which she believes to be unconstitutional, and oppressive to her, as a sovereign—the whole Union is up in arms against her, and the warlike Massachusetts steps forward, to "*clothe the President with extraordinary powers, in order to reduce her to submission;*" but when Massachusetts, or any other free State, *nullifies a clause of the constitution*, not one word is said, IT IS ALL RIGHT. Shame on you, shame on you *of the South*, who would endeavour to ridicule Carolina for being at least open and manly in resisting what she deems oppression, on the part of a government which is a hundred times stronger than herself; while the *mean* and faithless theft of private property, by the authority and *injunction* of sovereign States, you seldom talk of, and then always with at least becoming gravity. Talk not of *bluster*. Bluster is nothing in the scale with PERJURY! Is Carolina a *Hotspur*? Methinks we know of BELZABUBS.

The present agitation partakes of no intermediate course. The issue once made, there can be no neutral party. There can be no conservative party; every community must take up its position, *pro* or *con*. The question then recurs, is the *issue* likely ever to be made? It would be well for every man seriously to consider for *himself*, is it likely *ever to come?* Let the past be a guide for the future. If it is found, upon investigation, that there has been any *approach* to such an issue, for the last fifty years, we may take it for granted that there will continue to be one for the future, all extraneous causes remaining the same. Any one, having satisfied himself on this point, is then prepared to form an opinion as to the probable result of the present agitation. If any one thinks, as we do that the *issue must come*, let him consider the following suggestions.

When the present government was formed and the constitution finally adopted, every one will concede that the merits of slavery had no place in the politics of the country, neither was it ever mentioned on the floors of Congress, except in a dignified and courteous manner. The official intercourse between the Southern and Northern representatives and senators was then harmonious and conciliating.

All the civility and etiquette which should characterize the conduct of gentlemen, was then tenaciously observed. At that time, the slaveholding interest was undisturbed by Northern politicians, for the obvious reason, that they had it not in their power, and possibly were not disposed to do so. The Union was literally an experiment. There was no manufacturing interest, no mining interest, no peculiar local commercial interest, no California interest, to be made the darling care of Congress. The interest of agriculture identified, then, as now, with slavery, was the great concern of the country; and, as a consequence, the slaveholding States formed the most important section. They possessed greater wealth and a much greater extent of territory than the free States. The population of the two sections was about equal; but, only three-fifths of the slaves being represented, the North had a small majority of Representatives in Congress. We will directly see how that representation has increased. Each peculiar section of country had its own commercial emporium; each exported and imported for itself. In those brighter days, when the country was just emerging from its infantine struggle for existence; when every citizen, as he trod the soil of his State, felt the exalting consciousness of having consecrated it as his right, by his own blood and treasure; when *States' rights*, as well as individual rights, had been lately carved out with the sword; the Union of the States was a community of SOVEREIGNS, formed for honourable purposes, and Congress was an assemblage of *men* and *gentlemen*. In those days, the *State* was the sovereign, and Congress the agent, and the legislators knew the value of independence, for they had just earned it; they knew the worth of honour, for they were honourable. But now!

CHAPTER XV.

"A government, on freedom's basis built,
Has, in all ages, been the theme of song,
And the desire of great and godlike men.
For this the Grecian patriots fought;—for this
The noblest Roman died."

A BRIEF historical review of the rise and progress of the Union and the constitution, will "tend to show the genius and value of the government." As early as 1754, a Congress was held in Albany, at which *seven* States, or rather colonies, were represented. At this Congress, great efforts were made for the formation of a confederacy of all the colonies then existing, from New Hampshire to Georgia. It was unanimously resolved, by the assembled delegates, "that a union of the colonies was absolutely necessary for their preservation." A proposition to that effect was, however, rejected, not only by the crown, but *by every provincial assembly*. The colonies were "jealous of each other's prosperity, and divided by policy, institutions, prejudice and manners." So powerfully did these dividing influences operate in those early times, that Dr. Franklin, an eminent advocate of Union, observed, in 1760, "that a union of the colonies against the mother country was absolutely impossible, or, at least, without being forced by the most grievous tyranny and oppression." In another quarter, it is declared "*that the colonies had no principle of association amongst them, and that their manner of settlement, diversity of charters, conflicting interests, and mutual rivalship and jealousies, would render a union* IMPOSSIBLE."

In 1775, another Congress assembled, to take care of the liberty of the country; and, soon after, a confederacy of the thirteen colonies was agreed upon. It was accomplished, however, exactly as was predicted by Dr. Franklin, fifteen years before; it was *forced upon the colonies* by the tyranny of the crown. The direct and sole object of the union was resistance to a common danger. The absolute necessity of that union has never been doubted. But, as to any sympathy of interest, fellow-feeling, inducing a voluntary desire for union, their non-existence is evident, from the proceedings of those early Congresses. As an illustration of the fact, we have only to remember that, as early as June, 1776, Congress "undertook to digest and prepare articles of confederation;" but, notwithstanding the same danger threatened them all, and although they "were contending for the same illustrious prize, it was not until the 15th of November, 1777, that Congress could so far unite the discordant interests and prejudices of thirteen distinct communities, as to agree to the articles of confederation. And when those articles were submitted to the State legislatures, for their perusal and ratification, they were declared to be the result of impending necessity, and of a disposition for conciliation, and that they were agreed to, not for their intrinsic excellence, but as being the best system which could be adapted to the circumstances of all, and, at the same time, afford any tolerable prospect of general assent." These difficulties, which, in a time of such stupendous danger, could present such obstacles to union, have been lurking behind the constitution ever since its formation. It is true, sixty years ago these difficulties were few and surmountable, the constitution was new and powerful. But now these difficulties have increased and multiplied apace with population and territory, while the constitution has lost its power proportionately.

In 1786, some of the defects of the compact became so evident, that the legislature of Virginia made a proposition to the other States, for a convention of delegates, to devise measures for the regulation of commerce and foreign affairs. This proposition was responded to by five States, whose delegates assembled at Annapolis in September, of the same year. These delegates presented "a strong application to Congress for a general convention, to take into consideration the situation of the United States, and to devise such further provisions as should be proper, to render the federal government not a mere phantom, as heretofore, but a real government, adequate to the exigencies of the Union." Congress assented to the proposition, and, accordingly, a convention of all the States was called, to meet in Philadelphia in May, 1787. This occasion was, perhaps, the most solemn and eventful ever witnessed in America since the first settlement of the colonies. This convention "combined a very rare union of the best talents, experience, information, patriotism, probity and character which the country afforded." And, after a few months tranquil deliberation, a plan of government was decided upon, which now forms the Constitution of the United States. This plan was brought about by *compromise*, not only between parties having *different interests*, but between sections of country having *different institutions*, and *conflicting ideas of policy and right*, as well as statesmen "having widely different views of the principles on which a federal government ought to be constructed." But though there were many opposite opinions entertained by the statesmen who concocted this plan, it is certain they were all of opinion that it was an experiment, it was one of *anticipated value*, and that if practice and experience proved it to be of insufficient *practical value* it should then be abandoned for a better.

That the people who make a government have *the right* to alter or destroy that government; that, in the formation of a government, it may be proper for one party to yield to the other a disputed point, for the sake of unanimity and strength; but that, *when the government is formed*, it should be on sound principles, clearly set forth and distinctly understood; annd that, *after the government is formed*, it should be a government of principle, with the rights, powers and privileges of each component part fixed and determined, without any farther yielding of opinions by any party: for, where a right is defined, for one party to yield it to the counter claims of another is concession to usurpation, surrender to conquest, and immediately terminates the previous equality of the parties.

The plan was submitted to the States for their acceptance or rejection, and in 1790 it became the law of the land. The doctrines expounded at this convention, and the enlightened philosophy of the plan it suggested, are too well known to admit of any remark from us. It is sufficient to qualify the fact, that "the peaceable adoption of this government, under all the circumstances which attended it, presented the case of an effort of deliberation, combined with a *spirit of amity and of mutual concession*, which was without example;" by adding, that *the peaceful continuation of this government, as the nation grows rich, acquires power, population and territory, will require a spirit, not only of amity and mutual concession, but of forbearance, submission, equity and good faith, equally without example, and perhaps beyond the power of human nature to exhibit.*

It would, of course, be impossible to form a constitution, in which every contingency that could ever arise in the history of a nation, would be *expressly and individually* provided for. It would, therefore, be impracticable to frame a constitution which would require *literal obedience.* It was in consequence of this, that the old articles of confederation, which gave no power to government, but such as was *expressly* granted, were changed in the new, so as to obviate the necessity of *literal construction.* In the new articles, the word *expressly* is carefully omitted. So that when a question arises, as to whether this or that power is granted by the constitution to this or that branch of the Federal Government, it is to be decided, *not by the letter* ALWAYS, *but by a fair construction of the whole instrument, and a careful regard to the history of its formation.* Mr. Jefferson has laid down a general principle on the subject, which will never fail when strictly observed. He says: "The capital and leading object of the constitution was, to leave with the States all authorities which respected their own citizens only, and to transfer to the United States those which respected citizens of foreign or other States; *to make us* (that is, THE STATES) *several as to ourselves, but one as to all others.*"

Now, this compact is every where acknowledged to be as perfect as in the nature of things it can well be, and if it ever fails to effect that for which it was intended, it will not be the fault of the *instrument*, but of those in whose hands the instrument is placed. The constitution is unimpeachable, and the omission of the word "expressly," just alluded to, gives it one of its peculiar charms. But it is now evident, that *in order to arrive at a fair construction, the spirit of amity and mutual concession in which the instrument was created, must always actuate the parties construing it, to precisely the same extent as it actuated the parties framing it.* And the reason of this is, that a set of precedents have been established, which place it in the power of politicians who are dishonest themselves, to place a dishonest construction on the constitution, whenever sufficient latitude is allowed. An example of such precedents, is to be found in the wholesale surrender of her "rights, powers and privileges," by the Southern States, in that ill-advised and humiliating measure, called the Missouri Compromise.

In the early days of the Union, the people were accustomed to rely on forms, and to confide in written constitutions; in their patriotism, virtue and good faith, they never dreamt th the constitution, the creature of the greatest men of the age, could ever fall short of practical perfection. But sixty eventful years have passed since then. Every statesman of that day has long since been numbered with the dead. That generation has passed away, and a new people has sprung up in their place. Though the constitution they created is still the same, their offspring is a different race. New issues have sprung up, scarcely to have been anticipated, which cannot fail to bring to an early development, the principles of discord pointed out by such men as Franklin, and which have ever since been lurking in our system. It is now apparent that the construction, *that fair construction* which the constitution requires, can be so completely distorted, as not only to "give a new direction to the action of our system, but, leaving its outward and visible form unchanged, might derange its vital functions, and give it a morbid energy, an irregular, diseased and pernicious operation; that a constitution settled upon fair, mutual, and liberal compromise and concession, might become unfit for the very purposes for which it was organized, might break down every barrier which has been created to restrain it, might assume those very powers which were intended to be withheld, and which, if they had been granted, would have assured its rejection; and this, by the technical construction of some doubtful expressions." There was a time when the experiment involved in the constitution was hopeful and promising. In those brighter days, whatever political division of parties there may have been, each party was found in every portion of the country, and "asperity of feeling was every where tempered by daily intercourse in the city, the village, or the neighborhood." But now that soothing intercourse is inevitably disappearing before the destructive influence of geographical divisions, even in parties of the same politics. And if this must be, who is there to gainsay it? It is true, some faint echoes have been heard from the Northern press, and some surprising demonstrations made in the Senate by antiquated and disappointed demagogues, to the effect that the majority of the people of this Union would not allow the minority to depart from among them. The North will not allow the South to dissolve the Union. Preposterous! But more of this anon.

It is now more than twenty-five years that the North has been openly depriving the South of those rights, powers and privileges guarantied by the constitution. Every year injury has been heaped upon injury, wrong upon wrong. It took less than twenty-five years for Great Britain and America to separate from each other; and it took less injury to make the colonies revolt. But, within late years, injury to the South has been changed to degradation, and wrong to punishment. It is the natural right of *every free people* to withdraw from tyranny. The principle of self-preservation gave a sanction to the separation of the thirteen colonies from the mother country; the same principle will always sanction the separation of the South from the North, immediately as the government fails to to carry out the ends for which it was intended, even if there was no inherent right to do so. For "when a government established over any people, becomes incompetent to fulfil its purpose, or destructive to the essential ends for which it was instituted, it is the right of that people, founded on the law of nature and the reason of mankind, and supported by the soundest authority, and some very illustrious precedents, to throw off such government, and provide new guards for their future security." But self-preservation is not the only law upon which a dissolution of the Union would be sanctioned. It is a principle universally accepted, that all power is originally vested in the people; and all *free* governments are founded on their authority, and are instituted for their peace, safety and happiness. Now, if this be true, if the people are the source of all power in a free government, and if this be a free government; then the people, so far as the distribution of power is concerned, are the sovereign and supreme arbiters, and they

9

can give and take away at the will of the majority. And when the power which they have delegated by written constitutions, or otherwise intrusted to the care of agents, is turned against them, they have the right of separation or revolution, PEACEABLY IF THEY CAN, FORCIBLY IF THEY MUST. It may, therefore, be presumed—upon the ground that this purports to be a free governmeat, and that each State is an independent sovereign—that when the General Government fails of its end, it is the right of any State to separate from the government, provided it is the will of the majority of the citizens of that State. But if one State enjoys this right, another does also; it is, therefore, the right of any number of States to withdraw from the Union, when the majority of the citizens in each so will it. If, then, the Southern States think proper, to withdraw from the confederacy, they have the right to do so. And the only question, would be the ways and means.

The constitution, it is urged, binds the States to perpetual union. Where, then, let us inquire, does the constitution derive this overwhelming authority. We all know that after having been agreed upon in a general convention, it was submitted to each individual State for ratification. It was adopted by the voluntary act of each State, through the medium of conventions. It, therefore, derives its whole authority from the conventions of the people of the different States, held within their respective limits. Throughout the compact, the legislatures of the different States, as representing the sovereignties of those States, are regarded as the constituents and as the contracting powers. So much so, that the contract itself constitutes the State legislatures the organs for proposing amendments. But, in order to amend the constitution, they must have the right or power "to consider the good or evil of the existing constitution," and to put their own unbiassed construction on the requirements of the contract. Moreover, the powers of the General Government are limited; for *all powers* belong to the State governments, excepting only those delegated by them to the General Government, but no power belongs to the latter, except such as is granted by the former in the constitution. The Federal Government is, therefore, not a sovereignty, but the agent of a community of sovereignties. This being the case, it is the prerogative of any one of these sovereignties, or any number of them, to dismiss their agent, or cease to employ their agent, whenever it is made manifest to them that this agent is overstepping his prescribed limits. There can be no doubt as to the spirit and design of the *union*, the term "can have no other meaning in our constitution, history and transactions than the word *confederation*," and is totally unconnected with any idea of *indivisibility* or CONSOLIDATION, which persons may attach to the word. The union of the States rests upon a *covenant* entered into by them individually. And "when the terms of this covenant are supposed to be broken by any of them, as there is no common arbiter to decide between the parties, it is of necessity, that each State must judge for itself, and act as its own judgment may dictate. If in the honest exercise of this judgment any sovereign State declares the covenant broken by its co-States, and chooses to dissolve the Union thereby established for this cause, she has the perfect right to do so; and this makes secession from the Union as to that party only."

"This Union results from a compact between the States, to which they became parties in their sovereign capacities, with full powers and rights inherent in each, (as in all other compacts) to dissolve or to secede from such compacts, for breaches of any of its fundamental conditions or material stipulations, and of which each State of itself, and of necessity, must be the exclusive judge."

The right of secession never was opposed in the former days of the Republic. No man was bold enough to denounce such solemn truths, such unshaken principles of common justice, till General Jackson issued his proclamation in 1832, against the South-Carolina Ordinance of Nullification. "Until then," says '*Ran-*

dolph of Roanoke,' "I undertake to say, that in the whole history of the constitution, not a vestige remains of that invaluable right having ever been brought to question. Not a word recorded in the Madison Papers, casts a doubt upon the subject. Nothing that occurred in the Convention—nothing written in the Federalist—no construction of the constitution upon the powers delegated or reserved during the administrations of Washington or the elder Adams, ever brought it into doubt; while the very memorable instance I have already given to your Excellency, touching Kentucky's famous memorial in 1795, solemnly and boldly announcing her purpose of seceding from the Union, with the implications arising from the silence and acquiescence of Washington and his cabinet, of their concession of the right, carries with it overwhelming testimony in its favour. And in far more recent times, (1844–5) such free and bold constructionists of Federal powers, as Mr. John Quincy Adams, and large majorities of the two houses of the Massachusetts Legislature, resolved and declared in substance, that the annexation of Texas would be such a breach of the constitution, as to justify and authorize her secession from the Union, and it was her standing menace for a twelvemonth, that if Texas came into the Union, that Massachusetts would go out of it."

By the established law of nations, each party to a treaty construes it for *itself*, but it must allow other parties to do the same; and if the difference between their respective constructions is important enough, *the parties have the right, either to rescind the whole treaty, or to enforce the treaty by conquering in war.* Vattel says: "If one of the allies fails in his engagements, the other may constrain him to fulfil them; this is the right derived from a perfect promise. But, if he has no other way but that of arms to constrain an ally to keep his word, it it is sometimes more expedient to disengage himself from his promises and break the treaty. *He has undoubtedly a right to do this;* having promised only on condition that his ally should accomplish, on his side, every thing he is obliged to perform. The ally, offended or injured in what relates to the treaty, may then choose either to oblige the perfidious ally to fulfil his engagements, or declare the treaty broken by the violation of it." The sovereign aggrieved "is permitted to threaten the other to renounce the entire treaty—*a menace that may be lawfully put in execution*, IF IT BE DESPISED. These principles are general, sound, and not to be questioned. They apply in all cases, as well to confederations as to treaties. Each party must judge for itself, for the very good reason that no other can properly judge for it; it must judge on its own responsibility, at its own peril. If their judgments are contrary, and their opinions obstinately persisted in, then "war alone can arbitrate the event, or if a peaceful course be adopted, the whole compact is at an end."

But there is one truth which renders the right of a State to leave the Union more unquestionable perhaps than any other; it is to be taken in connection with the principles already laid down. It is this. In a question of *political power* between the Federal Government and a State, as for instance, whether the former has a right to abolish the slave trade between the several States, or whether Congress has a right to prohibit slavery in the territories, there is no power to decide but one or the other of the two parties, there is no common umpire, neither the Supreme Court, nor any of the other States have the authority to decide. It is then the business of either the Federal Government or of the State, to make a decision. If the Federal Government has the right, then it has a right to make any one of the States adhere to any law it may think proper to make. For if it, in the first place, assumes the power, then the State disputes the assumption, of course when the matter is brought back for *it* to decide it will confirm what it has already done. In this way its power would be unlimited. This would be consolidation in perfection. If, on the other hand, the State has the right to decide, *no abuse of the right is possible*; for when it disputes the assumption it only *acts for itself*, it says, you have assumed a power which I never have granted, you may exercise that power over other States if *they* are willing, but as for me *you shall not*. I AM A SOVEREIGN, I have agreed with other sovereigns that you should conduct *certain of my affairs* in common with theirs; but in this matter you are undertaking to conduct affairs which I have reserved for my own especial care. Therefore, either you must desist from this undertaking, or I must abrogate my contract with you. You will not desist? Then we are henceforth no longer connected. I cannot *make you desist*, but I *can* return to the state I was in before I bargained with you. *I can secede!*

Then comes the cry of force, that most ridiculous of all absurdities. FORCE *to bind a Union of* REPUBLICS? Why bayonets might as well be used to quell the waters of the sea. A union of States, in these days, is founded in a common interest, common sympathy, common destiny, common rights powers and privileges; not in force, not in soldiers, not in wars, not in VICTORIES! All the victories, all the conquests in the world can never make a union such as ours formerly was, or purported to be. They may make bloody revolutions, confusion, anarchy and despotism, but never a union of Republics. But this cry of *force* is all jargon. This is not a fighting age. The men of the present time have other matters to attend to. We feel no hesitation in asserting that no State or States of this Union, after seceding, will never have a gun fired after them *to bring them back*, unless it be such *pop-guns* as have grown rusty in the Senate, and can only shoot squibs and tirades across the floor.

CHAPTER XVI.

"Money and man a mutual falsehood show,
Men make false money,—money makes men so.

GENERAL GEORGE WASHINGTON, "*The illustrious Southerner*," in his farewell address, says: "It is of infinite moment that you properly estimate the immense value of your national Union to your *collective and individual happiness*." Be it remembered, our collective and individual happiness. Let us then proceed to make this important estimate. What has this Union done for the Southern States collectively and individually? And what is the present value of this Union to them collectively and individually? Does the value increase or depreciate?

We are told by foreign observers, parties quite disinterested as to our local concerns, and quite able to form correct opinions, precisely what impartial history would confirm, viz: that the policy of the United States has been to form manufacturing interests of her own, notwithstanding it has been generally considered averse to the interests of the Southern States. And although this policy has unquestionably advanced the NATION far beyond what could have been expected; yet when we come to consider what has been the effect of it on the *South* and *North respectively*, we immediately see that though the nation *as a whole* has been benefitted, the South *as a part* has been comparatively injured. Whilst the *nation* has made the most of its resources, and advanced to wealth with the most gigantic strides; the North has reaped the benefit of government, and the South has borne the burden. We are within limits when we say that for every dollar the South has lost by this policy, the North has gained ten. The produce of the South has called into existence manufactures at the North. The profits of these manufactures have been applied to building up new manufactures, villages and towns *at the North.*—Thereby accumulating capital and population *at the North.* Building churches making roads, establishing universities and seminaries *at the North.* Improving the market for some things, and creating a demand for other things, enhancing the value of property, increasing the general wealth, and *finally concentrating irresistible political power*, ALL AT THE NORTH.

So valuable has the Union become to the North, with respect to money and apart from other advantages, that from being fifty years ago, of no very great moment, it is now, on a moderate calculation, estimated that the annual *profits* of the North derived from its connection with the South, including only the items of freight, imports, exchange, manufactures and Northern capital employed at the South, is no less than *ninety millions of dollars* per annum, in round numbers. The Federal Government raises upwards of $30,000,000 per annum by taxing imports. Now without going into the question of the right of the government to levy these taxes, merely look into the *effects* of the tax. The great effect is to enrich one portion of the country by embarrassing another. Take the illustration given by a gentleman in Congress. Suppose rail road iron can be manufactured in England and sent to any part of our coast for $40 per ton. For that price, iron cannot be manufactured in America. Those districts of country, therefore, which contain iron and every facility for its manufacture, being undersold by England, petition Congress to assist them to cope with England by levying a heavier tax on English iron. The tax is laid, say $20 per ton. English iron then which could formerly be had at $40, now costs $60. Where do these $20 go? Not to the importer, not to the English manufacturer; it goes to the American manufacturer. And who pays it? not the Government, but the American consumer. For, American iron can undersell English iron at $60. Who, then, is benefitted by this tax? The iron monger. And who is made to suffer by it? All those who pay $60 when they formerly paid but $40. As soon as this tax is laid, additional capital and labour is employed in the iron business. This is beneficial to *iron districts*, and so far as the entire nation is concerned, it not only is a source of revenue, but serves to develope the mineral resources of the country. But this revenue and this development is at the expense of nearly two-thirds of the country. It may benefit one section, but it injures another. The burden of the tax is more or less "diffused over the whole country, but the benefit is limited to the manufacturers, and those persons who reside so near as to have thereby a better market; very little more than one third of the Union gets the benefit of the system, in exclusion mainly of the South and West." The State of Pennsylvania on the one hand reaps the benefit, but we question whether Georgia or Texas experience any material advantage from it. What may be said of rail road iron, may also be said of other manufactures which flourish under the protection of such a tax. This burden—falling as it does, chiefly on the South—has not been very generally complained of, for the following, among other obvious reasons: In the first place, owing to a rapid increase in the labouring population, and a consequent proportionate reduction in the price of labour, combined with the most astonishing improvements in machinery; the price of American manufactures has steadily declined ever since their beginning. *This circumstance* has acted very powerfully in reconciling men to the system, and has, in a great measure, caused them to *overlook the fact, that "though there is a gradual reduction of prices in the United States, yet it is still more striking on the other side of the Atlantic."* In the second place, this system has been submitted to by the South, because her good faith has been pledged that she would do so, and because she is true to her engagements. When the Federal Constitution was formed, the South and North entered into an agreement, which some call a compromise; in which the South agreed that a majority of Congress might impose taxes upon imports, instead of three fourths as was proposed.* By this agreement, the power to levy the tax passed immediately into the hands of the North, for she had a majority in Congress. In her turn, the North agreed that three fifths of the slaves should be added to the free population in the apportionment of representatives; that free importation should for a time be permitted; and that fugitive slaves should be delivered up by the non-slaveholding States. It can, therefore, be easily understood why the South has so patiently borne this burden, more easily, perhaps than it can be ascertained why so great a portion of the Northern States have *broken their faith* in regard to the delivery of fugitive slaves. This compromise has been sufficient precedent for many more, less worthy of the name and less likely to be observed in good faith by the North.

But this is not the only way, nor the least way in which the South has become a looser by its connection with the North. It was proposed last winter—when Congress had first assembled—to disburse for the next fiscal year $40,000,000; yet not *five millions* were to be expended in all the slaveholding States put together. The State of North-Carolina, according to Mr. Clingman, contributes $3,000,000 to the coffers of the General Government, but does not receive in return as much as $100,000; *not one thirtieth* of what she gives, and very little over *three per cent of the capital thus forever taken out of her hands to be given to the North.* And what is true of North-Carolina is true of other Southern States.

But let us make out the account in due form.

The *direct profits* from freight, imports, exchange, manufactures and Northern capital employed at the South, amounts, as already seen, to - - - - - - -		$90,000,000
In 1848, three fourths of the imports were based on the export of Southern produce. The duties on these imports amounted to $31,757,070; taking three fourths of this as the duty on imports based on Southern produce, we have Contributed to Government by Southern produce.	$23,817,801	
From the proceeds of the sales of public lands, the money paid into the treasury for the purchase of lands in *slaveholding States*, for the same year was - - - - - - - - -	900,000	
The amount contributed to the General Government that year was, therefore, - - -	$24,717,801	
Taking this as an average annual contribution of the South, and allowing for the increase of produce and trade, and the contributions of Texas, which were not considered in the estimate of 1848; we may put down as the contribution of the South this year, - - - - - - - -	$25,000,000	
But of all the money disbursed this year, not $5,000,000 will be expended at the South. But deduct - - - - - - - - - -	5,000,000	

And we have as the net contribution of the South to the Government, and by it to be expended at the North, - - - - - - - - -	$20,000,000
Add to this the profits of travellers fare, schools, Colleges, individual purchases, &c., not computed above, and all other incidental profits rising out of her union with the South, at least, - - -	5,000,000
And we leave as the *annual income* of the North, derived from its connection with the South, no less than - - - - - - - - - - -	$115,000,000

At the rate of five per cent per annum, this would be the interest of $2,300,-000,000. The Union then, so far as profits in money can be thus imperfectly arrived at, *is worth just so much to the North;* whereas, *it costs just so much to the South.* Estimating the free population of the North at 12,000,000, and that of the South at 6,000,000; the Union would have the average value, in money, to each individual of the North, of $191.66, and would afford an income amounting to five per cent of this; while it would cost each individual at the South $383 32, and would deduct from his income an amount equal to five per cent of that. So that for every hundred dollars the Union is worth to the North, it costs the South two hundred.

From 1790 to 1845, the tax on imports paid for goods in exchange for Sothern produce amounted to $711,200,000; while the tax on imports, paid for goods in exchange for Northern produce amounted to $215,850,097. For every ten years the tax on each individual, ranged, at the South from $10 to 35; while at the North it only ranged from $2 to 13. The North has received over $28,000,000 in pensions, the South but 7,000,000. From the formation of the government to the year 1849, the North received for collecting the customs $43,000.000, and the South $10,000,000. Yet the North paid but $12,000,000, while the South paid 41,000,000 of the amount. From 1833 to 1837 government expended but 37,000,000 at the South, while at the North the expenditure amounted to $65,000,000. Yet, during that period the South paid $90,000,000, in duties, and the North but $17,000,000.

Is there any wonder that the North can afford to pay a million and a quarter a year for abolition purposes? Is there any wonder that the North so loves the Union as not only to remain united with the land of slavery, but like a loving bear, to hug it so close as to produce suffocation and death?

Since the South so loves the Union as to pay this immense tribute to the North, for the *sweets of it;* is it surprising that the latter assumes the tone of authority. With one hundred and fifteen millions of annual tribute pouring into her lap, is it surprising she has power and wealth to COMMAND; is it surprising she does not *rule* even more strictly than she does, such generous tributaries? Ah, the wonder is; the *great* wonder is, that those whose fathers, seventy years ago, gave "MILLIONS FOR DEFENCE, NOT ONE CENT FOR TRIBUTE;" now give millions for tribute, but will not rise united for defence.

The amount above stated is not *all* the Union is worth to the North, neither is it half what it costs the South. To estimate every thing, would require more space, information and acuteness than we can bring to bear. The following items are only a few of those to be considered in the final estimate.

We must consider the enhanced value of property at the North, and the encouragement given to industry there, by the public works and improvements carried on by government with the treasure derived from the South.

We must consider the profits derived from foreign trade, driven from Southern to Northern ports, by the policy of the Federal Government.

The treasure annually drained from the South by the faithless course of Northern States in sanctioning and encouraging their citizens, in violation of the Constitution, to abduct slaves in whom Southern capital is invested.

The immense territory given by the South to the General Government, out of which States have been erected to put down the *independence* of the South and crush her institutions.

The stability acquired by the North through the Federal Government, from the superior counsels of Southern Statesmen over any thing that has ever emanated from the North.

We must consider the influence the government has acquired among the nations of the earth, owing to the domestic productions of the South having become necessary for the maintenance of millions of people who would otherwise be in want.

The blood of Southern soldiers that has been shed in defence of Northern soil, and in vindication of Northern rights, as the major part of the confederacy, and which it now appears is to reap the whole reward.

The odium which is constantly heaped upon Southern institutions by Northern prejudices, and the repeated humiliating concessions the South has made to the North under the name of compromise.

We must remember that what we contend for, is actual, real and visible, that it has "a local habitation and a name," that it has *life*, existence, it has length breadth and thickness, it has sense and action, every thing appertaining to sound, positive and actual reality, as well in theory as in practice; whereas, what the North contends for is a crazy abstraction, it is neither actual, real, nor visible, it has neither habitation nor name, neither life nor existence, neither length, breadth, nor thickness, nor sense nor action, nothing appertaining to sound, positive, or actual reality, either in theory or practice.

We must consider whether it is not infinite concession, nay *absolute surrender*, for any thing so *real and rightful* as slavery, to be COMPROMISED with such *unreal and wrongful* fanaticism as abolition or any of its offspring. Consider, then, the exorbitant and ruinous forbearance it has cost the South to submit to the palpable injury she sustains. *Consider these things, oh man of the South, and then ask yourself the question, What is the value of our National Union to our* "COLLECTIVE AND INDIVIDUAL HAPPINESS?"

What does the South gain by all these concessions and compromises? Absolutely nothing. Yes, nothing but abuse, contempt and deterioration. We feel fully authorized to say that the Union has been supported and relieved from debt, and the entire North, enriched, strengthened and defended, by the slaveholding States of the South, through the action of the Federal Government. Yet Southern people are denounced for all that is worthless and bad. Because the North appears to have advanced more rapidly than the South, it is the common fashion to suppose the Northern people are superior to the Southern in energy, industry and ingenuity. Facts, however, authorize a different conclusion. A few will be mentioned. But in calling them to mind, it should be remembered, that in every branch of industry the Northern people have all along been encouraged by the Federal Government, while those of the South had commerce driven from their very doors.

In the first place, Where is that boasted superior energy and perseverance so peculiar to the North? Is it developed in her rail roads—let us see. The road from Charleston to Hamburg, in the State of South-Carolina, was *the second* road projected in the United States; and for many years, was the longest continuous line of rail-road, not only in the United States, *but in the world!* This company introduced the *first locomotive* of English construction in America, and was *the first to undertake the construction of locomotives in the United States.* In 1848—the white population of the free States being more than twice that of the slave States—the United States mail was transported, *by steam power*, over 4,224,410 miles in the free States, while in the slave States it was transported, also by steam, over 4,488,792.* At the present time, there are 4,307 1-2 miles of rail-road completed at the North, at a cost of $135,000,000; and at the South, with less than half the population, there are 2,147 miles of road complete, at a cost of $44,000,000. Now, so far as rail-roads are concerned, is there any want of energy exhibited on the part of the South? Are we behind the North in this department, when we have the same proportionate extent of road, at a less cost; notwithstanding we have *fewer uses* for such roads? It must be remarked that the North—especially that portion of it where rail-roads most abound—is essentially a commercial and manufacturing country. The people there are called upon to travel from one town to another *on business*, and raw material must be sent to the factories, and fabrics must be sent back; imports must be sent one way, exports another; consequently greater facilities for transportation and travelling should be expected there than at the South, where the population is *stationary;* because it is agricultural, our people are not called upon to travel from town to town *on business*, we have no factories (or so few as may be omitted) to supply and receive from, and consequently no pressing necessity for a greater number of roads than we have. If a country has as many improvements of a given description, as for instance *roads*, as the community can use, what more is wanted.

In commerce, *the bona fide exchange of domestic for foreign produce, we are* NOT BEHIND THE NORTH. It is very true, our commerce is *different* from that of the North; ours is not so *profitable*, but it is equally *energetic.* If our people *do not pocket so much money* as those of the North, it is certain they *go through as much work.* It is the *modus operandi* of the business, and not the energy of the people that makes the difference in the profits. Without going into the details of freight, brokerage, factorage, or any distinct head under this branch of industry, we wish to show that though the North realizes more by her commerce, yet she is not possessed of more energy and industry than the South; and all the superiority she has acquired, in this department, comes from external causes and not from any superior quality of her people. During the year ending June 30th, 1848, the North exported domestic produce to the amount of $56,862,590; while the South exported $76,041,531. Considering the difference of free population, it appears that the South exports about *three times as much* domestic produce as the North. When the exports of *foreign produce* is added, the total exports of the North is 76,119,362, while that of the South is $77,917,074. The South still exporting twice as much as the North. Now, though we have no information as to how much is annually imported *from the North* by the South, yet we do know that the exports and imports of the whole of the States, during that year, were almost exactly to the same amount; and we also know that the excess of *imports over exports* at the North, was about the same as the excess of *exports over imports* at the South. The South sent to foreign markets as much more than it received *direct* from them, as the North received *direct* from foreign markets over and above what it sent. Where this surplus of Northern imports went, must evidently have been where the means of acquiring it emanated, and that was at the South. The ship which sails from the Southern port laden with cotton, does not return from Europe with goods for the Southern port from which it sailed; it returns to its Northern owner, freighted with European goods at a great profit. From the Northern port it sails to the South, either with *ballast* or

* American Almanac.

an assorted cargo of European goods and Yankee notions, to be sold at an enhanced price to the cotton grower. The commerce thus carried on is not confined to two chief parties. There are three. It is a triangular system of operations. And just so surely as it is true, that a straight line is the shortest distance between two of these parties, it is true that *the third party* lives on the profits which legitimately belong to the other two. Europe and the South are the two parties in the traffic to whom the whole conduct of the business belongs; the North is a foreign party in the exchange; she has been dropped in between the others by causes at war with the interests of those others, and lives, to grow rich and impudent, upon the profits she can wrench away from them. In this state of things, *the whole loss is suffered by the South*—and why? *Purely because the South has placed herself in the* COMMERCIAL POWER *of the North, to such an extent that she can never throw off that power without throwing off the* POLITICAL POWER *involved in it, and* THAT *she has never heretofore exhibited the least desire to do.* In order to keep up this triangular system of commerce, it is evident each party must receive from one of the other two a return for what it sends away, and that *return* must be an *equivalent*, or the party would sink under its losses and the commerce be ended. The South, then, evidently must import from Europe and the North, taken together, *as much*, if she does not more, as the exports to them; but with this disadvantage. In this three handed game, the South, in the first place, has to set the ball in motion; to do this it has to *create* the ball and then *apply the force* to set it rolling along the *first* line, which is the *chief* line, to the point in Europe. When it arrives at this point, it has the cost of freights, etc., added to its value. It is there metamorphosed and thoroughly prepared for another roll, with increased value to the extent of the cost of metamorphosing. It is then put on the second line and rolled along to the point at the North. By the time it reaches this point it has acquired another addition to its value, on account of freights, commissions, etc. Here it is cut open, unravelled, turned up, turned down, tasted, smelt, handled, and then boxed up again *if all is right.* Government *gouges* a large slice out of one side, and to make it even, the *agents* take a slice from the other. Then comes the remnant on its *third* voyage, *homeward bound, with the accumulated charges for* THREE *voyages,* THREE *sets of commissions, one metamorphose, two gouges, and a sample*, all for the unweary producer to pay for. Now when it gets home, all the machinery is overhawled, screws tightened, wheels greezed, and every thing *fixed* for another three handed reel round the world; and just as it is time to start again, a *small item* comes up for *wear and tear*, if you please, sir?

With these facts known to every body, it cannot be denied that though the South does not realize all the profits she should, yet she contributes the fundamental essence of the system; and as she is so *essentially* important, how can she be less energetic and industrious than the other actors in the scene. We have seen that the South exports more than the North; we have shown that she must import from all quarters, though it comes chiefly from the North, as much as she exports. It follows, therefore, that she really imports more than the North. But as she does this with a less population and a less capital, how is it that she has less energy, enterprise and industry?

Let us compare individual States. New York is the great exporter and importer of the North. Louisiana has that relation to the South. New York has a population at least *nine times* as large as that of Louisiana—all the slaves included. During the year ending with June, 1848, New York exported $38,771,-209 worth of domestic produce, and Louisiana exported $39,350,148 worth. This makes Louisiana, comparatively, more than nine times as large an exporter as New York, and nearly three per cent. larger absolutely. New York imported that year $94,525,141, and Louisiana $9,380,439. This, in proportion to population, makes New York about ten per cent. the largest importer. But taking the exports and imports together, can it be said that the commercial community of Louisiana is less energetic and industrious than that of New York.

Pennsylvania, with a population at least three times as great as that of Maryland, including slaves, exported $5,428,309 worth of domestic produce, while Maryland exported $7,016,034 worth. This makes Maryland nearly seven times the largest exporter. Pennsylvania imported $12,147,584, Maryland imported $5,343,643. This makes Maryland far more than twice as large an importer as Pennsylvania, in proportion to population.

The North is a great superior to us in manufactures, but all of her superiority to us in this respect, is fully counterbalanced by our superior agricultural resources. Moreover, her manufacturing interest, in many quarters, is near its culminating point, whilst ours yet glimmers in the twilight of dawn; and as ours rises to the meridian of success, hers must wane and gradually repose in the horison of decay. Her possession of factories is no evidence of superiority in her people, but rather conclusive proof of the prospering condition of agriculture at the South.

Education is a peculiar boast of Northern braggadocios. Let us see the foundation of this proud exultation. At the North, there are 61 Colleges, annually educating 6,057 students. At the South, there are 60 Colleges, annually educating 4,773 students. As far as *mere numbers* go, the advantage is on the side of the South. But on considering the endowments and general qualities of the Colleges, we are willing to admit that there are some at the North which are superior to any at the South. It is, however, one thing to have Colleges and another to have *students*—one thing to have a library and another to *read* it—and yet another to learn. It is completely out of our power to say how many of the students in these Northern colleges are sent there from the South. But from what we do know, we believe we are within limits when we say, that out of the six thousand students sent to them, at least one thousand are from the South, and return to the South when their term has expired. If, then, there is any superiority in education at the North, the South participates in it to quite a sufficient extent, and *pays handsomely for it in more than money.* The education of Southern youth at the North is matter of dubious policy. The benefit which may be derived from the larger libraries, aparatuses, museums. etc., etc., of the North, is apt to be counteracted by the pernicious effects of other causes. We believe that out of the 10,830 students in all the States, fully half the number come from the South; and as far as college education is any advantage, the South enjoys it in a superlative degree. It is, however, much to be regretted that the South has so completely adopted the erroneous and even injurious custom of sending her youth to be *educated at the North!* We have never been more forcibly struck with the error of this custom, than we were a few years ago during a protracted stay at the North, when we saw the sons of wealthy and influential slaveholders, planters, *educated* at the private school and living under the roof of an abolitionist, who openly, and on all occasions, pronounced through the ballot box his uncompromising hostility to the institutions of the South. Here was one of those occasions where the South lends its purse to support its worst and vilest enemies. It is a VITAL EVIL. Its continuance is suicidal. And what can be expected to flow from this state of things? If the private schools of the North, not to mention colleges, are so superior to those of the South, as to render the employment of active abolitionists a consideration of no importance, is it not high time the schools at the South were raised to a higher standard? But this is not the case. Southern schools are fully as competent as Northern schools; and no better proof can be desired than the fact that some of the brightest of the Literati of America have never entered a Northern seminary. Unfortunately, the truth is a reproach on the South. Nothing but *fashion and caprice* is the cause of the evil.

In theological schools, the North outstrips the South, the former having 32 schools with 1,072 students, the latter 10 schools and 245 students. Judging, however, from the morals of the people, the catalogue of crimes, and other evidences of the kind, the majority of these students must also be from the South, or being from the North, the fruits of their studies are destined to be severely taxed.

There are six Law Schools at the North and 200 students; six at the South with 215 students, not including those at the Alabama University, the number of which we have not been able to ascertain correctly. In view of this disparity, it is not wonderful that the Northern people are so profound in their construction of the Constitution, and so free from mobs, disorders and riots.

There are 19 Medical Colleges and 3,125 students at the North, and 16 Colleges and 1,439 students at the South. The great number of hospitals which are necessary at the North, on account of the misery, pauperism and dissipation of the *working people*, attract a great many students from the South, where, fortunately, there are not many hospitals and they but small. If the number of such students could be ascertained, it would surely be found that there are, in proportion to population, many more annually educated for the medical profession, *who are destined to reside at the North*, than the South.

CHAPTER XVII.

"Now's the day, and now's the hour,
See the front o' battle lour;
See approach proud Edward's power—
Chains and slaverie!

We have transcended the limits we had imposed upon ourselves, yet we have not gone over half the ground we intended. Our notes concerning the abolition agitation in this country and its connection with the English abolition party, which we had intended to discuss in a few additional chapters, we are obliged to omit on this occasion. Our story is but half told. Still we must leave off, not however before we briefly discuss *one more point*. What are we to expect for the future *in* this Union, and what may we expect *out* of the Union?

We will not stop to count up *all* the injuries we have sustained in the past, nor all we should expect in the future. We simply invite your attention, oh most patient reader! to the way our government works, the *legislative department* of our overgrown government. See how it serves the North and how it serves the South. Do not start when you hear this *warning voice*. *It is* ALL *truth*. THE POLITICAL INDEPENDENCE OF THE SOUTH, *in this Union*, IS DEAD. Did you hear those hundred guns yesterday, the last still louder than the rest? They were interring it then. Did you hear those loud huzzas? They came from the vultures that were hovering over the corpse when the grave diggers began to throw the sods upon the hollow sounding coffin. Did you notice that death-like silence which followed the hearse back to its place? The vultures were asleep. Those you saw were the sly Reynards and Grimalkins that had snuffed the odour of the carcass from the distance, they looked sour and gruff, for they had come too late to see the body, they only lapped up a few drops of blood that oozed out on the way. But hist! Did you hear that sob, that female sob, just as the preacher said "dust to dust?" Ah, that *was* a sob indeed. Poor woman, she was on the banks of that very river in her younger days, she stood smiling by the side of a cradle—there was an infant in it—she smiled and passed on. An age rolled on—but when she heard those guns, she knew the omen, she hurried to the spot; the cradle was old, empty and decayed, the infant had grown old, grey and bent with care, it wept bitterly, its name was *Justice*. The woman sobbed aloud, her name was *Liberty*. Did you see those few old men who kept themselves aloof, and seemed so sad and weary? They were the mourners—they were the only friends the poor deceased victim had to care for it in its dying agonies. They did "the best their circumstance affords," and "angels could no more." And did you see those ugly monsters with their snaky tongues, as they wound their way among the mazy crowd? They were the poisoners, their fangs struck the blow, they are *the Southern traitors!* But that one you saw far away, coiled up and asleep in the woods, he is the old king snake of all the vipers, age makes him drowsy. Do you hear that tingling noise as it swells up with the north winds and falls upon our ears with such sweet melody? It is the voice of revelry, the lucky heirs of the deceased are feasting themselves upon the spoils of their plunder. They are happy *now;* but bend your ear, listen well, *do you* HEAR IT? HEAR THAT! Hear the muttering! Hear the voices! Hear the clashing! Hear the tumult! Hark, hear that long wild blast!! 'Tis the trump of vengeance! *It is the South!!* Leap up and whoop an answer. That awful shriek which seems to rend the heavens like the stunning thunders of an angry God, is the cry for help *your country's help!*

"Rise fathers! *Rise! 'Tis Rome demands your help!*" Shake your grey locks in anger, that your sons may catch the spirit of your youth, and your daughters not *blush to call them men*. Speak out ye mothers, matrons of another age, tell out the virtues of your ancient defenders, stir up the ambition of your sons, lest they *kiss the rod that smites them.* Spring up, oh long deluded South! Cast off the fetters that are wound around you! Burst off the manacles that enchain your sovereignty. Throw off the yoke that galls your independence. Onward!

"Forward! let us do, or die!"

California is now a State—a free State. Her two senators and two representatives are now voting in Congress—voting with the North. We do not say one word as to the propriety of her admission. She is admitted, that's all we will here speak of. There has all along been a steady decline of political power at the South, and this decline has lately received an impetus which hastens it to ruin henceforth and forever. The causes of this decline are manifold; but the great leading cause is the nature of our pursuits. We here, of course, leave out of consideration the action of the Federal Government. The tendency of our pursuits is to spread a small population over a large extent of territory; the tendency of northern pursuits is to concentrate a large population in a small space. With the South, territory must increase with population, with the North it is not essential. The consequence is, that the population of Southern States has all along, after reaching a certain point, remained comparatively stationary, while that of the Northern States has increased rapidly. The effect of this is to give a greater increase to the representation in Congress of the North than that of the South.

According to the apportionment of 1790, Congress was composed as follows:

From the North, 14 Senators, 36 Representatives.

From the South, 12 Senators, 30 Representatives.

Since that time, 18 new States have been added to the Union; 9 free States and 9 slave States. One of the *then* slave States has now become to all intents and purposes a free state, viz: Delaware. So that out of the 31 States, there are 17 free States and 14 slave States. The population of the two periods, composes as follows:

	In 1790.	In 1850.
The North, - - - - -	1,930,808,	about 12,000,000
The South, - - - - -	1,875,799,	" 8,000,000

The Congress now in session, including the California members, and classing Delaware as she always votes, with the North, is composed as follows:

From the North, Senators 34; Representatives 143.
From the South, Senators 28; Representatives 90.

The North, therefore, has four times as many representatives as at first, while the South has but three times as many.

In 1790, New-York had 6 representatives and Georgia 3; New-York now has 34 and Georgia 8. Pennsylvania then had 8 and Virginia 10; Pennsylvania now has 24 and Virginia 15.

In 1802, Kentucky had 6 and Ohio 1; Kentucky now has 10 and Ohio 21. Michigan and Arkansas were both admitted in 1836. The former has three representatives, the latter one.

New-York and Pennsylvania together, had in 1790 but 14 representatives, they now have 58. Virginia and North-Carolina then had 15, whereas the nine States of Virginia, North-Carolina, South-Carolina, Georgia, Alabama, Mississippi, Louisiana, Arkansas and Florida, now have among them but 56 representatives.

These are isolated facts; now for their concomitants. Out of our 90 representatives, *thirteen* are from *territory acquired since* 1790, and out of our 28 senators, *ten* are from such territory; while out of the 143 northern representatives, only *four* are from new territory, and out of their 34 senators, but *four. The South then would not have the little power she now has, had it not been for the acquisition of these new territories.* The policy of the South has heretofore been to keep up her balance of power by acquiring new territory, out of which to form new States. She has, *heretofore* been aided by the North in carrying out this policy, because it was also essential to the prosperity of the North. That aid is now forever withdrawn, because new territory is no longer essential to the North. The policy which the South has heretofore pursued, is therefore forever, eternally and unalterably stopped—at least, as long as she is in *this Union.* What would have become of us long ago, had we not acquired this new territory? Look, and see. Suppose that Florida, Louisiana, Arkansas, Missouri, Iowa, Texas and California, had never been purchased or annexed. By deducting their respective delegates from the congressional list, the South would have but 20 senators and 77 representatives, while the North would have 30 senators and 139 representatives. The policy we have heretofore pursued has then clearly been the means of preserving us from this *dangerous minority.* But this policy is now *forever* cut off. For *it is a moral and a physical fact, an absolute truth, elaborately demonstrated in a debate of nine months, on the floors of Congress, that there will never be another inch of territory added to the present limits of the South,* SO LONG AS IT REMAINS IN THIS UNION. *No, not ever.*

Here then is *one* thing to be expected for the future, *in this Union. We are to have no more territory under any circumstances.*

The slave trade is abolished in the District of Columbia. This is the greatest triumph, the "rabid fanatics" have ever achieved. It is the great entering wedge for whatever else they may desire in all time to come, *in* the Union. Depend upon it reader, whoever you may be, if you survive a few years, perhaps one year, and this Union holds together so long, you will live to see the bill abolishing slavery in the District. The right to abolish the *trade* and the right to abolish the institution are inseparable, and the exercise of the one is just as sure to be followed by the exercise of the other, as night is to be succeeded by day. The early abolition of slavery in the District may then be regarded as a fixed fact. Now what will be the result of this measure? Who will undertake to say? Who that looks back upon the last thirty years, is prophet enough to tell us what we must expect during the next ten, or the next five, *in this Union.*

We have already expressed our belief in the doctrine, that however proper it may be in forming a government for parties having conflicting interests and opinions to compromise with each other, to the end that a clear and abiding compact may be formed; it is inexpedient and dangerous for such parties to depart from the course and spirit of that compact, to enter into *new* comprises *after the government has been agreed upon.* The violation of this doctrine was the first fatal error of the South. It was committed thirty years ago. The Missouri compromise, equitable though it may have been *as a part of the constitution, as a part of the* COMPACT. It was dangerous as a legislative measure. Right though it may have been as an *original agreement*, it was wrong as an implied legislative prerogative. Expedient though it may have seemed to avert an impending danger, it was a precedent which has been suicidal in its efforts. It was a sad error, for it was not strictly, it was *not at all* a constitutional measure. It was not constitutional, because it imposed a law which rendered nugatory a prominent clause in the Constitution. That clause of the constitution which provides for the admission of new States, imposes but one condition as to the nature of the laws and regulations of the new State, and that is, that they shall be *republican.* It has ever been admitted by the government that slavery is a republican institution, else *nine* new slave States never could have been admitted, nor five old ones existed under the compact. The Constitution then unquestionably provides that a slaveholding State *may* be admitted into the Union, under any circumstances which would secure the admission of any other State. But the Missouri compromise—as we will proceed to show—provides that, north of a certain line, a slaveholding State *may not* be admitted into the Union under any circumstances which would secure the admission of any other State.

In erecting a new State, there must be at least a given population, and by population is meant *residents.* These residents must have emigrated from some of the old States or elsewhere. Now if these emigrants, when about to leave their old homes, are going to a land over which there is no law, they carry with them what they please, and after settling there, they proceed from time to time, to adopt such measures, and agree upon such regulations among themselves as the nature of their circumstances require. But if they are going to a land where there is a law, and that law prohibits the introduction of certain property and certain customs, these emigrants dispose of such property, and leave such customs at home. In the course of time these people increase in number to such an extent, that their primitive government fails in answering the demands of society. A new government must therefore be formed, a State must be erected. A Convention is held and a Constitution agreed upon. Now in the formation of this Constitution, the people have a right to make whatever laws, and regulate whatever customs they please, provided only they be republican. So says the Federal Constitution. In the case first mentioned, where the people carried whatever property they pleased, this *constitutional right* is freely enjoyed, and if in forming their State Constitution they prohibit any species of property or customs, it is their voluntary act, at least in point of constitution and law. But, in the second case, where people cannot carry certain property with them, they do not freely enjoy the right granted by the Federal Constitution, to make whatever laws, and regulate whatever customs they please, for *the same law which prevented their carrying that property with them when they first emigrated, has ever since prevented such property from going there, and henceforth and forever will.* Here then the provision made by the Constitution is absolutely and forever rendered null by this law. Such was the Missouri compromise, as it effects the territory north of the latitude of 36° 30′. Is it constitutional? If slavery is prohibited in a territory, how is it to be expected that slavery will be admitted in the State formed out of that territory, and whose inhabitants are the non-slaveholding inhabitants of that territory.

This compromise was indeed hard to resist. The Government was then but thirty years of age; no sectional animosity had previously existed. It was believed by honest men, that the risk of overstepping the limits of the Constitution in this one particnlar, would be more than compensated for, by the final adjustment of this sectional jealousy, which it was supposed the compromise would effect. But short sighted man! The very measures which were expected to end, served but to commence the warfare of sections. It was not adopted until "almost every possible mode of reconciling the bitter animosities, sectional interests and prejudices, had been attempted in vain. John Randolph, of Roanoke, had even proposed that the Southern members retire home in a body, as having no longer any interest in an assembly which did not recognize their rights and privileges. The sentiment began generally to prevail. In this dark hour for the Union, there was, perhaps, no other hope than in the measure which was adopted. Whether it has been well for the South, however, or whether she did not, in yielding to the exigencies of the times, yield up a most important and sacred principle, which has been the occasion of all the subsequent injuries and aggressions that have been heaped upon her in the halls of Congress, might be worthy of consideration." The Constitution thus infringed, a strict obedience to it can not be expected for the future, *in this Union*. The rights and privileges of the South thus yielded, with the purest intentions though they may have been, can no longer be preserved unimpaired, *in this Union*.

It is but too true that "men commence with the control of things—they put events in motion, but after a very little while events hurry them away, and they are borne along with a swift fatality that no human sagacity or power can foresee or control." From the time of that *first great error*, the ascendancy of the North was secure. The South confided, but alack! the temptation was too strong, the North could not withstand it. Abolition petitions increased and multiplied in Congress. Those *insinuating* petitions upon which English abolitionists built their greatest hopes of success; those petitions which are like small drops of water upon the hardest marble, sure to conquer all resistance, were received and acted upon in the presence of the entire Southern Delegation, and even accepted for consideration by the votes of some. It is true, these little drops were for a time kept back, but only to burst forth anew with the pent up fury of a torrent. The House of Representatives repealed the rule prohibiting the introduction of these petitions, and the result has been an exterminating war against the political equality of the South; an ever-growing invasion of our sacred rights. We have then an exterminating war upon our equality to expect, for the future, *in this Union*. An ever-growing invasion of our sacred rights to expect, for the future, *in this Union*.

Although there has ever been a disposition on the part of individuals to attack our institutions, as the early formation of abolition associations testify, it was not until the "Emancipation Act" of the British Parliament had become the law of England, that any States, in their sovereign capacities, became avowed enemies in this exterminating war. Massachusetts lead the van. She suddenly remembered that South-Carolina had among her laws one which invaded "the hypothetical rights of her coloured citizens," although it had been in existence, and she had overlooked it fourteen years before. Her commissioned agents were sent abroad to vindicate those rights, but vindication was inadmissible. This was the signal for a general outbreak of State diplomacy of the most *amicable and conciliating* nature. And *now*, "the records of Congress teem with documents emanating not from fanatical individuals alone, *but from* SOVEREIGN STATES, irritating to our feelings, unfriendly in their bearing, embittering rank wrong by biting insults, and disturbing our tranquillity by agitations dangerous to our peace and safety." We have then these *State agitations* also to expect, for the future, *in this Union*.

These are but a few of the obvious hopes and expectations we are to entertain in the Union. What are we to expect out of it? It is certain we are to expect *none of* THESE *things*.

"The first resistance to aggression is always the cheapest and most successful. Every delay has to meet an accumulation of power and precedent, and gives a fresh argument for a renewal of wrongs, until the period is reached when there is no adequate remedy, except in a thorough re-organization." The first resistance to Northern aggression, as we have seen, was changed to *compromise*. This compromise caused delay—this delay occasioned an accumulation of power at the North, and a series of precedents on the part of the Federal Government, which have hastened us to the period, the present juncture, when *there is no adequate remedy, except in a* THOROUGH RE-ORGANIZATION. The crisis has now come. The question is re-organization, or submission to further aggression. If submission is preferred, then nothing is to be done. "Lay on McDuff," with all your heart. The South likes it, it cant have too much oppression, lay on more, trample it, crush it, it likes it, for it takes it very kindly, it submits very quietly. But if re-organization is preferred, then the sooner we set about it the better. Now what sort of re-organization is wanted; why such as will secure us our rights, equality and independence, to be sure. Where do you expect to effect this re-organization. In Congress—what! In Congress!! Yes, we must effect it in Congress, by amending the Constitution, compromising our differences, or some such "equitable adjustment." What folly! Go to Congress to adjust affairs? Why that would be nothing more than going to Congress to undo what it has been nine months struggling to achieve. Go to the spider to unravel his web—go to the bee to decompose its honey—call on the clouds to take back their rain—demand of the sun to withhold its light—call upon nature to remand her laws—summon the ancient sepulchres to yield up their dead—but never, oh most injured South, never go to the tyrants that oppress you—the brigands that rob you—the cheats that swindle you—the foes that master you; never, no, never, go to Congress more, for aught but *base submission*. Go bend your knee, go lick the dust and bow down before the *awful majesty of* CONGRESS; but never go there to be an equal. Know you not, that *there* you are degraded of your rank? Know you not your escutcheon has been defaced, your diadem cast away, your effects confiscated, your name disgraced, your pride humbled, your power subdued, your knighthood lost, your banner riven, your lance shivered, and that you are "*hors du combat?*"

Congress is surely not the place to effect this re-organization. For how can it be supposed that the very power which one day disorganizes for an avowed purpose, will the next day reorganize in direct opposition to that very purpose? And if Congress will not redress our wrongs, think you the respective States, whose Senators and Representatives have thus wronged us, think you that *they* will give us justice? No, not they. Well, if they will not it is certain no other power in this Union *can*. If then a re-organization of our political and State rights is to be effected, we must expect it, for the future, *out of this Union*.

If we would regain the POLITICAL INDEPENDENCE our fathers asserted on the 4th of July, 1776, we must expect it, for the future, *out of this Union*.

If we would regain the SOVEREIGNTY we had when our fathers contracted for the faithful performance of the mandates of the Constitution, we must expect it, for the future, *out of this Union*.

If we would secure the PROPERTY our fathers toiled to accumulate, that they might leave an heritance for us in our day and generation, we must expect it, for the future, *out of this Union.*

If we would transmit to our children the "LIFE, LIBERTY AND PURSUIT OF HAPPINESS," which they have a just right to claim untarnished from our hands, we must expect it, for the future, *out of this Union.*

If we would preserve A RESPECTABLE POSITION AMONG THE NATIONS OF THE EARTH, we must expect it, for the future, *out of this Union.*

If we would provide for our COMMON DEFENCE and our GENERAL WELFARE, we must expect it, for the future, *out of this Union.*

If we would ensure DOMESTIC TRANQUILITY, HONEST INDUSTRY, and all other comforts of society, we must expect it, for the future, *out of this Union.*

If we would retain for ourselves all that is desirable in this life, the approbation of posterity, and the smiles of him who made us what we are, and gave us what we have, we must expect them, for the future, *out of this Union.*

If you would, oh land of our birth! preserve your streets from desertion, your homes from pillage, your hearths from strife, your sons from infamy, your daughters from defilement, your people from pestilence and famine, your fields from desolation and decay, your cities from tumult, conflagration and massacre, your soil from anarchy, carnage and blood—if you would preserve your *very self* from the ignoble charge of POLTRON PERFIDY! Look—look with the fixed eye of power and resolution, immaculate, beyond the crumbling ruins of a dismembered Union, which now comes crashing down upon your devoted head.

We must not be amazed. We must not be alarmed at the great work that is before us. Our immortal fathers were but a handful, yet they could throw off the yoke of mighty England. We are millions, and can we not at least, secure, protect, defend the legacy they left? Are we so wedded to one sweet-sounding word, that we are no longer men, but servile sycophants? Surely not. Life is not yet so dear, or peace so sweet, as to be purchased at the price of chains and slavery.

We cannot be astonished at our case. The evil has grown with us, and with us it has become but too familiar. It is scarcely seventy-five years since our tenacious fathers lifted up their heads at the mere semblance of danger, and "augured misgoverment at a distance, and snuffed tyranny in every tainted gale." But *now*, it requires no gale to waft tyranny to us, it requires no snuffing to catch the tainted breeze; no distance is between tyranny and us; it is upon us, it is around us, aye the tainted odour tingles in our very nostrils. The patriots of that day were *deliberate*, *firm*, *united* and *candid*. Even so must we be, oh people of the South! We must at this time, above all other times, be men who

"know our rights, and knowing, dare maintain them."

In our primitive assemblies, our town meetings and our county meetings, we must first understand distinctly, and be of *one opinion* as to what are *our rights.* We must then understand, and be of *one opinion* as to what *are our wrongs ; on these two hang* ALL THE DIFFICULTIES OF THE CURE. If we are of one opinion on these two, it is certain *we will be of one opinion* AS TO THE REMEDY. But in weighing the merits of our remedy, we must be careful to remember the *action* that must follow and the *end* that we aim at. Let every man have deeply impressed upon his mind, what the popular Mr. Quincy remarked, in Boston, at one of the primitive meetings of the people, before a blow was struck in that great revolution of 1776—"It is not the spirit that vapors within these walls that must stand us in stead. The exertions of this day will call forth *events*, which will make a very different spirit necessary for our salvation. Look to the *end.* Whoever supposes that shouts and hosannahs will terminate the trials of this day, entertains a childish fancy. We must be grossly ignorant of the importance and value of the prize we are contending for—we must be equally ignorant of the power of those who are contending against us—we must be blind to that *malice, inveteracy*, and insatiable revenge which actuate our enemies, to hope we shall end this controversy, without the sharpest conflicts—to flatter ourselves that popular resolves, popular harangues, popular acclamations, and popular vapour, will vanish our foes. Let us consider the *issue.* Let us weigh and consider, before we advance to those measures which must bring on the most trying and terrible struggle this country ever saw." *Oh Friends, Countrymen, Southrons! By the shade of* WASHINGTON, JACKSON, *your defenders in war; by the shade of* JEFFERSON, MADISON, CALHOUN, *your counsellors in peace; in the name of* LIBERTY, TRUTH, JUSTICE, *your birthright; in the name of* GOD, *your master; let us invoke deliberation, firmness, courage, justness, candor, love and harmony among you*, IN DEVISING THE REMEDY.

"Firm, united, let us be,
Rallying round our liberty."

"Great nations cannot be held together under a united government by anything short of despotic power, if any one part of a country is to be arrayed against another in a perpetual scramble for privilege and protection, under any system of protection. They must fall to pieces; and if the same blind selfishness and rapacity animate the fragments which had occasioned the disunion of the whole, there will be no end to the strife of conflicting interests." It is this truth which, being put into practice, has dismembered this Union; and it is this truth which demands of the whole South UNITY. *Unity for the sake of defence. Unity in devising the remedy.*

As to what the remedy should be, we cannot undertake to say *for others.* But for us, we proclaim SECESSION, *the rightful remedy.* We have seen what our institutions are. We know how old our customs are, how well approved they were in the olden time by holy men—by Deity; We have seen how they became intailed upon us; how proper, equitable, economical and politic they are; how indispensable they are. We have seen what principles have been enlisted to abolish them in a foreign country. We know what power there is arrayed against us on their account. We understand that it is to deprive us of them, that we, as a political community, are degraded, wronged, insulted and pilfered. We know their value, and we know the value of those who would despoil us of them. We know the value of slavery, and we know the value of the Union. We have the bane and the antidote. There is *Union and Abolition* on one hand, and *Disunion and Slavery* on the other. Which of the two shall we choose? Reader! we can not tell what you and other men may think, but as for us, *give us* SLAVERY *or give us death!* We can not tell what you may think as to the *remedy*, but as to us, we look upon *secession*, the *prompt, positive and unqualified secession of each State, independent of the others, in its capacity as sovereign, supreme sovereign, supreme arbiter of its rights and powers, to be the only step which can lift us out of the mire we are in. It is the sole, the rightful remedy.* The Declaration of Independence was issued by the *Representatives of the United* STATES *in Congress assembled.* The *credentials* of the members of the Convention of 1787, which formed the *Union*, declare them to be delegates from the *respective* STATES. This Convention was, therefore, an assemblage of the *independent sovereign* STATES, in their independent sovereign capacity. "The union or confederation which then took place, was *a union*, not of the whole people, but *of the separate* STATES, and accordingly the name adopted was THE UNITED STATES." In all the business of this Convention, the votes were taken by *States;* but a majority of *States* was not alwas a majority of *people*, or of *representatives.* This Federal

Union and the *Constitution* which formed and binds it, *are each and both of them, the creatures of the* SEVERAL INDEPENDENT STATES *whose representatives were there assembled.*

The Federal Government, consisting of three co-ordinate branches, is the AGENT of the *confederated* STATES, created, *by them*, for certain purposes and no others, with certain powers and no others; therefore, all purposes and powers not delegated to this agent, are *reserved* and *belong to* the several independent States, and them only. Moreover, this *Government* is not based on a compact *to which it was a party*. IT WAS NO PARTY TO THE COMPACT. Being no party to the compact, it has *no power* OVER IT. "It is *not* a power pre-eminent and superior, but an agent *only*, *subordinate to the several* INDEPENDENT SOVEREIGNTIES, *that by common consent gave it existence* FOR COMMON PURPOSES." These sovereignties may *alter*, *modify*, *abolish* and *reinstate* this agency. They remain as before, INDEPENDENT OF EACH OTHER, AND ALL OTHERS. They are not *merged and absorbed in the* FEDERAL GOVERNMENT! That agent is not the government of a nation ONE AND INDIVISIBLE! "It possesses no control over the several States of the Union *beyond what the Constitution has given it* FOR COMMON PURPOSES—but *is* STRICTLY *and* TRULY AN AGENCY *invested with* LIMITED POWERS, *which it* CANNOT HONESTLY EXCEED. *Those powers are to be* FOUND IN THE CONSTITUTION, AND NO WHERE ELSE." They must be exercised solely with a view to the TRUSTS for which they were granted. "Whatever is done by the Federal Government *within* the authority delegated, *is binding on* ALL THE STATES and the people of the States: *what is* NOT *done under and by virtue of, and within the* PLAIN AND OBVIOUS MEANING OF THE AUTHORITY CONTAINED IN THE CONSTITUTION," IS USURPATION. *Usurpation is* TYRANNY, *and Tyranny the desert of* COWARDS.

Usurpation by the Federal Government can lead to no end but consolidation, and *that* IS RUIN. "Disunion is a bad thing, says Mr. Jefferson, *but* CONSOLIDATION IS WORSE."

The powers delegated to the *Federal Judiciary*, do not include "*a question between the Government of the United States and any* STATE, *growing out of the* RESERVED RIGHTS OF THE STATES."

There are two cases in which the Constitution has made provision for the course of Congress, *in a question between* THAT BODY *and any* STATE *or* STATES. "Where Congress is in doubt whether a power claimed, be constitutional or not; and where a power not granted is desired. In those cases, a Convention of States can be called by Congress, and the powers doubted or denied may be given, *if two-thirds of* THE STATES *consent;* and this is the fair and regular course of proceeding. If Congress neglect or refuse to put in force this salutary provision of the Constitution, but proceed in a steady career of usurpation, passing laws which the Constitution does not justify, and closing their ears to the memorials, remonstrances, (*protests*,) and appeals of the minority—what is that minority, or any independent State, *party to the federative compact*, to do in such a contingency? For every RIGHT *there is* A REMEDY. What is the remedy in this case?" There is *but one.* And *that* is the RIGHT ONE. If remonstrances, protests and appeals *will not be heard*—SECESSION MUST! If THEY *can not avail*—SECESSION CAN. AS THEY *have not*—SECESSION WILL.

If any one, at this late day, should ask, if the South has income and capital enough to dissolve the copartnership and set up in business for itself. Let him be assured *she has* even an abundance. Besides the vast treasures she annually contributes to the Federal Government, to be expended at the North, notice the financial affairs of the several State Governments at the present time.

The total debt of the free States amounts to - -	$116,775,235
" " " slave " " - - - -	94,477,197

The total ordinary annual income of all the free States is	$10,716,865*
" " " " " slave States is	7,069,619†

In proportion to population, the debt of the slave States is rather larger than that of the free States, *but in it is included the debt of the late Republic of Texas*; if this debt be deducted, the debt of the slave States will be found rather less, in proportion to population, than that of the free States. The ordinary income of the Southern States is, comparatively, much greater than that of the Northern States. In the payment of their officers and public functionaries, the Southern States, can afford to be nearly twice as liberal as the Northern.‡

The ordinary annual expenditure of the Northern States, (exclusive of debts, free schools, &c.) is - - -	$2,756,700
The ordinary annual expenditure of the Southern States, (exclusive of debts, free schools, &c.) is - - -	$2,501,952

It must be remembered, in considering these numbers, that none of the States, probably, levy more taxes than are just sufficient to meet their expenses. So that they afford no accurate criterion as to how much they could command, if circumstances required more. They only show what the people are accustomed and willing to do under ordinary circumstances. Like straws, they show how the wind blows. Here, also, it must be rembered, if the States separate, the *credit* of the South is not likely to suffer as much as that of the North, for the reason that our domestic products are so much more valuable.

In 1830, all the ordinary expenditures of the United States—with a third more population than the South now has—were $13,000,000. Now, including all our exports, as well to the North as to foreign ports, the annual amount is put down at $170,000,000,§ and the return imports at $200,000,000. This at the low duty of 10 per cent., would yield a revenue of $20,000,000—twice as much, perhaps, as the South would require for her *ordinary* expenditures; but *three millions less than she now pays to the federal government, over and above what is returned to her by the government.*

Putting down the whole amount of our exports, of *staples alone*, (including those sent to the North,) at the moderate sum of $130,000,000, and the return imports at the same amount, at a duty of 30 per cent., which is less than the present duties on many articles, we would have a revenue of $40,000,000, and no increase of prices would ensue on manufactures. "We might therefore spend as much as the government of the United States ever did, in time of peace, up to the beginning of General Jackson's administration, and still have on hand $25,000,000 to devote to domestic purposes."‖ These $25,000,000 could, at the rate of 5 per cent., pay the interest on a debt of $500,000,000, if, on account of separation, we should require a loan to that amount. We need not, then, be uneasy on this score.

As we have dared thus publicly to defend a measure, the *popularity* of which is doubtful *even now*, when the necessity for it is obvious, the reader may be disposed to inquire if we have any plan by which the measure may be consummated. We answer, yes! But we will inquire, have *you* a plan? If you have, compare it with ours, reason upon them both, and adopt that which, to your better judgment, may seem best. We are not *wedded* to ours; we trust you are not wedded to yours. This is a time when *pride of opinion* should be smothered in its first efforts. Let none of us, Oh, men of the South, however wise, experienced and

* Iowa and Wisconsin not included. † Missouri not included.

‡ These numbers are collected from the American Almanac and other sources.

§ See "The Union," the Past, etc.

‖ See the Speech of Mr. Clingman, in the House of Representative, Jan. 22d, 1850.

influential we may be, indulge the idea, hurtful as it would be on this issue, though harmless in matters of minor importance, that we know better what should be done than other people. If we have already formed our opinions, let us candidly compare them, *in a logical manner*, with those which may be advanced by others.

In the first place, Congress is not the power to dissolve the compact. As Congress did not form this union, so Congress cannot dissolve it, *de jure.*

In the next place, a combination of States, AS SOVEREIGNS, should not dissolve the compact. A combination of one set of contractors, to destroy a compact, to which another set of contractors are parties disposed to keep the contract binding, is not a manly or independent course. There was no combination of States, as sovereigns, in forming this Union, so there should be none in dissolving it. But, be it remembered, as there was consultation and advisement, a proper interchange of views and opinions between the *people of the several States, as parties interested*, in the formation of this Union, so there may properly be consultation, advisement, and exchange of opinion, in dissolving it.

In the next place, each sovereign should go out of a confederation in the same way, on the same footing, and with the same degree of independence with which it entered that confederation; otherwise, that sovereign has deteriorated, degenerated, lost power, lost caste, lost respect, lost *something*. As each State joined or came into the Union, so, also, should it go out. Then, as each State came into this Union upon its own responsibility, independent of all the other States, and without a *necessary* regard to the *previous or anticipated* action of any other State, so also should each State go out of it.

In the next place, as the events which have brought the Southern States to the inferior position in which they have been lately placed, and to the dangerous position in which they now stand, have been the result of thirty years repeated aggressions on the part of the Northern States, through their authorized representatives, in the federal legislature, and the concerted action of their private citizens, as well as the formal proceedings of their governments, and as they have, during these thirty years, been again and again appealed to, warned, solicited to desist from their obnoxious measures, *all to no purpose*, it becomes each Southern State, in whatever course it may pursue, in order to guard against those further and more dangerous events which must, in the nature of things, necessarily follow those gone before, not to rely on them for any *retraction* which it may be supposed they would make, *if again appealed to.* As *they* are the responsible powers, which have deliberately and repeatedly disrobed us of our rights, honours and immunities, it would be degrading in its effects, servile in its essence, degenerate in its spirit, and cowardly in its appearance, for us, after having, in convention, solemnly declared that certain events would render certain proceedings, on our part, necessary for the preservation of our birthright, now that those events have transpired, in more monstrous shapes than ever had been expected, for us to shrink from carrying out those proceedings, or to *qualify those proceedings, when carried out, by an appeal or proposition to them for any favour, compromise, or other things than those which we claim as our* RIGHT, AND HAVE DETERMINED TO TAKE.

Based upon these obvious principles of honourable independence, which must find an echo in the breast of every enlightened freeman, the following plan, by which this Union should be dissolved, may not be altogether impracticable or improper.

Let each Southern State send its delegates to the adjourned meeting of the Nashville Convention, which meets about the middle of November. The members of this body will weigh our rights and weigh our wrongs; they will consult calmly, candidly, logically, and freely with each other; they will agree upon and recommend to the people of the States they represent, such a course as they may think best. Their recommendation should then be submitted to the people of the several districts, by their respective delegates, at the earliest opportunity afforded for holding a primary meeting of their constituents. At these meetings, the recommendation of the general convention will either be agreed upon or rejected, in part or in whole At the same time, the recommendation should be submitted to the governor of each State. This functionary should convene the legislature and submit the matter to their consideration. But before the legislature can have assembled, these primary meetings will have been held. Now, each of these meetings, if in their judgment they deem it expedient, should address a memorial to the legislature, thus about assembling, praying that body to take the necessary steps, and without unnecessary delay, by which *to effect an honourable, equitable, independent and unqualified secession of the State from the Union.* This is the first great step to take. Secede first. Settle disputes afterwards. Proclaim your rights first. Maintain them afterwards. If you cannot maintain your rights in the Union, it is certain you can do no less out of it. By this time the new Congress will be in session. Any business, then, which the State legislature may have to arrange with Congress can be accomplished without delay. The first item of which, perhaps, would be to recall the senators and representatives from that body. The secession of any one State having been accomplished, let it look around to arrange its foreign relations. The first thing, under this head, will be to communicate with such other States as may also have seceded. With all such a confederacy should be formed, for "the common defence and general welfare." Exigencies, however, may arise, which would require *immediate assistance and co-operation*, the one from the other. In this case, an *alliance* may be formed, for the time being, under a treaty. When there is more tranquillity, a permanent compact may be formed. When each State secedes, it should notify the government which it is about leaving what claims it sets up to public property, territories, etc., etc. If the seceding States determine to claim a part of the territory belonging to the present government, and a part of California, unconstitutionally taken from them, let them claim every inch lying south of latitude 36° 30′. Let them claim all of this, or none. *It is a claim not only moderate in itself, but fortified by a law of thirty years standing, a precedent of binding authority*—THE MISSOURI COMPROMISE. This compromise, though, as we have already maintained, impolitic and unconstitutional in itself, is nevertheless the law of the land. It is a precedent, binding *by time, consent and usage*, though it be *unconstitutionality legalized.* The parallel of latitude, 36° 30′ should be proclaimed the Northern boundary of the territory of the new republic, from Missouri to the Pacific, or else no territory shold be claimed at all. This, however, supposes that all the Southern States secede; if, therefore, only a part of them secede, the proposition perhaps would not hold.

By such a course, the South places itself entirely on the defensive. She does nothing more than what she has a right to do; nothing more than what she is forced to do; nothing more than what she should do; nor does she claim more than what is hers. It will be for the North to decide whether we shall have peace or war. If she is disposed to accede to our claims, we will have peace; if she refuses them, we must have war. But not a *civil war*. It is a monstrous error to suppose that a dissolution of the Union would, in any event, cause a civil war. A war between such great countries as the South and North, the one entirely arrayed against the other, partakes of none of the features of a civil war. Civil wars, mobs and massacres may be expected when one class of a community is arrayed against another class, in the same community, living in the same cities and the same districts. In some of the revolutions of France, when fratricidal blood was made to gurgle under the feet of delirious mobs, there were civil wars. But in the American Revolution, there was no civil war, properly speaking. It was a regularly waged war, between Americans and Britons. So in the event of a Southern Revolution, it is impossible there can be a *civil war.* If war does come, it will be an open, vigorous and determined war, between two *great nations;* the one defending all that is sacred, the other the Lord knows what.

In conclusion, Oh, men of the South, let us remind you how the noble Brutus reasoned, on the march to Philippi:

"You must note beside,
That we have tried the utmost of our friends,
Our legions are brim full, our cause is ripe,
The enemy increaseth every day,
We, at the height, are ready to decline.
There is a tide in the affairs of men,
Which, taken at the flood, leads on to fortune;
Omitted, all the voyage of their life
Is bound in shallows and in miseries.
On such a full sea are we now afloat,
And we must take the current when it serves,
Or lose our ventures."

THE END.

www.ingramcontent.com/pod-product-compliance
Lightning Source LLC
LaVergne TN
LVHW021408110826
845150LV00007B/1832

* 9 7 8 1 4 2 5 5 1 1 4 5 6 *